Who's That Girl

Also by Thea Glassman:

Freaks, Gleeks & Dawson's Creek

Who's That Girl

THE UNTOLD, DEFINITIVE HISTORY OF *NEW GIRL*

Thea Glassman

ST. MARTIN'S
PRESS
NEW YORK

First published in the United States by St. Martin's Press,
an imprint of St. Martin's Publishing Group

EU Representative: Macmillan Publishers Ireland Ltd, 1st Floor, The Liffey Trust Centre,
117–126 Sheriff Street Upper, Dublin 1, D01 YC43

www.stmartins.com

Designed by Steven Seighman

The Library of Congress Cataloging-in-Publication Data is available upon request.

ISBN 978-1-250-38113-2 (hardcover)
ISBN 978-1-250-38114-9 (ebook)

First Edition: 2026

10 9 8 7 6 5 4 3 2 1

To Anthony Rizzo and the Chicago Cubs for all we've been through.

And to Ben, for the same thing and so much more.

Introduction

WHEN LIZ MERIWETHER WAS IN her twenties, she went through a bad breakup. One of her guy friends found her crying on Sixth Avenue in New York City, picked her up off the pavement, and whisked her over to a nearby diner. He ordered a plate of french fries and did his best Daffy Duck impression to cheer her up.

If Meriwether had called one of her girlfriends, they would have cried with her. But in that moment, her broken heart needed a different kind of soothing, someone who would good-naturedly wave away the ache with humor, tough love, and an impressively spot-on impersonation of a cartoon character.

"Oh!" she thought at the time. "Male friends are different and kind of good in a way."

When it came to matters of the heart, the guys in Meriwether's life offered a very specialized support system. They were on hand to decode texts and Facebook messages, offering a handy road map to navigating the all-too-confusing world of dating. In turn, she accompanied them to weddings and ran interference when they attempted to date women she knew.

Little did Meriwether know, as she sat in that diner with her friend, just how formative a moment it would be. Later, a transplant in the strange city of Los Angeles, she'd step into producer Peter Chernin's office to offer up a television-show pitch. It was a take on *Modern Family*, Fox's biggest sitcom at the time, and as she rattled off an idea for another multigenerational show, Chernin stopped her. "Listen, write what you know," he said. "Write about the people you know, write about your friends. Ninety-nine percent of things fail, you might as well fail doing something you're proud of."

Meriwether thought about her guy friends. She flashed back to her days in New York City, a wonderfully dark, dirty, and intense place, where nights were spent watching subversive comedy shows on the Lower East Side. Los Angeles was filled with happy, healthy people who seemed really jazzed about exercising. Equally confounding was the corporate culture of Hollywood studios—a foreign land where box-office numbers, quotas, and ratings reigned supreme. Meriwether moved to Laurel Canyon, a cinematically stunning neighborhood filled with craggy mountains set in the Hollywood Hills. But she wanted to re-create the feeling she had hanging out with her male best friend in his spectacularly gross Brooklyn loft alongside his two roommates. Man, did she miss that place, which had come to feel like home.

Meriwether decided to call her show *Chicks and Dicks*, with the understanding that the title might need to change because, she conceded, "this isn't France." As she dreamt up a burgeoning nostalgia-tinted world, she thought about a valuable piece of advice that entertainment executive Jonathan Davis once offered her.

"Pilots are like a Trojan horse," he said. "You want to explain the show in a nice, easy package that everyone can get. Then you hide all the weird, crazy shit that's in your head for later, slowly rolling it out throughout the course of the season."

Meriwether took that sneaky suggestion to heart. Her premise could be neatly summed up as a reverse *Three's Company*: a young woman named Jess—fresh off a bad breakup—moves in with three single guys.

"The tone of the show is edgy humor surrounded with love—ledgy," she pitched. "It's me guest starring on *Entourage*. It's Bridget Jones forced to live inside a Judd Apatow movie. It's Jonah Hill wearing Spanx."

Possible taglines included:

"Three guys. One girl. No grown-ups."
"Three guys. One girl. Trying to have *Sex and the City*."
"Three guys. One girl. Totally not a porn."

Her idea worked. At twenty-nine, she landed a pilot with Fox, hooking them on a tidy, rom-com-like concept that would be packaged up on butter-yellow billboards touting the buzzy new show as "adorkable." Just beneath the surface, all the weird, crazy, wonderful stuff was yet to come. It started slow at first, and then took off at breakneck speed, taking the classic hang-out show and bending it in a far more interesting, surprising direction.

New Girl was an anarchy of a series, where the actors were invited to help mold and shape their characters, turning them into genuinely likable, three-dimensional people with foibles plucked from their own imaginations. Improvisation was warmly welcomed on set, and it was often the smaller, off-the-cuff tangents that made it into an episode, the kinds of delirious moments that the cast thought wouldn't possibly be aired . . . and then promptly were.

Writers would sometimes write hundreds—yes, hundreds—of alternate jokes for every joke that appeared in the script. Episodes could stretch ninety-five pages long, more than triple the typical page count. Beneath those overstuffed scripts was a burning, single-minded focus on making the show as good and funny as possible, even if it meant that Meriwether spent many nights sleeping at her office, slipping inside a puffy purple sleeping bag for a few hours of shut-eye.

Those long evenings, both on set and inside the writers' room, gave way to unexpected comedy gems and the development of fictional romances audiences not only rooted for but deeply, *fully*, *madly* obsessed over. (We'll talk about the hallway kiss quite a bit.) *New Girl* managed the nearly impossible: creating a hangout show that was sweet but not saccharine, comforting yet sharply witty, and populated by genuinely strange but relatable characters.

Along the way, there were growing pains and plenty of experimenting—from struggling with their biggest will-they-won't-they storyline to defining what, exactly, the show was. Staggeringly impressive ratings dipped and the series went from the coolest on the block to oft-ignored by viewers, poked at by critics, and eventually landing on the brink of cancellation. It was only after its quiet exit from the air in 2018 that the comedy found a surprising afterlife a few short years later, becoming what so many series strive for and so few are able to do. *New Girl* found its foothold as a comfort rewatch, joining an elusive stable of shows that fans welcome into their homes during the mundane moments, the dark moments, and everything in between.

This is the story of arguably the last great network hangout show, which left the air just as streaming took a tight grip on narrative TV. It exists as a relic of the shows we loved growing up, but with a little more chutzpah and a whole lot more experimentation, tucked somewhere between the cozy days of network television and the exciting realm of what was to come.

Who's that girl? She's so much more than the frothy labels critics once pinned on her, and her roommates were much, much more than the typical ensemble of TV pals. Entering their world meant stepping into a surreal comedy planet filled with woodland musicals and pet bowls for humans. It was also a place where your heart kicked rapidly at lines like "Not like this," and a lump formed in your throat every time the group showed up for each other during life's lowest moments ("LAXmas," "Wedding," "Oregon" . . .).

Welcome to apartment 4D, the best downtown Los Angeles loft there is or ever was. Feel free to rock a lot of polka dots, take a weekly selfie with your cat, and read a really insane book about zombies.

1

Chicks and Dicks

Yeah, I think you *should* sing all the time.

—JESSICA DAY

AHEAD OF THE 2008 PRESIDENTIAL election, Meriwether was sitting in a church basement in Ohio, trying to help get Barack Obama elected. She was working as a volunteer at the time and typed out an email to some of her New York friends in hopes of getting them involved. Her note was both dirty and filled with obscenities, featuring an abortion joke and a dig at Ohioans.

When her bosses got wind of the email, Meriwether was pulled into a back room. After reading her words back to her, they asked if she thought it was funny. Meriwether had two options in that moment—pretend the email wasn't amusing and avoid any consequences or stand by her jokes. "You can fire me," she thought, "but I won't tell you it's not funny." Meriwether was promptly let go.

As far as writing origin stories go, this makes for a pretty good one. Not only did Meriwether's knack for comedy cause her email to quickly circulate around the campaign office, but her commitment to the joke was resolute. It was, as she'd later say, her stand-up-to-the-world moment.

The writer's true origin story, though, happened in a far less grabby manner, one state over. Growing up, she put on plays in the basement of her home in Ann Arbor, Michigan, casting her brother in various roles or strong-arming her friends into starring in adaptations she wrote of books. Her first real onstage production was *Oliver!*, playing an orphan eating gruel and then, in a reprisal of the show, as Mr. Bumble, the evil head of the orphanage. Much to her chagrin, the string of male parts continued to plague her throughout middle school—the annoying result of being tall for her age. She played Captain Hook in *Peter Pan* and Gollum in *The Hobbit*, while her adolescent theater nemesis snagged all the female leads.

Meriwether's TV allegiances lay firmly with *Friends* (she loved Ross and Rachel), *Dawson's Creek* (the whole Dawson/Pacey/Joey love triangle), and, above all else, *My So-Called Life*, the 1994 drama that explored the pains of adolescence. Starring a thirteen-year-old Claire Danes as Angela Chase, it was the first TV series that took young people seriously, realistically exploring the complicated emotions that come along with being a teen girl.

Meriwether started dressing like Angela, wearing flannel shirts and developing a crush on a guy much like the show's heartthrob, Jordan Catalano, complete with a gas-station attendant jacket and leather choker necklace. For the first two years of high school, she was an outspoken student, who called out people in her class when they were being sexist. Then she got her braces off and someone on the soccer team wanted to date her. She swapped flannels for baby tees but remained a self-proclaimed theater nerd at heart. Summers were spent at Interlochen Center for the Arts, set on the leafy shores of northern Michigan, where she was introduced to Stephen Sondheim by fellow camper and future musical superstar Josh Groban, who loaned her a CD of Broadway's *Sweeney Todd*.

Meriwether traded Ann Arbor for New Haven, enrolling at Yale University. She lived on campus in a tidy brick building above Durfee's Sweet Shoppe and was the director of the improv group the Viola Question. Back in high school, a visiting writer once delivered a lecture to her class and told them, "A lot of people say they're writers, but not everybody is actually writing." Meriwether took that sentiment to heart. She was putting pen to paper, writing—among others—a ten-minute avant-garde play called "The Touch, The Feel," in which the main character, played by her classmate Zoe Kazan, talks to cotton.

Meriwether's growing list of credits earned her a write-up in the *Yale Daily News*. She sat atop a pile of pillows in her room as she gave her interview, face framed in honey-blond hair, wearing a cutoff T-shirt and black-rimmed glasses. While munching on gummy peach rings, the young writer shared that she loved the "in-between stuff" of storytelling, when you weren't quite sure if it was funny or sad. As she looked toward her postgrad future, Meriwether aspired to be like the celebrated playwright and poet Gertrude Stein, who hosted weekly salons for artists and writers in her Paris apartment.

She set about pursuing her Stein-esque dreams in New York City, working as a receptionist at a real estate investment management company by day, while establishing herself as an up-and-coming voice in the local theater scene. Her name quickly became synonymous with weird, funny, and subversive work—like the play *Heddatron*, an updated version of Henrik Ibsen's *Hedda Gabler* featuring robots. She would go to every performance, sitting in the back risers of Soho's HERE Arts Center and taking studious mental notes, clocking what made people laugh.

It would turn out to be a play about dirtiness and grief that caught the attention of a Fox network executive. After college, Meriwether wrote *The Mistakes Madeline Made*, the story of a young woman working a soul-crushing job as a personal assistant who decides to stop bathing following the death of her brother. "Is dirty living a political act?" the play asked. "And is clean living even possible in these times of unrest? An unlikely story of love and dirty people."

The ten-minute play was performed at 45 Below, a theater space in the East Village, and earned positive reviews from critics, including *Variety*'s Marilyn Stasio, who suggested that there was a bright future for the young playwright. "Girl rage is powerful in Elizabeth Meriwether's absurdist comedy *The Mistakes Madeline Made*. In a prickly, funny production by Naked Angels, that rage is every bit as hilarious as it is scary and sad," Stasio wrote, adding, "Meriwether's gift as a playwright is her ability to take what is familiar and real and view it through the distorted lens of absurdism."

That play landed her a pilot deal with Fox before she even had the chance to purchase Final Draft, the industry's go-to screenwriting software, for her computer.

Suddenly, she was quitting her receptionist job and moving to Los Angeles for a high-profile TV gig. At twenty-six, she zipped around in a golf cart on the Fox lot in sunny Southern California, tasked with hiring a crew and creating her very first TV show. The pilot, called *Sluts*, was loosely based on Meriwether's own life as a postgrad twentysomething living with her roommates in Manhattan. A precursor of sorts to Lena Dunham's *Girls*, *Sluts* would have likely found a comfortable home if it had been snagged by a cable network, where characters and their lives could exist in messier, edgier places. Network TV—maybe not so much. The very concept of her female characters seemed to baffle executives, who couldn't quite wrap their heads around three-dimensional women with sexual desires.

So many of the network notes questioned whether her characters could be smart and also enjoy sex so much. When Meriwether told people about the pilot she was working on, there seemed to be even more confusion, along with the same nagging question: "Who is going to watch a show with only girls in it?" (Cover your ears, Carrie Bradshaw.)

Sluts didn't end up making Fox's lineup. Jason Winer, who directed the pilot, suspected that Fox never intended to put the show on the air. Network TV was still considered king in the mid-2000s and could afford to finance multiple pilots without believing deeply in all of them. By making the *Sluts* pilot with a group of young, edgy creatives, Fox could say they were doing cool stuff without actually airing the cool stuff.

Meriwether felt lost in a strange city, living a nomadic existence and hopping between Craigslist sublets. When she was invited to a Halloween party, she decided to dress up as a slutty Alvy Singer from *Annie Hall*, donning a curly red wig for the occasion. Meriwether quickly learned that people didn't do ironic costumes in this part of town. Everybody, in her estimation, looked hot and perfect. She was supposed to get set up with a guy that night, but when he took one look at her dressed as Alvy, he turned right back around.

Meriwether drove around the city, jumping from one meeting to the next, her car steadily filling up with bottles of water from each meet and greet. At one point, she was hired to attend a comedy roundtable for the *Transformers* sequel and pitched a joke about a soldier telling another soldier that he's gay right before the aliens attack. Michael Bay, the franchise's director, didn't laugh. As they headed out for the day, Meriwether overheard a writer discussing the earnings he had made from the session. "Hey, now I can retile my pool," he said.

"These aren't my people," she thought to herself.

Meriwether kept trying to find her corner of Hollywood. One of her many meetings was with famed director Ivan Reitman, who pitched her the idea of writing a movie script off the title *Fuckbuddies*. He was interested in a film that explored relationships in the digital age of texting and Facebook messaging, where commitment waned and loosely defined romances flourished.

That idea Meriwether liked. She herself was in an on-again, off-again six-year situation that she found herself frequently pulling away from. This was a chance to put a different sort of female character in a romantic comedy: the rare fictional protagonist who didn't want a relationship. She wrote a script and a glittery A-list cast was attached, including Natalie Portman, Ashton Kutcher, Mindy Kaling, and Kevin Kline.

As her film took shape, the studio expressed concerns about the strangely foreign dynamic that they saw playing out on the page. "Are women going to relate to her?" Meriwether was asked. "Is she going to seem, like, cold, and, I don't know, *damaged*?"

Evidently not.

The film, which was renamed the far more family-friendly *No Strings Attached*, landed in movie theaters winter of 2011 and scored an impressive $19.7 million opening weekend. The receipts also told an interesting story—among its top five highest-grossing peers, which included *The King's Speech* and *True Grit*, Meriwether's film was the only romantic comedy. It was also the only movie written by a woman.

The success caught some in the industry by surprise. "It's a so-called 'chick flick' because of the subject matter, but it had appeal for both men and women with the whole idea of being 'friends with benefits,'" *Hollywood.com* analyst Paul Dergarabedian wrote. "For it to do $20 million is fairly impressive, considering it's rated R and January's not a hotbed of huge grosses, unless you're *Avatar* and you're holding over."

As Meriwether's star rose in Hollywood, she befriended three screenwriters—Dana Fox, Diablo Cody, and Lorene Scafaria—with the combined credits of *Juno*, *What Happens in Vegas*, and *Nick & Nora's Infinite Playlist* under their belts. The foursome affectionately dubbed themselves "the Fempire" and wore tiny matching heart pendants with dirty inscriptions etched on the inside. They'd ride in white limos together anytime one of them had a movie premiere and meet at laptop-friendly restaurants to punch out pages while sitting side by side.

Their kinship earned a write-up in *The New York Times*, under the headline "An Entourage of Their Own." These writers, journalist Deborah Schoeneman posited, were the "boozy, all-woman answer" to a very specific breed of men who had taken over Hollywood, including the *Entourage* crew and tight-knit Judd Apatow universe, where raunch, silliness, and the joys of boyhood spilled onto every script page.

"There are so few slots for us in Hollywood," Cody told the *Times*. "Sometimes you hear the lobsters-in-a-pot metaphor—if the lobsters cooperated, they could get each other out. We're cooperating. We refuse to just lie there and boil."

A funny thing happened the year Meriwether's first film came out.

Bolstered by the surprise smash success of *Bridesmaids*, a 2011 comedy written by Kristen Wiig and Annie Mumolo and starring an all-female cast, there was a sudden interest in stories about women, by women. In a wonderfully fresh twist, *Bridesmaids* allowed its characters to be just as slapdash, flawed, and gross as their male comedy counterparts. Yes, there's a beautiful representation of female friendship in there but also, at one point, Melissa McCarthy poops in a sink.

Bridesmaids nabbed an industry-shaking $26.2 million during its opening weekend. Of that audience, 67 percent were female—proof that women wanted to see funny stories about themselves on the screen. An alarm bell went off in Hollywood. "You could practically *hear* studio heads screaming in staff meetings, 'Where's our *Bridesmaids*?!'" producer David T. Friendly wrote in a *Hollywood Reporter* op-ed.

Suddenly, the previously ignored names of female writers were being bandied about on rewrite lists. "Their spec scripts, once relegated to a desk drawer, are being dusted off and, for the moment, the powers that be, the people who actually greenlight movies, have decided that—guess what?—women are funny even when disgusting!" Friendly wrote.

Around when the tides were beginning to change, even marginally, for women in Hollywood, Meriwether stepped into producer Peter Chernin's office for her next TV pitch. He waved away her multigenerational sitcom idea and asked her to write something more personal, sending Meriwether back to the basics. Who were the people in her life whom she most wanted to write about?

She thought about her guy friends and one in particular jumped out. The pair had developed a surprising bond after her ex-boyfriend and his ex-girlfriend started dating. He was an alpha-male type who slept around and was so different from her other friends, whom she lovingly described as weirdo dorks. He'd tell her about the women he hooked up with and there was a comfort level there. She could share, he could share, and there were no romantic implications.

The original idea for the show took shape in her mind as a straight version of *Will & Grace*, inspired by her friend and their relationship. The show's world needed more people, so she got busy populating it, dreaming up an ensemble cast of guy roommates as she pulled from her own experiences spending those postgrad years at her friend's Brooklyn loft.

Even as the industry began to shift its perspective on greenlighting female-led projects, television execs were still zeroed in, with sweaty determination, on the male demographic: hook the guys into watching and all those eyeballs could lend themselves to a syndication deal. "That is the business model: you get men to watch it, you make money," Meriwether told journalist Joy Press for her book *Stealing the Show: How Women Are Revolutionizing Television*. "We had meetings where they were telling us we basically had to appeal to men." So, perhaps, it wasn't all that much of a coincidence that the initial concept for *Chicks and Dicks* surrounded her heroine with multiple guys—and a quieter friendship between two women was tucked within the edges.

Meriwether decided to name her lead female character Jess, a young woman who wants to belong in the world of *Sex and the City* but secretly prefers the missionary position and finds complicated underwear stressful. Her Craigslist roommates are Nick, a bartender who's closed himself off to love, and Schmidt, best described as "Larry David stuck in the body of the Situation." Coach was originally written as an overweight jock who had peaked in sixth grade and signs off his emails with "The Coachness." (Only the latter feels accurate to who that character would become.) "What I was really interested in with this show was showing these male characters who are just as insecure and emotional as any woman," Meriwether would later say.

And then there was Cece, Jess's oldest friend, with the backstory that the pair met when they were awkward teens and have stuck together ever since. Jess often gets "hot-girl advice" from Cece, which, Meriwether explained, only works if you're very hot: "Like the infamous: 'Just call him!' No. You never just call him."

While developing her cast of characters, Meriwether examined commedia dell'arte, an early form of European theater that featured stock comedic characters. She was trying to teach herself how to create an ensemble of fictional people who were different from one another and had their own comedic energies and engines.

She was also watching a lot of *Green Wing*, a British sitcom that featured a love triangle between doctors. Caroline, the center of the triangle, is a surgical registrar who has two men competing for her heart: the charming and highly lusted-after Dr. Macartney and the jerky but ultimately endearing Dr. Guy Secretan. The men were so wildly different and Meriwether found herself inspired by those dichotomies as she built the characters of Nick and Schmidt, who would ultimately become the show's central odd couple.

Included in Meriwether's pitch was an early note that Nick and Jess would have a crush on each other, despite the fact that he drove her crazy with his cynicism and she drove him nuts with her candy-coated optimism. Meriwether liked that dynamic of light and dark between them. She also looked to the future for Jess—noting that her arc on the show would be to learn to stand up for herself while becoming confident in life and love.

Ahead of pitching her idea to Fox, Meriwether met with executive producer Katherine Pope, who was the president of television at Chernin Entertainment. The pair took their seats at Hugo's, a West Hollywood eatery, the day after the *No Strings Attached* premiere.

"Your hair looks so pretty! You look so good," Pope told Meriwether, who had gotten a blowout for the big event.

"You will never see my hair look like this again," Meriwether informed her.

The writer, Pope observed during their meeting, was so intrinsically herself—vulnerable and honest. She had all the swagger of someone who knew how good she was, juxtaposed with awkwardness and insecurity. Something about that combination really spoke to the producer. As they discussed pitching *Chicks and Dicks* to Fox, Meriwether confided in Pope that she was feeling nervous ahead of their big meeting.

"I'm so uncomfortable," Pope remembers her saying. "I don't want to look people in the eye."

"Here's the deal, honey," Pope told her. "Just walk in and read your pitch pages."

So Meriwether did exactly that. She stepped into a roomful of executives armed with her pages and read them out loud, word for word. As she rounded out the pitch, she told her audience, "When your heart's breaking on the side of the road, sometimes you don't need a girl to come tell you that men suck. Sometimes you just need a man to shrug and say, 'I'd still do you.'" Then she offered a final, shrugging salute. "Thank you for listening and go with God."

The executives bought *Chicks and Dicks* on the spot. At twenty-nine, Meriwether had her own TV show, one that—unlike *Sluts*—looked like it *might* actually make it through the gnarly trenches of pilot season alive.

Excited as they were about her idea, the execs didn't think Meriwether was ready to take on this show entirely on her own, so they hired writing partners Brett Baer and Dave Finkel to work alongside her. Baer and Finkel were already fixtures in the industry, with credits that included *30 Rock* and *United States of Tara*, and previously worked with Meriwether on an unaired comedy starring Artie Lange.

The writers set about figuring out where, exactly, their show lived. The answer, they decided, was that this would be a pilot about four people who come into each other's lives when they need one another the most. These characters were on a journey of figuring out who they were while making each other better in the process. As Meriwether put it: "I really wanted to write a show about people who are at a time when they should be moving forward but are in a weird, stuck, heartbroken, slightly immature place in their life."

The writer ended up feeling a little disappointed when her *Chicks and Dicks* title didn't make it past the pitch document and was replaced with the far more network-friendly *New Girl.* In a vastly populated pilot season, with so many shows jockeying for eyeballs, it would have been nice to have a title that caught people's attention. Plus, would a show with the word *girl* be alienating for male viewers?

She felt good, though, during her first sit-down meeting with Fox president Kevin Reilly, who offered up some surprisingly heartening words about Jess. Meriwether walked into their one-on-one, nervous that Reilly would tell her that Jess needed to be more "normal." Instead, Reilly told Meriwether he wanted to make sure they protected this character. "I want to make her unique, I want to do everything I can to make sure this still feels like you and your voice," he said. It was a surprisingly magical sentence to be uttered by a person with so much sway over *New Girl*'s future. Jess would get to be exactly how Meriwether envisioned her: the leading lady's messy, off-kilter best friend, who usually only got a quarter of the screen time in movies and TV shows, now promoted to top billing. This was her time to shine.

Before putting pen to paper, Meriwether watched the beloved '80s sitcom *Cheers* and CBS family comedy *Everybody Loves Raymond.* She was awed by how *well* the writers had structured their stories. As she studied the episodes closely, Meriwether tried to figure out how, exactly, sitcoms were made. She was thinking beyond traditionally shot sitcoms, too, her mind going back to *Freaks and Geeks,* a canceled-too-soon, single-camera show that followed the lives and growing pains of high schoolers in small-town Michigan. Meriwether was struck by how seamlessly the show managed to blend comedy and emotion, finding the "in-between stuff" she loved so much. She wanted that feeling for her show.

So, really, it only made sense that she decided to cold-email *Freaks and Geeks*' pilot director Jake Kasdan to see if he might be interested in taking on the all-important task of bringing *New Girl* to life.

Kasdan had thought he was largely done with television. Four years back, he'd written and directed a film called *The TV Set,* which offered an insiders' look at the frustrating process of pilot season. It was an unflattering portrait to be sure, and he suspected that the movie wasn't going to get him TV gigs anytime soon. Plus, how could he ever top the experience of *Freaks and Geeks*? Kasdan had turned his attention to the big screen, directing comedy hits like *Walk Hard: The Dewey Cox Story*, when the email from Meriwether popped up in his inbox.

Her note was sweet and the script was *funny*. He handed it off to his wife to read and he could hear her laughing from the other room. Kasdan fell fast for Meriwether's writing and found himself making a surprisingly snap decision. He would brave pilot season once more for this show.

When Meriwether and Kasdan sat down for the first time, Kasdan offered his vision for *New Girl*. At the time, the most popular single-camera TV shows—*The Office* and *Modern Family*—were shot mockumentary style. Kasdan wanted to step away from that arena, and the typical sitcom style in general. The world, he suggested to Meriwether, should be cinematic in the way that it was lit and shot, allowing audiences to feel like they were watching a movie rather than a TV series. From a purely technical perspective, that entailed using an 85mm lens, which created a shallower depth of focus, akin to feature films. (More traditionally shot sitcoms, like *Friends*, *Seinfeld*, and *Cheers*, were filmed with 35mm lenses.)

As he later impressed on guest directors, *New Girl* should look like a Sandra Bullock romantic comedy, mirroring films like the bright, poppy *Two Weeks Notice*. Jess, after all, was a romantic-comedy heroine in her own right and needed to exist within a space that was fitting for her genre.

Kasdan was also interested in bucking the traditional sitcom strategy of sticking diligently to the script, inspired by his time working with producer and director Judd Apatow on *Freaks and Geeks*. While shooting the show, Apatow often found unexpected moments during filming, shooting the pages as written and then, the camera still rolling, calling out alternate lines and jokes to the actors to deliver on the spot. Their show ended up shooting so many takes—a staggering one million feet of film—that Kodak sent a case of champagne as a thank-you.

Not only that, but Apatow had emboldened his young actors to improvise and pitch ideas. *New Girl* would keep that spirit alive, opening up the floor so that performers could take their own crack at the comedy in the scene. They wouldn't be improvising storylines or episode arcs—that would be the writers' jobs—but they'd be invited to come up with their own character moments and flourishes while filming.

Of course, in order for *New Girl* to make that kind of spontaneous comedy work, they'd need great comedic performers who were nimble on their feet. If Kasdan had learned anything about casting pilots, it was to hire truly funny actors who inspired the people who wrote for them. Finding that specific breed of performer mattered more than splashy names and the overall commercial appeal of the show. It was even more important than the script itself. Sometimes, lightning can strike, and a project, amid the hell that is pilot season, could actually transcend it all and lead to something pretty special.

And so they set about trying to find those magical actors, the ones who would make audiences come back again and again for more.

2

Finding Apartment 4D

I am not a successful adult. I don't eat vegetables and/or take care of myself.

—NICK MILLER

MERIWETHER WAS IN HER CAR, turning down Crescent Heights, a sleepy, tree-lined boulevard in Los Angeles, when an agent from Creative Artists Agency called. "Zooey Deschanel might be interested in doing TV," he said, causing her to yank her car to the curb in excitement. That simple, teasing sentence felt like a miracle. "She *has* to be in this show," Meriwether thought to herself.

Like the majority of film stars at the time, Deschanel had never fancied herself doing television. With mainstream movie hits like *Elf* and indie darlings *500 Days of Summer* and *Almost Famous* under her belt, the actress had found a comfortable foothold on the big screen. Then, as she approached the end of her twenties, a group of movie studios began cutting their slates. Smaller comedies and indies were being gutted to make room for bigger blockbusters and action films, which made Deschanel wonder if her film career was over altogether. She stopped acting for a year and toured around the country with her band She & Him, a duo that consisted of herself and indie folk artist M. Ward.

With films evolving away from smaller, more intimate stories, Deschanel found herself gravitating toward television with a new kind of interest. As she watched *30 Rock* and *The Office*, which were leading the forefront of smart, half-hour shows, she thought to herself, "Maybe I'd like to do something like this." When the script for *New Girl* was handed off to her, Deschanel was mid-negotiating a small arc on *The Office*. Meriwether's pilot put a swift brake on those conversations.

Here was a female-centered comedy in the tradition of the greats like *Roseanne*, *The Mary Tyler Moore Show*, and *I Love Lucy*. It wasn't totally joke-driven like most sitcoms and there was real emotion in there. Yes, it would be a huge commitment if *New Girl* was picked up. Yes, there was this firm delineation in Hollywood where movie actors weren't crossing over to network TV. And yes, as a film actor, it was a really big risk to make the move to television. But if *New Girl* had been a movie script, she would have taken it in a heartbeat.

Plus, Jessica Day, a kind, unapologetically quirky teacher with a penchant for out-of-the-blue singing, reminded her a bit of her thirteen-year-old self, who was optimistic and excited all the time. For Deschanel's eighth-grade talent show, she had chosen to sing the showstopping "Shy" from *Once Upon a Mattress* in front of an auditorium of a thousand students. The song starts out timidly, gradually climbing until Deschanel was belting the word *shyyyyyy* like a huge Broadway number.

Jason Ritter, one of Deschanel's classmates, watched in awe from the audience. "It was a real sort of Zooey coming-out," he later said. "The rest of us were all trying to sort of find out who we were and to be cool, and she was just like, 'This is who I am. I already figured it out. I'm this. Like it or don't.'"

The actress was taken by the chance to be a major driving force behind a show's comedy, as opposed to one setting up the punch lines. So often, the scripts that arrived on her desk were for girlfriend roles, there to tee up the other actor rather than instigate the jokes. Jess got just as many opportunities to deliver funny lines as the guys did in the pilot, if not more.

Deschanel was on board, lending a headline-grabbing name to the show. Fox network executives were delighted—*beyond* delighted—and were about to pool a surplus of brainpower, resources, and money into making sure their pilot was a hit. Now came the time to fill out the rest of apartment 4D.

* * *

By the time casting director Seth Yanklewitz arrived home from his interview with Meriwether and executive producer Katherine Pope, he already had an incoming call from the duo.

"We really love you," they told him. "But we're just a little worried . . ."

Yanklewitz jumped in and finished their sentence. "That I don't know all the UCB actors . . . ?" he asked, and began rattling off names to prove he did. UCB was shorthand for Upright Citizens Brigade, a comedy theater and school in New York City and Los Angeles that featured improv shows with some of the industry's brightest up-and-coming talent. (Ilana Glazer, Abbi Jacobson, Donald Glover, and Aubrey Plaza are all alums.) *Those* were the kind of actors who would need to populate the world of *New Girl*—performers who were quick on their feet, open to collaboration, and excited about the live theater of it all. Yanklewitz had a packed Rolodex ready to go.

Auditions would take place on the west side of the Fox lot, in a small 1930s bungalow that once housed Shirley Temple's dressing room. Deschanel wanted to be there for each one, reading the role of Jess alongside the actors who made it past the first round. It wasn't an idea that her agents necessarily liked—she wasn't going to be paid to sit in on those casting sessions—but Deschanel didn't care. There was something intimidating about walking into a room full of writers, producers, and directors. Maybe if she, a fellow actor, was the person reading opposite them, performers would feel more comfortable. Plus, she'd have a better sense of whom she had chemistry with.

The crew munched on Deschanel's homemade rainbow-sprinkle cookies and got to work.

Finding the right fits for apartment 4D would be a long, arduous process, with Kasdan and Meriwether continuously trying to keep the material fresh and funny. "What if the character were more like this?" Kasdan would throw out to actors, some of whom returned to the building again and again. "What's it like when he's angry? What's it like when she decides *not* to say something aloud and says something else instead?" Meriwether did her part, too, returning home every night to punch up the material and write new sides for the actors, in hopes of keeping the pages alive day after day. And then there was Deschanel, walking over to the actors after they were done with the scripted scene and riffing with them.

Mercifully, some people walked in and . . . were just *it*. Such was the case when a struggling actor named Jake Johnson arrived at the bungalow. Auditions had not been the actor's friend—he'd been going into casting rooms since the age of twenty-four and struggled to land roles. As he once put it, he was experiencing "five fails a week."

The thirty-two-year-old, who grew up in the suburbs of Chicago and studied dramatic writing at NYU's Tisch School of the Arts, had roughly ninety-five dollars to his name when he auditioned for Nick Miller, the loft's cranky bartender. Johnson had a fan in Meriwether, who first discovered the actor when she was sitting in her friend Max Winkler's childhood bedroom as he edited his rom-com *Ceremony*.

Johnson played a supporting role in the movie, though it had been a near miss casting him. He was deemed "too intimidating and scary" by the film's financiers, which prompted Winkler to set up a meeting between Johnson and those skeptical backers. Johnson borrowed a suit—he didn't own one at the time—and Winkler told him to gel his hair back. Needless to say, he charmed them all. Johnson's special sauce, as Winkler put it to me, is that a lot of women have a crush on him and a lot of men want to have a beer with him. "It's this very rare star quality that just doesn't exist a lot," he said. "You usually get one or the other."

Johnson played a drunk in the film and modeled the character after a close relative who was one of his favorite people growing up. He was a drinker who told the same stories over and over again, would pause in the middle, forget what he was about to say, shrug, and everyone would laugh. On drives home from Christmas and Thanksgiving, Johnson would do impressions of him for his mom and siblings to make them laugh. He brought that imitation back for *Ceremony*, and as Meriwether watched him in the dailies, she was taken by his performance. Johnson was such a natural actor and when he told jokes, she didn't see it coming from a mile away.

Johnson was cast as Greta Gerwig's love interest in *No Strings Attached*, marking the first time he had ever been asked to play a romantic character. When *New Girl* got the greenlight, Meriwether decided to reach out again.

They just picked up my show, Meriwether texted Johnson. Would you be willing to read for it? This was in the early days, before Deschanel was even attached, and the pair met to do a read-through in an office on Hollywood Boulevard. "Can I rework this monologue with you and pitch you ideas?" Johnson asked Meriwether. Nick had originally been written as the straight man to Jess and Schmidt, each wacky in their ways, and the actor wanted to figure out how to make the character weird in his own right.

Johnson pitched the idea that Nick had panic attacks during sex, would get very sweaty, and was really bad at everything. He liked playing people who had big flaws—it was easier to be funny that way.

The actor was called in to do chemistry reads with a few performers who had been narrowed down to play Schmidt. When Johnson arrived on the Fox lot, he was met with a handful of potential Nicks, all in hoodies, and a handful of Schmidts, most of whom were roughly six two and blond. One guy stood out from the *Baywatch*-esque crowd, with dark hair and a definitively less preppy vibe. His name was Max Greenfield and Johnson liked reading with him—really liked it.

The pair, Johnson recalls, were true opposites. Greenfield's performance was way more presentational and his jokes finished with hard lines. Johnson filled in around Greenfield, improvising and waiting for a screwup so they could go off script. As they read together, everybody in the room laughed. "Oh, this is working for people," Johnson thought, noting how easy it was working opposite Greenfield.

"Nice to meet you," he told the actor afterward. "I really hope we get to do this together, man."

Johnson was brought back in again for a chemistry read with Deschanel, his potential love interest. As the two read opposite each other, the connection was undeniable. There was just *something* about the pair of them. Yanklewitz had overseen countless auditions at that point in his career, and sometimes he'd comfort himself by thinking, "We can get them there, later in the series, it'll work."

Not Johnson, and certainly not Johnson and Deschanel as a pair. There was an effortlessness to the actor's take on Nick Miller, and Pope remembers asking him to read his scene several more times. Not because it was necessary, but because it was genuinely fun to watch him in action. He seemed to have this character in his bones.

They asked themselves one nagging question: Was he handsome enough for Fox?

It was 2011, and there was an assumption that male love interests needed to look like they had been ripped out of an Aaron Spelling drama. Johnson, they all knew, was such a charismatic guy but didn't quite fit that cookie-cutter mold. (This all feels insane to write now, knowing exactly how much of an intense, wholehearted crush Nick Miller would become to one and all.)

Johnson, along with two other actors, was brought in to read for the heads of Fox. Any concerns about whether or not he fit into some sort of quintessential-TV-star box were immediately thrown out the window. "Oh yeah, that guy is a star," Fox president Kevin Reilly said. He was in.

Johnson's favorite Schmidt equally charmed the audition room. Max Greenfield, who had a few TV credits under his belt including a recurring role on *Veronica Mars*, *Greek*, and—lest we forget—young Sandy

Cohen on *The OC*, was on the cusp of quitting acting altogether when he walked in to read for *New Girl*. He had just had a child and was starting to wonder if it was time to say goodbye to his dreams of performing. "At what point does this become selfish?" he asked himself. "You don't want to become a dad who is running around and saying, 'I just got a callback to be a guest star on *The Middle*.'"

After testing for so many shows and not landing roles, Greenfield was worried he wasn't employable as an actor. He found himself ricocheting between two different thoughts—on the one hand, he kept getting so *close*, one of these jobs was bound to happen. On the other hand, maybe this just wasn't supposed to work out.

Greenfield reached out to his friend Todd Milliner, a producer on the TV Land comedy *Hot in Cleveland*, and asked about the possibility of getting a job as a writers' assistant. Maybe he could start at the bottom and try to work his way up, since acting didn't seem to be in the cards.

A month later, he had an audition for Schmidt, the hair chutney–applying, driving moccasins–wearing occupant of apartment 4D.

As Greenfield read the pages for Schmidt out loud, a ripple of surprise ran through the audition room. The casting team had pictured Schmidt as a Waspy, douchey guy but here was Greenfield, who was bringing something so much more interesting to the table. He softened the edges of the character with an unexpected warmth and he was surprisingly needy—so *very* emotionally needy. Meriwether hadn't pictured that facet of the character, but watching Greenfield in action gave her an epiphany. "Of course!" she thought to herself. "This is why we love this guy, because he wants to be better. He doesn't want to be a douchebag: he just can't help it."

While Meriwether mulled over the sharp turn Schmidt had taken, the idea for a douchebag jar was being born. She decided that there should be some sort of jar in the loft, which Schmidt would be required to deposit money in anytime he did something cringey, a nod to the audience that he was capable of change. Or, at the very least, some level of self-awareness.

Later that day, as the group went through the headshots of every actor they had seen, they pulled up Greenfield. "I don't think he's what was on the page," Pope remembers them saying. "But he's *so funny*." Greenfield didn't know it at the time, but halfway through his audition, everyone in the room had privately come to their own conclusion. He was their Schmidt.

One of the trickiest pieces of the casting puzzle would be Cece, Jess's best friend. The character was based on Meriwether's own very glamorous friend Cece, whom, as Pope remembers it, she always felt a bit like a Beverly Hillbilly around. Fictional Cece was scripted as a high-fashion model, so Yanklewitz started there. "I auditioned all of the Victoria's Secret models," the casting director recalled, "and it was just apparent that they could not act and certainly couldn't hold up to the comedy group I had assembled here."

As Yanklewitz pushed forward, he flashed back on an actress he had met two years prior. Her name was Hannah Simone, and she had auditioned for a role in the Fox series *Nevermind Nirvana*, which chronicled the story of two Indian-American brothers and their relationships with their families and romantic partners. Yanklewitz liked her—she was hysterically funny and beautiful. He dug through his old files and found her headshot.

Simone had a blank acting résumé at the time. She had started out her career as a human-rights and refugees officer in London and then moved over to VJ hosting for Canada's MuchMusic channel. Now she was hitting the pavement in Los Angeles, trying to book roles. It was an unusual time to be auditioning in Hollywood as a South Asian actor. In 2008, *Slumdog Millionaire* had landed in theaters to uproarious success. The film, which featured an entirely South Asian ensemble, went on to score eight Oscars, along with becoming a critical and commercial hit. "All of a sudden, there was this desire for South Asian cast," Simone recalled.

The actress got to the network-testing level for both *Nevermind Nirvana* and *Outsourced*, a pilot about a workplace in Mumbai. When she didn't land either, she went back to her apartment, a little one-bedroom on

Third Street in Los Angeles, and thought, "Well, that was it. How many all South Asian casts are going to happen? That was my one chance."

Then, a glimmer of hope. Yanklewitz's office called to ask her to come in to audition for the role of Cece in a new Fox show. When Simone read the script pages, she immediately connected with the young woman on the page. The actress prided herself on being a really good friend. She loved that Cece is immediately protective of Jess when she meets her new Craigslist roommates, explaining that she will "crazy murder" them if they let anything happen to her friend. "Yeah," Simone mused. "That's what girlfriends do."

She decided Cece would be bored. Bored of Schmidt, who is trying desperately to impress her by proudly yanking off his shirt. He wouldn't get a big reaction from her, she'd heard it all before, it's a yawn. When Simone arrived for her audition, she discovered that the walls were mercilessly thin. She could hear each actress—well-known actresses—reading for the part of Cece. They all had the same take on the character and none of their versions of Cece matched up to what Simone had in mind. "I'm not going to book it," she thought. "I'm doing a 180 of what I hear through the wall from these very professional working actresses."

Everyone who came in to read for Cece had played her up in an almost exaggerated fashion. Simone was the first person to try something different. Her version of Cece was dry and totally deadpan, refusing to give Schmidt even an inch of attention. "She had that vibe which was exactly what Liz was going for, which is, like, beautiful women don't have to try that hard," Pope remembers. "She doesn't have to work overtime, she's barely acknowledging that he's there."

Amid the *New Girl* audition process, Simone went off to shoot a YouTube series called *H+* in Chile, alongside actress and future *Outlander* star Caitríona Balfe. Simone played a poor, barefoot woman who was the surrogate for Balfe's character's baby. The pair, who became fast friends, discovered they had both auditioned for the role of Cece. It was Simone, though, who got called in to test for *New Girl* while they were shooting.

She raced back to Los Angeles, sand still in her hair from the Chilean desert.

Simone did her studio test and her network test and was told she'd need to wait twenty-four hours or so until she got the news. She spent the day at her friend's apartment in Marina del Rey with her phone beside her. She decided there was no way she was going to get the job—she had a blank résumé!—but it was nice, in that moment, to live in the beautiful possibility of it all.

After hours and hours of waiting, Simone's friend suggested they throw in the towel. "You know what? It's obviously not going to come now. I mean, it's nighttime. Let's just go for a walk."

"Yeah," Simone agreed. "I'm going to leave my phone because if the call does come late at night, it's probably going to be a no."

She added, "Let's just go and live this dream that it's possible for a little longer."

They walked down to the marina and stopped at the corner store for a little bottle of amaretto and a newspaper. Upon returning, the two discovered that they had been locked out of the apartment. Simone lay on the floor of the hallway and read the newspaper until a locksmith showed up three hours later. She picked up her phone to discover roughly forty text messages, emails, and several Facebook messages. When she called her team back, they were so angry and happy at the same time. On the one hand, she should have been by her phone during this important day. On the other hand, she booked it. She had gotten Cece.

Simone wrote a letter to Meriwether, thanking her for casting a South Asian actress. Cece hadn't been written specifically for a South Asian woman, nor had there been any other South Asian women who had tested for the role. "You have no idea what you've done, the ripple effect you've done by kicking the first domino," she explained.

The writer responded, Simone recalled, in the way only Meriwether could. "Oh," she replied. "I just cast the funniest person."

When it came to Coach, Yanklewitz set his sights on Lamorne Morris, a performer trained at Chicago's storied improv school, Second City. Like Simone, he struggled to find his footing in Hollywood, hopping from one audition to another and sleeping in his car when he had to. At one point, Morris told his mom he was done—that Los Angeles wasn't for him and he was moving back to Chicago to teach improv. She sent him all the money in her savings account and told him not to give up. "Pay your rent and figure it out," she said. "You're not quitting."

Morris's breakthrough came with a commercial audition, when he was running late and didn't have enough time to prep. The actor quickly rehearsed the lines in his head during the walk from his car to the waiting room, but when he arrived and someone called "action," his mind went blank. He couldn't remember a single world. So he started improvising. To his delight, the room *loved* it. Not only did he nab that job, but he had lined up three more commercial auditions by the end of the week. And they all had the same note: "Do the thing you did before. Just make stuff up."

The actor would go incredibly big and take risks during auditions, sometimes purposefully making a choice that he knew the casting director wouldn't like. "Even if it's not what the director or producers had in mind, at least it's something that will separate you," he told himself. "It could get you a callback." Morris was learning that the weirder and more creative he got, the more rewards he reaped. It had worked during that fateful commercial audition and it worked when he was auditioning to be a BET VJ, back before his days in Los Angeles. "I got [that job] by being as weird and silly as possible," he'd later tell *The Washington Post*. "Everybody else was being really cool. I could not pull that off if I tried."

Morris booked Twix, Miller Lite, 7 Up, and spots for the Las Vegas Convention and Visitors Authority, which Yanklewitz watched and they all really made him laugh. "I gotta find this guy and get him in," the casting director thought. "He's so weird and so funny." Coach's audition scene involved the character attending a Halloween party in cutoffs, so Morris arrived for his audition in a tiny pair of 1970s-style shorts that left very little to the imagination. His legs were slathered in Vaseline and he paired his bottoms with a crop top.

Yanklewitz had some feedback. "You're the funniest person I've seen," the casting director said. "But you gotta come back with normal clothes on." It was an eye-opening moment for Morris—he had genuinely thought he was supposed to come in dressed as the part.

The role of Coach would come down to Morris and Jerrod Carmichael, an actor and comedian who would go on to create and star in *The Carmichael Show*. Carmichael, Yanklewitz recalled, freaked out over the show's seven-year contract. "He flew out of town and no one could find him," the casting director said.

Morris, meanwhile, was also struggling with making a weighty, potentially career-altering decision. The actor was up for a role in the CBS comedy *The Assistants* and the producers really, really wanted him. So much so that when he read for them, one piped up, asking, "We hear you're testing for *New Girl* tomorrow. Can we ask you to tank that audition?"

Privately, Morris wanted *New Girl*. Not that *The Assistants* wasn't funny but . . . *New Girl* had *Zooey Deschanel* in it. The next day, Morris was sitting in the courtyard on the Fox lot with Yanklewitz, when his agent called. "Shit," Yanklewitz said. He knew what was coming. CBS was going to make Morris an offer. Morris's agent tried to nudge Fox into putting in their offer first, but it was a hard no. So Morris said yes to *The Assistants*, finally putting a clean end to pilot season.

Well . . . not quite. After Morris signed his contract with CBS, Fox reached out again. "Hey," they said in an email to Morris's agent. "If we make Lamorne an offer now, would he accept it?" They were an hour too late.

With Morris out of the picture as Coach, Pope turned a laser focus on a comedian named Damon Wayans Jr. She had been impressed by Wayans Jr.'s audition, which involved him yelling at Jess in an attempt to get her to stop crying. Pope loved how, amid his stern shouting, he was so clearly a good, sweet guy. The actor had found the perfect balance of playing this strong, no-nonsense presence in the loft, while mixing in a warmth and vulnerability. Plus, she liked seeing the dynamic between Zooey as Jess and Wayans Jr. as Coach, with Jess so ably piercing the hard shell around his character.

The actor, whose father is Damon Wayans of *In Living Color* fame, hadn't set out to be a comedian. Yes, he had the early chops for it—frequent *New Girl* director Max Winkler, who went to the same high school as Wayans Jr., remembers hearing from so many people "The funniest person that has ever come to this school is a guy named Damon Wayans Jr."

Still, Wayans Jr. initially steered clear of the family trade, enrolling in Otis College of Art and Design to study animation. A year later he dropped out because of the course load: there were eighteen units and barely any of them were art-focused. Wayans Jr. found his affections shifting from illustrating to writing, starting a job as a punch-up writer on the ABC sitcom *My Wife and Kids*, where he stood on the sidelines and would offer up alternate jokes between takes.

Wayans Jr. started doing stand-up, initially under the name Kyle Green, hoping to avoid comparisons between himself and his dad. Still, the physical resemblance was undeniable and people would call out, "You look just like Damon Wayans!" from the audience.

The young performer began opening for his dad on the road, which offered up even more comparisons. Once, when they were in Boston, Wayans Jr. got on stage in front of thousands of people, approached the mic, and heard one person yell, "You better be funny." It was an intimidating experience for the burgeoning comic.

When Wayans Jr. got the call for *New Girl*, he was waiting to hear if *Happy Endings*, the ABC ensemble comedy he had a starring role in, was being picked up. If Fox was interested in casting him as Coach, he'd be hired in second position, which meant he could shoot the pilot but should *Happy Endings* get the green light, the *New Girl* crew would lose the actor.

Pope was pregnant at the time and had been trekking out to casting sessions as the crew desperately tried to find a replacement for Morris. She was five days away from giving birth and had one mission: *Get the network to approve Wayans Jr.* Yes, it was risky hiring someone who might have to leave to do another show. But privately, Pope didn't really care. She was so confident Wayans Jr. was the right fit for the role that taking a risk with him felt like a no-brainer. What was Fox going to do—cancel *New Girl* if Wayans Jr. ended up leaving?

"Let's make sure we have the absolute best version of the pilot now so we can get to the next step," she told everybody. "We should be so lucky to get that next step."

Blissfully, Fox was on board with Wayans Jr., and the occupants of apartment 4D were, at long last, ready to move into the loft. Around the corner—the joy, thrill, madness, and deep growing pains of Season One had only just begun.

3

The Pilot

Let's take the *Lord of the Rings* references, let's put 'em in a deep, dark cave where no one's gonna find them, ever.

—SCHMIDT

ZOOEY DESCHANEL ARRIVED AT COMPOSER Michael Andrews's studio armed with a chorus for the show's theme song. Her sunshine-covered bop of a tune was designed to give viewers a sense of not only who Jess was but what to expect when they entered the world of *New Girl* for the first time. She wanted it to feel upbeat and uplifting, while buckling the audience in for the new adventure her character was about to embark on.

It would need to be supercatchy, poppy, and colorful, too—like the short, snappy "Love Is All Around" from *The Mary Tyler Moore Show* and the sweeping instrumentals of *That Girl*. The two banged out a theme song in a day that was the melodic embodiment of Jess—warm, endlessly optimistic, vintage, and ready for an exciting journey ahead.

The original sequence was supposed to be a massive musical number filmed at the Museum of Contemporary Art in downtown Los Angeles, featuring hundreds of dancers performing a flash-mob sequence. It was scripted as such:

EXT. LOS ANGELES STREET-DAY

A city street. People walk by on their way to work. A light, bubbly jazzy song starts to play. Suddenly Jess appears whimsically dancing along to the music. She's euphoric—a ball of optimism and energy. People on the street don't know what to make of her. As the song plays, she sings to the passersby and continues to dance.

JESS

Hey sunshine! Whatcha doing?
Hey sunshine! Where ya going?

A DIFFERENT PART OF THE STREET

Jess dances into frame, following an unsuspecting BUSINESSMAN with a briefcase. She dances very close to his body, but he never flinches or looks up from his BlackBerry.

JESS (CONT'D)

You get down and make a frown, she's gonna come and turn it around!

A DIFFERENT PART OF THE STREET

Jess dances into a SCARY GANGSTER-TYPE GUY who looks

like a "real" person on the street, then surprisingly joins Jess in the dance—a time-step tap dance.

JESS (CONT'D)

She's a shot in the arm,
A twinkly eye . . .

AN OPEN PLAZA SPACE

Jess dances across frame with a full body dance, crazy arm movements, 1920s flapper legs.

JESS (CONT'D)

It's like a lollipop with legs just fell out of the sky! Who's that girl?

Jess unwittingly dances right into a large fountain. Not letting that stop her for a moment, she pops back up and does the big finish . . .

JESS (CONT'D)

That's Jess!

There wasn't enough money or time to orchestrate such an elaborate opening so they decided to go with a much smaller, contained idea—Jess cheerfully singing as she's surrounded by a magical world of props, including fluffy cotton-ball clouds and bright blue cardboard buildings, which the guys wheel around to reveal they're back at the loft. The song ends with them holding up bright lime-green signs that read NEW GIRL. No cool flash mob . . . but it did get to the heart of what Baer, Finkel, and Meriwether set out to achieve: something fun and colorful.

As Andrews sat with Deschanel in his studio, he was taken by how charming she was, with a cool edge. Plus, she was a movie star, and at that time, movie stars really weren't doing television. He had a good feeling about this upcoming pilot. "Be careful," he told Deschanel. "You're going to be doing this show for a long time."

When Debra McGuire, the costume designer for *New Girl*, first read the show's pilot script and pictured Jessica Day's look, Crayola crayons came to mind. A big, fresh box of crayons that, when you opened the lid, delighted your eyes with a rainbow of bursting colors. Because that was Jess in a way, McGuire thought. She was such a vibrant person. In those early days of shooting, the costume designer bought vintage clothes for the actress, digging her way through the LA secondhand shop Wasteland and embracing a 1950s silhouette, with fitted bodice tops and flowing skirts. She also turned to Kate Spade and Shoshanna as regular staples for Jess's wardrobe, while finding standouts from budget-friendly brands, like a peacoat made by H&M and the occasional Forever 21 piece. Shoes were typically ballet flats or sensible kitten heels, which would be useful for Jess's frequent dips into physical comedy. Deschanel was given black-rimmed glasses, just like the ones Meriwether wore in real life.

McGuire thought of the character's style as an updated version of Ms. Frizzle, the kindhearted science teacher from the *Magic School Bus* series, who was always decked out in whimsical, ultrabright dresses. As Schmidt later described it, Jess looked like "a drawing of a best friend that an eight-year-old would make." She even wore dreamy, colorful matching pajama sets that McGuire custom made from scratch, inspired by the vintage shape of a man's pajamas and covered in the very things you might find in scenes from children's coloring books: giraffes, balloons, turkeys, and puffy clouds.

Meriwether and Deschanel, alongside makeup artists Jorjee Douglass and Robin Glaser, decided that Jess's look should feel vintage French, akin to Jean Seberg in the 1960 Jean-Luc Godard film *Breathless*, with long, thick eyelashes and a flick of a cat eye. They also wanted that Lucille Ball vibe, where—even when she was in her pj's—she had on a full set of lashes and lipstick. Oh, and big hair. *Lots of it.* "Let's go over the top with everything," Douglass remembers being the ethos. "Make it a comedy."

When it came time to build out the world of *New Girl*, Kasdan turned to production designer and frequent collaborator Jefferson Sage. Sage was hired to construct the show's sets, two of which would be the heart of the show: the Griffin, the bar the whole gang frequented, and apartment 4D, where much of the series would hang its hat.

Before he began his search for the Griffin, Sage met with Meriwether to get the lowdown on what kind of bar she envisioned. "Well, this is where I drink and it feels like it's probably one of those," she said, before offering up a few spots in the city. The production designer kicked off his quest to find the perfect bar, weaving his way through kitschy, divey watering holes dotted throughout Los Angeles.

On the list was the Prince, a far more elegant locale, tucked away behind a ruby-red door amid a slew of beige buildings in Koreatown. The restaurant, built in the 1940s, felt like slipping back into old Hollywood, where dimly lit booths might have once been frequented by women holding long cigarette holders. Decked out in rich red walls and oil paintings, the Prince had a smoky, ornate feeling dripping from every corner. Sage was sold on the space and particularly taken by the horseshoe-shaped bar in the middle, which would allow them to easily shoot Nick, the bartender, interacting with his friends while he worked.

As the production designer searched for the perfect apartment 4D, Sage found himself instinctually heading to downtown Los Angeles. There was an exciting feeling in the air there, where old factories, trucking depots, and warehouses were being converted into sprawling living quarters. He took photos inside those newly minted apartments and would bring them back to Kasdan. "Look at these windows!" he said excitedly. "Look at the light you get."

As much as they wanted to shoot in a real-life apartment, none of the loft layouts made sense for filming, so Sage pieced together elements from the spaces he had checked out on his research trips. During one scouting session, he found himself inside a loft with big factory windows and peered outside. All around were flattop warehouses, telephone wires, and sky. In the distance, downtown Los Angeles stretched out in front of him. "Oh my God, this is LA," he thought. "I've never seen it from this vantage point." That's how the residents of apartment 4D should see the city, too, as young people on the fringe of it all, Sage decided.

After roughly four weeks of prep, executives at Fox wanted to see what Sage, Meriwether, and Kasdan had been up to. By that point, the network was deeply invested in the *New Girl* pilot, a fact that was both flattering and exhausting. The writers had already caught some flack over the fact that the characters didn't seem very far along in their professional lives. "Can everyone just be good at their jobs?" execs asked. Meriwether, Finkel, and Baer pushed back. Viewers weren't meeting these characters at the best point of their lives—they were a little broken, and it was important for the audiences to feel that. Amid all the feedback, Kasdan saw himself as the guy holding the football tightly and trying the best that he could to get it to the end zone.

Kasdan, Meriwether, Sage, and a group of executives gathered in a conference room to check in on the production design. Sage watched as his model of the set was examined, along with all the research he had put into the project. It became clear—almost immediately—that the execs weren't happy. Not just about the model but, Sage noticed, about the show itself. They seemed to be questioning the pilot they had bought and all of that frustration and back-and-forth had culminated in this meeting.

"Why are they living in a loft?" one of them prodded. The model didn't fit the well-worn rubric of the typical living-room and bedroom sets on ensemble shows like *Friends* and *Seinfeld*. Sage felt all the work he had done slipping away from him. He had spent a whole chunk of their prep time on this set and if this concept got vetoed, everything was derailed. He was close to shaking.

Kasdan, who was thirty-six at the time, was typically the youngest person in these meetings. At five foot six, he wasn't a particularly physically dominating presence and, Sage recalled, it could be easy to underestimate him. But at that moment, he quietly stepped into the conversation. He asked a few leading questions that seemed to flummox the perturbed executive, and Sage was asked to leave as they continued their conversation.

The next day, the production designer approached Kasdan. "So, the meeting," he began. "Are we . . . ?"

"Nothing's changed," the director responded.

"*That* is how it's done," Sage thought to himself.

As the production designer began building out the loft, he focused his attention on the centerpiece of the living room: a large sectional where the roommates would congregate. Sage settled on a used leather couch from the secondhand furniture store Casa Victoria, which featured low seating that would force the actors to really sink into the cushions and lean back. It was all about creating the feeling of a comfy space where friends could unwind at the end of the day and, in turn, a place where audiences would feel safe, swept up in the familiarity and ease of this fictional apartment.

Elsewhere, Sage was inspired to create an industrial bathroom, like the ones used by workers at former trucking centers, packed with rows of lockers and a big shower. It would be yet another way of making Jess feel like a fish out of water in this drafty, unfamiliar loft. Her bedroom featured the same fixtures as the rest of the apartment—exposed brick walls and a beam ceiling—with the aim to make the big space feel overwhelming for this newly single young woman who had just moved into a home with three strangers. Still, Sage wanted the room to look like Jess had added her own touch to it, picking out gauzy, colorful lampshades, light floral rugs, and painting the walls a turquoise green.

When the loft was ready, Kasdan brought the cast into the space for the first time and Sage hung around the stage, on hand to field any questions. Slowly, the actors drifted in one by one. They weren't in their exact costumes and makeup yet but quick approximations of what was to come. Without being asked, the group all gravitated toward that big brown couch, nestling into those deep cushions as Kasdan pulled up a chair.

"Fuck," Sage thought, in awe, as he watched them instinctively find their way to their seats, the lights switched on around them. "There they are." It had worked. Apartment 4D was ready for its occupants to officially move in.

Freaks and Geeks was Kasdan's first time directing a pilot. While collaborating with creator Paul Feig and executive producer Judd Apatow, the trio decided that episodes should present themselves as forty-eight-minute minimovies. "Every episode of *Freaks and Geeks* will look and feel like an independent feature film," a visual manifesto for the show read. "The 'documentary' style is transparent. When asked about his acting philosophy, James Cagney said, 'Stand up and tell the truth.' That's all we need to do."

Kasdan brought that same ethos to the *New Girl* pilot, setting out to bring the cinematic experience to network TV. They'd film on location when they could and find spontaneous moments outside the script, which would make apartment 4D feel like it existed beyond its sitcom walls.

The week before shooting the pilot, Kasdan sat all the actors down together. "Who's been a series regular on a single-camera comedy before?" he asked. Nobody raised their hands.

"It's no joke," Kasdan told them. "It's really hard and the hours are tough." It was a fair warning of what was to come, when days would stretch into the morning's wee hours, with the cast and crew bleary-eyed and exhausted, driving home from the Fox lot at daybreak. But for now, the actors were excited and eager, aware of what a huge opportunity this was after years of hopping from one audition to the next, facing rejection after rejection.

Johnson, in particular, found himself entering strange, uncharted territory. After learning that he had landed the role of Nick Miller—along with the pay rate that he'd be making for the pilot—he and his wife drove to one of his favorite Mexican restaurants to celebrate. Visions danced in his mind of the kind of appetizers he was going to order once they arrived.

"I've got some television money coming," he decided. "I'm getting sides, I'm getting extra guacamole. Fuck it. I'm going to get that weird pitcher of margarita. I'm not getting one, I'm telling the waiter—'Do the whole thing!!'" As he thought about his appetizers, so wrapped up in the fantasy that he barely said two words to his wife, Johnson's manager called. The actor picked up his phone with a cheerful "*hellooo*," expecting he was about to get a congratulations.

"Everyone's excited about you playing Nick Miller," his manager began. "They're looking to shoot in six weeks and Fox would like you to lose ten to fifteen pounds."

Johnson had thick skin. It took a lot to offend him. So, when he got upset over the conversation, it wasn't because of the feedback—it was because he knew he wasn't going to be able to eat the meal he had been so excited for. When he and his wife arrived at the restaurant, Johnson asked for a green salad with chicken and no dressing. "When they give you something," he grumbled to himself, "they *gotta* take something back."

Upon arriving on the *New Girl* set, Johnson cut way back on his eating. He shoved power bars in his mouth, restricting his diet so much that Deschanel once made him a plate of food. "You've got to eat," she told him. (As Season One went on, Johnson decided to ditch the expectations and go back to the way he was. "Fuck it," he told himself, "I'm done. I don't care that much. . . . A body is a body, give me a break.")

The pilot opens on a tight shot of Jess, speaking directly into the camera as she details a recent horrifying breakup. We flash back to her in a cab, heading home to surprise her boyfriend, Spencer, with an uncharacteristically sexy present: a striptease complete with a bow over her crotch and a cheerful song. Spencer, it turns out, is not alone. Just as Jess whips around, trench coat down, we see that he's with another woman.

Flash forward, and we're back with Jess in the present day. "So, that happened," she says, with an attempt at a casual, half-hearted shrug. "That's why I need a new apartment." Pause. "I'm sorry, what was the question?"

The camera turns to reveal three guys staring back at her. "Do you have any pets?" one of them, wearing a half-zipped maroon hoodie, responds, bemused.

Those opening moments featured so many devices you're not supposed to use all at once, Kasdan remembers thinking. There's a flashback, a voice-over, a phone call, and a flash-forward, a series of storytelling crutches that were being piled one on top of the other. And yet, as he watched the sequence unfold, it felt so alive and funny and painful. Over the span of less than two minutes, the audience knows who Jess is, understands the setup of the show, and gets an immediate feeling of the tone—a romantic comedy with a self-aware, off-kilter twist. After all, how many TV shows open with the protagonist earnestly deciding her stripper name is Rebecca Johnson? Or actually, wait, no, Boobies Johnson. Two Boobs Johnson!

After some trepidation and through gritted teeth, the guys decide that they'll invite Jess to be their roommate, despite the fact that she sings her feelings and sobs aggressively on the couch. (Side note: this episode would be the first and last time we'd see Jess wearing disheveled loungewear. "Um, no, pajamas," Deschanel remembers telling Meriwether. "They're cuter.")

Originally, the script called for Jess to scream-sob along to "My Favorite Things" as she watched *The Sound of Music.* When the film's estate learned that, later in the episode, the guys would belt out their own version of the classic tune and change the lyrics, they pushed back. It became abundantly clear Meriwether wasn't going to get the permission she needed and she scratched out the reference, replacing it with the seminal song from *Dirty Dancing*, "(I've Had) The Time of My Life." That was all fine and good until associate producer Megan Mascena started digging a little deeper. She assumed the *Dirty Dancing* clip—along with the song—had gotten clearance, as is the case for all music and film footage used in TV shows.

"Who has the paperwork for this?" Mascena asked offhandedly.

"Oh, we haven't started that yet," she was told. Mascena had what she could only describe as a heart attack.

She reached out to the film's star, Jennifer Grey, for permission, and got a blissfully quick sign-off. Patrick Swayze had passed away from cancer in 2009, so Mascena began the process of getting his estate to agree to the scene being used. *New Girl* would go on to feature that song two more times over the course of seven seasons. The second time, they were told, would need to be the last time. The third time, Mascena remembers, they paid "up the butt for it."

As Meriwether found her footing during those early days, she quickly learned that the key to a successful ensemble pilot lay in the well-defined dynamics between each of her characters. It was something of a mathematical equation, which required tabulating how each of the men related to Jess over the course of twenty-one minutes. "Does every character have a really separate relationship with Jess, and separate relationships with each other?" she asked herself.

The writer skillfully used a scene of Jess sobbing on the couch to help set up those relationships. Coach, completely unaware of how to handle emotions, tries to yell at Jess drill-sergeant style and then slinks away, horrified, when he realizes he's made things far worse. Schmidt puts on his den-mother hat and offers to take her out on the town, while also sternly informing her that he does not want to hear any of her *Lord of the Rings* references. Nick stays far, far away from Jess's sobbing. He's hunched in the kitchen, with zero idea of how to deal with her feelings.

Early on, Kasdan offered Meriwether some valuable advice: cast actors you love and write to their strengths. As Pope remembers it, Meriwether had already put so many truthful pieces of herself into Nick and Jess, which bled easily onto the pages of the pilot. The writer embedded her romantic side into Jess, along with her tendency to not totally understand "guy rules" when it came to dating. Much like Nick, Meriwether was holding on to fantasies of what a relationship had been. While she did also hide in her sweatshirt at times, she actually based Nick's tendency to tuck himself into a hoodie on a fellow Obama volunteer who would put his hood up when they were doing data entry so no one would bother him.

Johnson and Greenfield's dynamic, meanwhile, was quickly and organically seeping its way onto the page. When Greenfield arrived in the makeup trailer, he was freshly exercised, morning coffee consumed, and eye masks already applied. Johnson grumpily trundled in wearing flip-flops, a Coca-Cola in hand and sleep in his eyes. Makeup artists Jorjee Douglass and Robin Glaser would hand him a hot towel and a toothbrush to get ready for the day, ribbing him by asking, "Why didn't you shower?" Sometimes he'd wear a ripped-up Patagonia jacket with no shirt underneath. (As Coach later said, when Nick makes a similar fashion choice, "I mean . . . it's a clean look.")

To further cement their odd-couple dynamic, one day, both Greenfield and Johnson arrived on set for haircuts. Greenfield was wearing a cape, which he ripped off when his hair was done to reveal he was wearing very little underneath. "What are you doing, dude?" Johnson yelped. "Why are you naked??"

"I don't want to get hair on my clothes," Greenfield replied.

The writers would later joke that the relationship between Nick and Schmidt wasn't a bromance, it was a full-on romance. And indeed, as episodes went on, it was clear that the pair loved each other in ways guys didn't usually get to love one another on TV, even if Nick grumbled his way through Schmidt's romantic overtures and anniversary parties. The pair were a hat tip to the long-standing creative partnership between Baer and Finkel, who first met doing sketch comedy in Los Angeles and went on to work as a writing duo on *30 Rock*, *United States of Tara*, and the

Friends spin-off *Joey*. "The guys I work with, my partner Dave—it is a real marriage," Baer would later say.

As the pilot kicked into gear, Greenfield was nervous about the likability factor of his character. The script called for Schmidt to rip off his shirt multiple times, obnoxiously ogle Cece, and try desperately to get into a sceney Wild West party. "There's a good chance that I'll never work again after this," Greenfield thought.

The actor approached Kasdan with his concerns. "Let's just try to make this character as not-douchey as possible," he said.

"Well, just don't play him douchey," the director responded.

Greenfield decided to find the deep vulnerability in Schmidt, a trait that would quickly seep into the writing of his character as episodes went on. In his approximation, Schmidt was less of a jerk than a sad little boy looking to be accepted. And as he went through early costume fittings, that vision became even more clear.

Greenfield was trying on different outfit options for the Wild West party, landing on an ensemble that consisted of a black button-up shirt decorated in heavy tassels and a large belt buckle, when an epiphany hit. He looked so silly and the outfit made him look, in his estimation, just unbelievably weird. "*Oh*, he's that guy," Greenfield thought. "He's a ridiculous idiot."

The pilot ends with Jess getting stood up by her date and the guys rushing over to make sure she's okay. It's there that Nick, potentially the least emotionally developed of the bunch, shows a shade of thrilling and unexpected kindness by busting out a rendition of "(I've Had) The Time of My Life" to cheer her up. The guys awkwardly follow suit, begrudgingly at first and then wholeheartedly.

Kasdan was pleased that the scene—as big and broad as it was—also felt grounded.

The singing wasn't great but it wasn't *cartoonishly* bad. They got most of the lyrics wrong but the tune was recognizable and there was an earnestness to the performance that made the moment feel real, like these guys *genuinely* wanted to try to cheer up their new friend. Anyone tuning in was handed a thesis statement for the show in just a few short minutes with that musical number. Life could be crappy but these characters were going to be there for each other through the bad and the really, really bad, to make everything a little bit brighter and well worth laughing at.

Wildly enough, the original script called for Nick and Jess to *almost* kiss as the episode came to a close. In the scene directions, Meriwether wrote, "Jess and Nick exchange an awkward high-five that brings their faces awkwardly close together. We think they might kiss, and, instead, Jess licks Nick's nose. After a beat:

JESS

(singing)

I just licked your nose. That was weird for me too. Why did I do that? That's Jess!

Thankfully that was scrapped—the sexual tension needed way, way more time to build—and in its place, the pilot closes back at the loft, with the whole gang together on the sectional. Schmidt tries to comfort Jess by reassuring her that he would still "do" her and she thrusts a finger in the air, declaring, "Jar!" That small moment was far better than any kiss tease with Nick. Right now, it was more important that the audience understood Jess was officially in the fold of the loft and that this foursome was about to embark on a warm, strange adventure together.

Steve Welch, *New Girl*'s editor, remembers Meriwether being initially shocked by the way television was made. The actors wandered onto set at 7 AM bleary-eyed, did a half-speed run-through of the script, and then started shooting. Meriwether was used to the world of theater, where rehearsals were extensive and nobody saw a final performance until it had been fully worked out. She seemed overwhelmed as she watched the pilot unfold. "These scenes don't work," she told Welch. "None of this is right."

"Don't worry," he reassured her. "This is what editing is for."

Back in his edit bay on the Fox lot, Welch watched early footage of the opening scene. When the bow fell off of a naked Jess, he remembers thinking how unexpectedly risqué the show felt. He came from working on *Malcolm in the Middle*, a family series starring a young Frankie Muniz. This all felt like such a different world. He loved the singing scene, too. The guys serenading Jess with "(I've Had) The Time of My Life" after she had been ditched was so sweetly charming.

Directors usually get a few days to watch the first cut of their episode before anyone else on the creative team, giving them some extra time to tinker with it. Kasdan often found those early cuts rough to watch—his director's brain immediately went to what wasn't working and what wasn't quite there yet.

For the first, and potentially only, time in his career, Kasdan watched an early cut of an episode without complaints. "Oh," he thought. "This is a knockout." He watched it again. Okay, sure, there were little things here and there that would need some work but, still, he was struck by how strong it was, a rarity in the often rushed and stressful process of pilot season. It was a strange feeling to have. They had something really special on their hands.

* * *

Shannon Ryan, Fox's executive vice president of marketing, was on a plane en route from New York City to Los Angeles when she first floated the word *adorkable*. It was a phrase that she and her friends used to affectionately describe their nerdy crushes in high school. Maybe it could be a fitting moniker for their heroine as they rolled out ads for their new show?

Joe Earley, her boss, was instantly sold. The key art for a marketing campaign is often the most challenging—you have *one* brief shot within a static visual to pique a potential viewer's interest. The word *adorkable* might be their ticket to capturing the coveted, fleeting eyeballs of passersby. The marketing team came up with the slogan "Simply Adorkable," which would be printed in red block letters on a plethora of billboards, the sides of buses, and bus stops. Front and center was Deschanel, beaming and wearing a lime-green mod dress.

Alternate key art was also shot of Deschanel alongside the rest of the guys to try to pull in male viewers. Bright-yellow billboards could be found all throughout Los Angeles boasting the tagline "Boys will be boys. Jess will be Jess."

The underlying message was threefold:

- ★ If you love Zooey Deschanel, here she is in this great show.
- ★ If you love ensemble comedies, we've got that, too!
- ★ This is a show men and women can watch together.

Privately, the *New Girl* crew had their concerns about the "adorkableness" of it all. As Welch watched the Fox marketing team throw themselves behind the catchphrase, he started to worry that the campaign was going to kill the show before it even began. "This isn't going to attract the right people," he thought. "It's not necessarily who we were writing the show for." Baer, meanwhile, took issue with using the word *simply* to describe Jess. This character wasn't going to be wrapped up in a neat package, he thought. She was going to have edges and corners and missing pieces.

Early on, Meriwether attempted to be publicly diplomatic when asked about the catchphrase. At a cocktail reception, she told a reporter from *Grantland* that she had "never really seen the character like that." Pressed more on the issue, she allowed, "Yeah, sometimes I hate it."

There would be an added assumption that Meriwether, being both the show's creator and a frequent wearer of Jess-like black-rimmed glasses, was an avatar for her main character, adorkableness and all. In all honesty, though, she thought of herself more like Nick—on the quiet side, self-deprecating, and with a slightly darker view on the world.

Despite mixed feelings behind the scenes, Fox's marketing strategy was working. The chatter around *New Girl* was becoming undeniable. One *Vulture* article released ahead of the premiere noted that the show was getting much more attention than CBS's *2 Broke Girls*, another freshman comedy that seemed to be vying for a young female audience. The answer, writer Jillian Goodman suggested, could be found on Deschanel's Twitter. The star was using her account, with its 600,000 followers, to interact with fans, post her own musings, live-tweet the premiere party, and boost tweets from the *New Girl* Twitter account that, at the time, clocked in at only 13,804 followers.

The actress lived in the Hollywood Hills and would drive her Toyota Prius down Highland to Santa Monica Boulevard on her way to work on the Fox lot. She was sitting in traffic one day when a guy came barreling toward her car and began pounding on her window, sticking his finger at a building covered—top to bottom—in an image of her. The network was putting Deschanel's face everywhere. She got tinted windows after that.

To add extra buzz, Fox decided to release the first episode on Hulu, Fox.com, and iTunes two weeks ahead of the broadcast premiere, a first for a network sitcom. Screenings were held in select cities including, one night, at an old smog-check center in Culver City. *New York* magazine writer Jada Yuan was on the scene that evening, profiling Deschanel ahead of *New Girl*'s release. "I'm not gonna lie. She's the reason I've had bangs for seven years," Yuan overheard one guest whispering, eyeing Deschanel.

That evening, the DVD kept freezing, causing an awkward hush to fall over the room, ice cubes in drinks clinking. After the second freeze, Deschanel called out, "Enjoy this moment, everybody! If it doesn't start again, we'll do it live!" Finally, the technical issues were resolved and the episode played all the way through. The actress stayed until the bitter end that night, doling out hugs to guests and stopping to chat with the show's publicist about an upcoming promotional trip.

"Don't worry," Deschanel said. "I am going to go to New York, and *I will sell this show.*"

The night that *New Girl* premiered, Meriwether dozed off in her office. She had been working late into the night and crashed from exhaustion. At 5 AM, a colleague woke her with the news. The pilot had pulled in 10.1 million viewers, making it the highest-rated show on prime time. Fox won the night with three key demographics—18–49, 18–34, and teens. Not only that, but *New Girl*'s pilot marked the most-watched premiere of a Fox scripted show since *The Bernie Mac Show* debuted in 2001.

The show was picked up to series and Hannah Simone sat in her apartment quite literally basking in the glow of the moment. A giant digital billboard for *New Girl* had been hung right outside and it pooled through the window, bathing the space in yellow light. Nothing felt real after that point, she remembers. The biggest dream of her life had come true.

The cherry on top was the critical reception, which was warm and promising. Of course, there were the critics who had complaints, particularly *The Washington Post*'s Hank Stuever, who declared, on the subject of Jess, "Boy, has she pulled the bangs over everyone's eyes with this atrociously cutesy sitcom . . . Worse still, she sings. 'Did you just make up a theme song for yourself?' one of her new roommates asks. Yes, she did; plug your ears."

Others, though, saw potential for something special down the road. Alan Sepinwall, then a critic at *Uproxx*, offered glowing feedback, deeming *New Girl* the best comedy of the fall season. "I genuinely enjoyed it from start to finish, rather than having to squint real hard and try to picture what it might look like once the producers figure out what to do with their stars," he wrote.

In so many ways, this could have been the rare fairy-tale television story from start to finish. And then Damon Wayans Jr.'s TV show *Happy Endings* got picked up for another season.

4

Welcome to the Loft, Part I

I've done things. I wrote half a book about zombies.
—NICK MILLER

WITH *HAPPY ENDINGS* OFFICIALLY RENEWED, Wayans Jr. was obligated to return to his old show, leaving Coach and the *New Girl* crew behind.

Meriwether, as a result, had to act fast. Losing Wayans Jr. meant roughly 80 percent of her pilot would need to be reshot with another actor in his place. Aside from being costly and time-consuming, the pilot had been such a success that Kevin Reilly, then the head of Fox, didn't want to risk redoing it. "I don't want you to reshoot the pilot," he told Meriwether. "I want you to introduce a new character in the second episode and explain why this other character left."

Being forced to fold a new guy into a show that—by name and concept—was all about a *new girl* sent a collective shiver down the spine of everyone involved.

Adding to the nerves over the loss of Coach was the mounting pressure to keep the tremendous momentum of *New Girl* going. A TV show's second episode, Kasdan told me, is notoriously the hardest of the entire series. You're trying to re-create the magic of the pilot, which had gotten months and months of attention, only this time, there's a week to get it all done and you're already planning the third episode . . . which, by the way, starts shooting the following week! Yes, it was so thrilling that *New Girl* had been picked up after its ratings windfall, but now an urgent question hung in the air: "*What's next?*"

Casting director Seth Yanklewitz was quickly sent back to the drawing board. He was tasked with finding an actor to play a brand new character named Winston, without totally knowing who Winston was. The casting director's mind shot back to Morris, who was so good in his Coach audition. CBS had decided not to move forward with the actor's television show *The Assistants* so there was hope, this time, that they could actually get him.

"Guys, come on," Yanklewitz told the group. "We wanted Lamorne originally, he's the most talented person out there, and he fits this whole world." Privately, Jake Johnson was going through that exact same thought process. The actor knew how funny Morris was—he had seen him in one of his many commercials—but didn't have any sway when it came to casting. What he did have, though, was access to many, many closed-door conversations that had gone down about this new character. After listening to those back-and-forths, he thought he had a pretty good sense of what they wanted.

Johnson got a hold of Morris's contact information and called him. "Dude, come to my house," he said. "I know we don't know each other but, like, it's *gotta* be you, man." Morris took Johnson up on his offer, driving over to his home in Atwater to run Winston's scenes together, drilling into the audition pages over and over again. "I'm not positive," Johnson told Morris as they got to work, "but this is *literally* what they've been saying in the auditions."

Yanklewitz would end up testing a few actors for the role of Winston, but Morris felt like the most natural choice. Meriwether agreed—she had been continually taken by the actor during his revolving door of auditions. He reminded her of a young Eddie Murphy and she loved his comedic energy, which felt manic . . . in a great way.

Morris wasn't the only new guy on the block. After the pilot was picked up, Meriwether, Baer, and Finkel got to work putting together a writers' room—a hodgepodge of talent including Kim Rosenstock, a playwright with an MFA from Yale School of Drama, Berkley Johnson, a longtime writer on *The Tonight Show with Conan O'Brien*, and J. J. Philbin, who cut her teeth on *Mad TV* and *Saturday Night Live*.

Before their interviews, each potential writer was placed in a room to watch the pilot and then instructed to meet with Meriwether, Finkel, and Baer to offer their thoughts. When Nick Adams arrived for his interview, he could already feel the mounting buzz around this new Fox show. His last job had been working on the NBC sitcom *Perfect Couples*, which, despite having a stacked comedic cast of Mary Elizabeth Ellis, Olivia Munn, and David Walton, came and went after one season with very little fanfare. As pilot staffing kicked in, Adams kept hearing about *New Girl*, which was *the* show everyone wanted a job on.

There was a rare, thrilling potential for job security in this new project. TV writers joining brand-new writers' rooms are usually faced with the typical nagging questions: Will the show get picked up? Is it going to be canceled after just a few episodes? The fact that *New Girl* had Zooey Deschanel in it, Adams thought, meant it actually had a good chance to keep going.

Plus, he was struck by how different the pilot felt from other TV shows at the time. Network television was so male-centered. Here was a show that revolved around a young woman, created and written from the perspective of a young woman. That felt exciting. It also just *looked* visually striking. Unlike so many sitcoms before it, there was a cinematic quality to the way *New Girl* was shot. And it took audiences out of the studio and onto locations, grounding the story in the real world.

With a staff hired, the newly formed group of *New Girl* writers gathered for the first time in a sleek white building on the Fox lot, decked out in glass windows and rows of balconies, that would later double as Schmidt's office. As they settled in for the first day, the room addressed their biggest, most glaring issue: Who was Winston and what were they going to do with this new character, who had replaced Coach out of the blue? "It was one episode," Adams remembers Berkley saying as he tried to reassure everyone. "I know it feels like a lot, but it's just the pilot."

The writers decided to explain away Coach's absence by slipping into the script that he moved to Santa Monica. (In the scope of LA terms, the Arts District and Santa Monica make for a decently long-distance friendship.) Winston, in the meantime, would start out as a shaky sketch of a character who mimicked echoes of Coach's jocky blueprint. The writers introduced him as a childhood friend of Nick's, who had been away playing professional basketball in Latvia. One early scene called for Morris to shoot a basketball into a toy hoop that hung in the loft, a small nod to the audience of who this character was. Meriwether began to question if an athletic persona was quite the right fit for Morris after he struggled to get the ball in the hoop, take after take.

"We have to change this character," she thought to herself.

The writers decided to shift gears and focus on Winston's career, sending him on a soul-searching journey that spanned a nanny gig and sports radio. As they experimented with different versions of Winston, Morris felt like he was part of a sketch-comedy show, trying on a new character in each episode. As he worried more and more that his lack of material would get him kicked off the series, he would jokingly, and not-so-jokingly, say to Meriwether, "I don't want to move to Santa Monica, don't let me move to Santa Monica."

Looking back, Adams suspected they could have just had Winston work at a bank and called it a day. But at the time, there was a laser focus on trying to figure out what made him unique. Jess was odd in her own way, as were Nick and Schmidt and, later on, Cece. In the beginning, Winston was the rational voice in the loft, the reactor instead of the instigator, which left very little for Morris to play with. It became clear that there was one central question that needed to be answered: What was Winston's particular brand of oddity?

Out of all of the cast, Morris seemed the most wide-eyed about being the star of a big network TV show. Early on, first assistant director Michael Risoli caught the actor frowning and asked him what was going on. Turns out, his tooth was really bothering him and he didn't have a dentist to go to. Morris was startled when, suddenly, the entire production crew was getting to work on not only finding him a dentist but getting him an appointment that very afternoon.

"Oh my God," Risoli remembers him saying. "I can't believe all of you are working on this."

Despite anxiety around Winston and the pressure of living up to the pilot, *New Girl*'s second episode, "Kryptonite," in which Jess is forced to reunite with her ex-boyfriend, was the top-rated show in its category, beating out reliable hits like *NCIS* on CBS and *Dancing with the Stars* on ABC. Fox swiftly ordered eleven more episodes, bringing Season One to a whopping total of twenty-four episodes. As *The New York Times*' Bill Carter put it, the network's supersized order served as "a signal that Fox wants as much *New Girl* as it can get."

* * *

Ahead of shooting his first *New Girl* episode, "Wedding," director Jason Winer studied the pilot. He was struck by how the shots were set up. There's a tendency for broadcast pilots to spend extra time getting as much footage as possible of the actors, which can lead to a lot of single shots, with the camera trained on one actor at a time. But *New Girl* avoided that. The show only had about twenty minutes to get the audience to fall in love with these four characters, and it did so through a slew of scenes that included all of them in the same frame, allowing the connection between the group to breathe and grow.

Winer used that very same technique for "Wedding." The premise involved Jess, Nick, Winston, and Schmidt attending nuptials where Nick's ex-girlfriend Caroline is in attendance. Nick, still bruised from the breakup, orchestrates a scenario where Jess pretends to be his girlfriend so he doesn't fall apart around Caroline. Their tactic works almost too well—Caroline starts cozying up to Nick and flirting with him, getting his hopes up before she promptly crushes them by revealing she has a boyfriend.

Nick falls apart after that, getting wildly drunk and planting himself in a photo booth. What unfolds from there shows not only the potential spark between him and Jess but the strength of his new roommate, who—up until that point—was presented as so breakable, the person whom the guys always needed to uplift and support.

"Hey," Jess says to Nick, as she squeezes in next to him. "She has a boyfriend."

"Yeah."

"She shouldn't have been flirting with you all night. You can't be her backup lane. You have to let each other go."

Nick doesn't say anything and Jess continues, with a gentle sternness, "So, now you have to make a decision—am I going to stay locked in a photo booth for the next hour? Or am I going to get out there, take my shoes off, and dance my face off?"

The two were sitting so intoxicatingly close together, and Winer didn't want single shots. He filmed the pair in a two-shot, allowing the audience to feel the chemistry bubbling just beneath the surface. The characters had such a great Spencer Tracy—and—Katharine Hepburn—like sexual tension, Deschanel realized while shooting that episode, there's a little bit of hatred and love all wrapped into one. It felt special, she thought, a kind of rapport you didn't see very often.

The next scene caused the network to quickly bump "Wedding" up in its schedule.

Jess, Nick, Winston, and Schmidt find themselves together at the end of the party, each dejected and rejected in their own ways. Nick realizes that he and Caroline will never get their happily ever after. Jess is stung by how dismissive the guys have been toward her, trying to box her into some sort of socially acceptable character for the evening. Schmidt's chances with his dream crush have been dashed. Winston has no idea what his professional career holds.

As Phil Collins's "A Groovy Kind of Love" starts to play, Nick beckons Jess to the dance floor. He's been a jerk to her, and as a way of making amends, he starts doing the very move he knows she loves so much: a slowed-down version of the chicken dance. Jess, surprised and delighted, joins him, and Winston and Schmidt quickly follow. They dance the chicken dance in a sea of purple lights, the night feeling a little less bad.

Winer really wanted to use a crane for that last shot, sweeping above the roommates as the evening came to a close. Cranes are expensive, so the director put in an impassioned pitch to producer Erin O'Malley. "I really want to go up, up, up at the end of this," he said. "I think it will make this ending dance feel big and special." Winer wanted to offer up the same kind of drug that the ending of the pilot had.

O'Malley agreed and Winer set up his shot in the ballroom of a hotel next door to the Fox lot. Just above them, there was a striking chandelier, giving the whole room a glittery, romantic feel. Winer directed the camera to move up in one smooth motion, delivering a sweeping view of the whole party and ending on that chandelier, which left the audience with a little sparkle.

As he watched the dance unfold from behind the camera, Winer found himself giggling. He was giddy. Not just because the scene was funny (he was particularly pleased by how Greenfield was committing to the slow chicken dance) but because it was all coming together, in its own wonderfully strange way—the odd rhythm of the dance to the music, and the story dovetailing together. Clear as a whistle, you could *feel* the love and support among this group of friends, which was exactly what the show was all about. It was also a reminder, courtesy of Meriwether, that this was not a show about a weird girl surrounded by a bunch of guys saying, "You're weird." This was a chance to move that narrative aside and let them all be oddballs together.

The first season would be all about trying to figure out what, exactly, the show's identity was. "I don't know? Is this it? Is that it?" the writers asked themselves, jumping from the slapdash and absurd—Nick and Jess almost having a three-way with their grumpy landlord—to sweet, unifying moments, like the guys backing Jess up as she stands up to her jerky ex-boyfriend. Then they decided to poke the boundaries of the show even further, going just about as dark as *New Girl* would ever get.

"Injured," which aired in March 2012, didn't start out as an episode about cancer. It began as a *Downton Abbey* parody that morphed into a story about Nick's parents coming to visit. In the original script, the pair ends up having very loud sex, with the kicker being that his dad is *also* named Nick, so he's forced to listen to his mom scream his name in the throes of ecstasy. The network didn't respond well to either of those options, leaving the writers to quickly scramble for a different concept. They came up with this:

Nick gets tackled too hard by Jess in a football game, forcing him to go to the doctor, which he hates to do. There, it's discovered he has a lump in his neck that he needs to get biopsied in case it's cancer. The possibility of his life-threatening illness brings the gang together and also drives a wedge between Nick and Jess, as both share some hard truths they've been thinking about each other.

At first, the writers figured an episode entirely about a cancer scare would be too intense, and decided to lighten the load by featuring a crazy B plot that involved Russian models. There was still something off about the script, and when the pages were handed over to Kasdan, he plucked out the glaring issue.

"You know what the problem with this thing is? Here's the story," he said, before pointing to Nick's cancer plot. "All five of these people would be weighing in on their friend's situation, there's enough comedy over here. Trust yourselves."

The writers decided to commit to an episode that didn't dance away from Nick's emotional journey with silly B plots about models. As the gang collectively prepare for Nick to get his biopsy test the next day, they spend the evening in the Griffin, performing impromptu raps ("Nick Mill-ah, Nick Mill-ah, he's the illest of the ill . . .") while getting progressively drunker. At the same time, tension begins to mount between Nick and Jess. Jess tries to make Nick, who is high on pain pills, feel better by telling him a Daniel Boone joke. Nick informs her that she's not allowed to speak at his funeral. "My funeral is my time to shine!" he declares.

(That moment was inspired by a real conversation Meriwether had with her good friend Matteo, when the pair got drunk together one night in New York. Matteo told Meriwether that he didn't want her to speak at his funeral, a statement Meriwether found hurtful to her core—but also undeniably funny.)

"I don't want Daffy Duck voices and feelings sticks," Nick explains to Jess. "You don't know how to be real. I can't have you trying to cheer people up."

Jess looks down, clearly crestfallen. "I know how to be real," she says softly. Nick, very nonsoberly, moves on from the conversation as he gestures to the space above his head. "Am I wearing a hat?" he asks.

The gang's bar time is cut short when Jess steps in to challenge Nick's criticism of her. "You want me to get real and stop being cutesy or whatever?" she says. "Fine, let's get real. You don't do anything. What did you want to do? I mean, isn't there something you wanted to accomplish?"

"I've done things. I wrote half a book about zombies."

"Okay, just tell me," she replies, softening. "If you could do anything, what would you do?"

"You know, I'm the guy who—I can't just jump into something if I don't know what's going to happen, I never have been that guy. Like, if everybody went into the ocean and jumped in the water . . . well, I'm the guy on the beach guarding the wallets."

That whole bar scene ended up being one of Steve Welch's personal favorites to edit.

"I'm going to shut my door," he told Meriwether. "I'm going to have a bottle of whiskey, I'm going to stay all night, and I'm going to cut this scene." Welch did just that. He pieced together a wealth of different takes and runs, drinking his whiskey in solidarity with the late-night, boozy occupants of the Griffin.

Welch marveled at the sheer focus of the fivesome as he sifted through the footage. Despite the hazy drunkenness of the scene, each of the actors knew exactly what they were doing with their bits, including Greenfield, who perfectly balanced showboating with agonizing over Nick's health. At one point, Morris sat down at the piano and started playing. He was miming, so Welch—who doesn't play piano—pulled out a little iPad piano and went to town. He messed around with the tune until he was satisfied, doing several takes and then splicing them together.

It was one of the few scenes Meriwether watched in the editing room that she didn't want to touch. "I'm scared to unravel it," she said.

After the bar, the gang heads to the beach, with Jess giving Nick the opportunity to try something he's always wanted to do, even though it's scary and unknown. He jumps into the ocean while everyone else hangs back guarding the wallets. The experience is terrible. He hates it—it's very cold—but still, he *did* it. They filmed that scene on a chilly evening in Santa Monica and the night stretched on, past the fourteen hours that was allotted for the cast and crew to work. "We almost all got fired," first assistant director Michael Risoli recalled.

By the end of the episode, it's revealed that Nick doesn't have cancer. As he goes to pay for his visit—offering the receptionist a mixture of paper money, change, and a check that has a "sixty/forty chance of clearing"—he discovers that his friends have chipped in to cover the bill. It's a simple moment that delivers the same satisfying magic of the "Wedding" episode. The foursome is there for Nick during an uncomfortable time in his life and it's not a schmaltzy reveal, just kind and emotionally satisfying.

Fox didn't want to air "Injured" in the slot it was originally intended for and shoved it to later in the season. ("What are you doing? "Please don't do this!" was their original response to the episode.) When it finally aired, the storyline caught some critics by surprise.

"Injured" earned praise from *AV Club*'s Erik Adams, who delighted in the "emotional heft" of the episode. "'Injured' nails emotional cues that were out of *New Girl*'s range at the beginning of the season," he wrote. "I'm taking an immediate shine to the episode because I like that the show can pull off a half hour that mixes pathos and humor as capably as 'Injured.'"

Adams also posed an interesting question. "Is it just me," he asked, "or does it seem like *New Girl* uses opportunities . . . to talk about the show itself?"

Why, yes. The writers were absolutely doing that. Nick's criticism of Jess was a thinly veiled mirror that reflected the criticisms lobbed at *New Girl* since it premiered—and the sharp jabbing Deschanel experienced prior to that. Critics had plenty to say about Jess, the actress who played her, and the way both existed within their respective worlds. As the show hit its stride mid-season, Meriwether geared up to offer her rebuttal.

5

Welcome to the Loft, Part II

I *have* touched glitter in the last twenty-four hours.

—JESS DAY

THREE MONTHS BEFORE *NEW GIRL* premiered, a Tumblr post penned by comedian Julie Klausner began circulating around the internet. Titled "Don't Fear The Dowager: A Valentine to Maturity," the piece criticized adult women who acted like "little girls" and "manic pixie Muppet Babies." While the essay didn't call out Deschanel by name, it did include an embedded tweet from the actress, which read, "I wish everyone looked like a kitten."

"There's so much ukulele playing now, it's deafening," Klausner wrote. "So much cotton candy, so many bunny rabbits and whoopie pies and craft fairs and kitten ephemera, and grown women wearing converse sneakers with miniskirts. So many fucking birds."

She added: "The larger issue is that it is a lot easier for men—or even guys or bros—to demean us, if we're girls. It's much harder to bring down a woman, or to call her a moron, when she's not in pigtails and Ring Pops."

In turn, Deschanel challenged the idea that girliness was considered a nonthreatening attribute. "I mean, I can't think of a more blatant example of playing into exactly the thing that we're trying to fight against. I can't be girlie? I think the fact that people are associating being girlie with weakness, *that* needs to be examined," she told *New York* magazine. "I don't think that it undermines my power at all."

More of the same criticism tumbled in. *The New Republic* published an article titled "Enough Quirkiness! Why I Can't Stand Zooey Deschanel," which took issue with the fact that the actress presented herself as an "adorable oddball," poking fun of her for such (deeply inoffensive) things like her harmonica playing and a doodle she'd drawn of a robot gardening. There were plenty more articles and blog posts targeting Deschanel for being, in their approximation, too cutesy, too quirky, too kooky, too feminine.

When *New Girl* debuted, *The Washington Post*'s review declared that Deschanel was playing a part meant for someone "about a decade younger" and gave the show's pilot a resounding *F*.

It all felt like a double standard to Meriwether. There was this idea that any form of immaturity and/or embracing of girlhood in a female character couldn't be seen as funny. Meanwhile, Judd Apatow movies, then the hottest theater ticket in town, frequently featured stories about men who acted like boys, which was often used both for comedic means and as a helpful vehicle to explore the character's growth.

Whenever Jess was accused of being "too this or too that," Meriwether thought about Diane Keaton, who had helped inspire her protagonist. "She's so massively, heart-wrenchingly funny, and she is never just playing one thing," Meriwether said. "Funny women aren't feminist symbols. Funny women are honest women. I guess that's also true for men, but no one ever asks me if my male characters are presenting a negative image of masculinity."

Something about Jess hit a pain point for critics, who seemed to view the character—and Deschanel—as an offense to feminism. It's no wonder that, in 2013, the internet was set ablaze when Deschanel declared herself a feminist—and a "fucking feminist" at that.

"I'm just being myself," she told *Glamour*. "There is not an ounce of me that believes any of that crap that they say. We can't be feminine and be feminists and be successful? I want to be a fucking feminist and wear a fucking Peter Pan collar. So fucking what?" Articles were swiftly written accompanied by big, bold headlines—"Zooey Deschanel Is a Feminist," *The Cut* declared, with writer Kat Stoeffel pointing out that the actress had put a "refreshing twist on the lady mag staple 'I'm not a feminist, but' quote." She also applauded Deschanel for pushing back on a question about wanting kids. "That is so personal, and it's my pet peeve when people press you on it," Deschanel replied. "And it's always women who get asked! Is anybody saying that to George Clooney?"

In an article headlined "Zooey Deschanel declares her feminism," *Salon* reporter Mary Elizabeth Williams noted that "after an appalling rash of high-profile women, including Marissa Mayer, Carla Bruni, Katy Perry and Melissa Leo apologetically insisting that they refuse to call themselves feminists, it turns out that the kewpie from the sitcom is the one bold and confident enough to announce [it]."

Looking back on the negativity once leveled at her, Deschanel told me, "There were a lot of people who were kind of making fun of me. . . . I have a good sense of humor but I was also like . . . I graduated cum laude from high school, I went to Northwestern, I'm not dumb just because I like to craft."

Meriwether ended up penning the episode "Jess and Julia" in response to all the negative noise, a decision that, to this day, touches Deschanel. In it, Jess butts heads with Nick's new girlfriend, Julia (Lizzy Caplan), a decidedly unfrilly lawyer, who tells a dismayed, cupcake-making Jess that she's "not really a dessert person." When Jess asks Julia to help her get out of a traffic ticket she got while braking for an injured bird, Julia lets slip how she really feels about her.

"You never know, the judge might buy into this whole thing," she says, gesturing to Jess. "Your whole thing, with the cupcakes and the braking for birds and bluebirds come and help me get dressed in the morning. The big beautiful eyes, that makes you look like a scared baby. I'm sure that gets you out of all kinds of stuff."

The two end up going head-to-head by the end of the episode, with Meriwether allowing Jess to go off on her detractors. Yes, she tells Julia, she *does* brake for birds. *Yes*, she does rock a lot of polka dots. And yes, she *has* touched glitter in the last twenty-four hours.

"I'm sorry I don't talk like Murphy Brown, and I *hate* your pantsuit," Jess tells her. "I wish it had ribbons on it or something to make it just slightly cuter. And that doesn't mean I'm not smart and tough and strong."

Before storming off, she concludes, "I'm about to pay this eight-hundred-dollar fine and my checks have baby farm animals on them, *bitch*."

Triumphant as the moment was, Meriwether didn't make Julia the villain of that episode. Despite the fact that, by design, it's a retort to Jess's critics, the audience also better understands Julia and her insecurities. We get why she finds Jess threatening—Jess is someone whom Nick might turn to when he needs support and offers something Julia feels like she can't deliver. Amid the anxieties of a new relationship, this is all terrifying and deeply relatable stuff.

Yes, there were detractors, but there were also the women who had fallen in love with Jess and her unapologetic ability to march to her own drum. At a PaleyFest event, young girls handed Deschanel their ukuleles to sign. Another asked the actress to autograph her microphone. A schoolteacher stood up at the event and shared that her seventeen-year-old daughter looked up to Deschanel and her "überadorkability." "I hope you stay around," she told the actress.

"This is progress in some way," Meriwether said to *Entertainment Weekly*, when asked about the young women who were responding to her protagonist. "From now on, I want to see more new, great, weird, fucked-up women on TV."

At the same time, the writer—while still embracing what made Jess Jess—was interested in seeing her evolve and grow as a character. That meant strategically curating her love interests in Season One, each of whom would help nudge her in the direction of discovering what she wants and needs from a partner. The writers had put careful thought into whom her first boyfriend should be, deciding that it would be interesting to match her up with a male version of herself. They'd assign the character all of Jess's singsongy earnestness while dialing that volume up several notches louder.

Enter Paul Genzlinger.

Played by Justin Long, Jess's new love interest was a teacher at her school: an intrinsically sweet person who sings, plays the fiddle, and doesn't quite know how to hang out with Jess's guy roommates in any sort of cool or organic way. As the writers developed Paul, the character shaped into someone who would crawl under Nick's skin in very specific ways. Deschanel and Johnson had such a clear, palpable connection, but it felt far too soon to touch that yet. Instead, they turned their attention to Paul and Nick. Paul bothers Nick. He doesn't like the fact that Paul makes small talk about the autumn nip in the air or calls his beer a "pumpkin ale." Of course, Nick dislikes Jess's boyfriend for other reasons he doesn't quite understand yet, too. Jess has to beg her roommate not to be mean or make his "little turtle face" around Paul.

Few guest stars embraced *New Girl*'s openness to improvisation like Justin Long. The actor would sit in his trailer ahead of shooting, diligently working on his scenes and thinking about what he wanted to do and how he wanted to do it. He took an immediate shine to Johnson, Morris, and Greenfield, and would try in earnest to milk any opportunity to talk to them in scenes, even if there was nothing scripted between their characters.

Take the time Paul arrives at the loft to pick up Jess for a date. It was supposed to be a simple scene between himself and Deschanel, but Long couldn't resist trying to say hi to the guys in the background, attempting to throw some lines at them, as they threw lines right back. Each time, Deschanel seemed to be getting—he *hoped* playfully—annoyed, and with every take, she opened the door less and less until she finally just offered Long a sliver of her face, so it would be too much for him to crane his neck and talk to the guys.

Johnson and Long's biggest scene took place during a drive to the store to pick up walnuts in the episode "Thanksgiving." The two actors ended up improvising a large chunk of it, with Long ad-libbing lines along the way, like, "Oh, Mr. Copycat, that's where I get my copies made!" Johnson, Long noticed, always passed the comedy ball, asking a question or making a statement that he knew would set up his scene partner to say something funny. He was never chasing his own jokes, and rather seemed to have a clearheaded image of the whole scene ahead of time, along with the nooks and crannies of what would make it as amusing as possible. "I could do this all the time," Long thought as the two pretended to drive around Los Angeles with a green screen in the background.

On set, Long leaned into physical comedy. Sometimes it was small, like making the choice to escape out the elevator door at the *exact* same moment it closed, leaving him alone with the corpse of the gang's neighbor Mrs. Beverly. Or it could be over-the-top wild—like the time Long made the unscripted decision to launch himself over the couch after discovering said dead body. It was a big move, to be sure, especially because there was no padding on the other side, but Johnson, Greenfield, and Morris always laughed when he made big moves.

Berkley, who wrote the episode, loved it. Others . . . maybe not so much. "This isn't *Three's Company*," someone cracked when they saw the cut, and the heroic bit of action improvisation got edited out. Long was a little bummed when he watched the episode and saw that the couch flip hadn't made it in. He had put his body through quite a large tumble.

The crew would have to stifle laughter when Long entered the room to greet the guys and then—again unscripted—said, "What's up, Washington." (Additional mispronunciations of Winston's name he tried out included "Winstons" and "Wimbledon.") What didn't make the cut was Morris, as Winston, correcting him, and Long, as Paul, continuing to politely challenge him on his own name. At one point, he also made the choice to call Nick Nicholas. Long figured Paul would want to be respectful to Jess's roommate by bringing out the grandeur of his full name.

Jess and Paul become an official couple following the "Thanksgiving" episode and, shortly after, attend a Christmas party together. The whole group was walking up the set of stairs that led to Schmidt's office when Long tripped on one of the steps.

"Okay, let's go again," Winer, who was directing the episode, called out, assuming it was a mistake. Next take, Long tripped on the same step again. Then it happened again.

Winer realized that the actor wasn't accidentally slipping, he had made a character choice to do so. The director found himself getting frustrated—he was trying to film the scene in one shot and he felt like the tripping was distracting for the other actors.

Later, he saw the take. "No," he thought. "It makes it interesting. It's hilarious." (Go back and watch that scene. You'll catch a millisecond of a trip and have a new appreciation for the full-throated commitment Long brought to making Paul Genzlinger as awkward as possible.)

Long taught Johnson an important lesson while he was guest starring on *New Girl*. Johnson had been so afraid he'd get fired in those early days and terrified that the town would turn on him. "It used to be—it's less so now that there's new things like podcasts and independent media—but there were gatekeepers," Johnson recalled. "There were like eighteen people and if those eighteen people didn't like you, you didn't get to live your dream. And if those eighteen people—who were not funny and who were not übertalented—if they decided you weren't it, your dream is over, go back home, get on the Greyhound, and get the hell out of here."

It was wild for Johnson to see Long just . . . not care about all that. This is supposed to be really fun, he told Johnson, and it's okay if sometimes people are a little mad at you. His outlook seemed to be "I'm here to make you guys laugh, to make the audience laugh, and make people in this room laugh. I'm not kissing ass." Johnson took Long's perspective to heart and, as he told me, "I will always love him for it."

Paul and Jess have sex for the first time in the episode "Bad in Bed," leading to a comedy of errors that involves Mae West impressions and near-death choking. Turns out, Jess is insecure about her sexual abilities after her ex cheated on her, which leads her to go way overboard with Paul, dirty talking in old-timey accents, pretending to be a lumberjack, and donning a complex starfish lingerie set. Deschanel experimented with several voices, trying to figure out which one sounded the most bizarre coming out of her mouth. She settled on what can perhaps best be described as an older woman from the 1920s with a cold. Long didn't expect that voice to come out of her mouth and he quickly tried to shield his face with her back so the camera wouldn't catch him laughing.

It's all broad, outlandish comedy for sure, but Jesse Peretz, the director of the episode, remembers wanting to find the grounded emotion behind it all. The scene needed to land in a real way, with the audience feeling Jess's insecurity and vulnerability, along with Paul's decision to play along because he genuinely likes her. The crux of the humor, Long felt, was in two people performing being comfortable about something they're absolutely not. There was also something heartbreaking about it, too, he thought.

Every week, *Vanity Fair* writers Bruce Handy and Juli Weiner would weigh in on the latest episode of *New Girl*, offering a male and female perspective of each new chapter. Handy applauded the show's rare spotlight on women and their awkwardness around sex, a narrative that was oft ignored.

"I love the idea of an episode about female sexual anxiety, after how many Woody Allen and Anthony Michael Hall and Jon Cryer and Matthew Perry and Jason Biggs and Steve Carell and Michael Cera movies and TV shows devoted to male sexual anxiety," he wrote. "Even on *Sex and the City*, the frankest series about sex in the city I can think of, did the women ever worry about being bad in bed?"

Paul ends up not being the right fit for Jess. Sweet and amiable, he doesn't offer the spark and friction she needs to go the distance with him. For the first time, she finds herself in the power position of a relationship, feeling her way around an uncomfortably new dynamic. "I am *always* the one who loves more," Jess tells Nick. "That's my thing." We see her inching one step further away from the person we met in the pilot and one step closer to who she'll become.

As the writers' room developed Jess's next boyfriend, Meriwether wanted to nudge the character even further out of her comfort zone. "Let's have her fall for someone who it's hard for her to be with, or challenges some part of her character," Meriwether decided. She had grown concerned that her protagonist was getting too much of what she wanted.

The result was Russell, a sophisticated father played by Dermot Mulroney, who would've fit comfortably as a Cary Grant–esque character in a 1940s screwball comedy. He's debonair, wears expensive suits, lives in a beautiful house, and doesn't text Jess—he calls her. Though the outline was all there, the writers didn't have a full grasp on Russell until the very first table read, when Mulroney opened his mouth to speak.

His voice, Adams remembers, was so deep, so gravely, and hit a different register from anyone else in the cast. "Oh, that's a *man* talking," one of the writers declared. They decided to play up Mulroney as the grown-up in the loft, who would serve to not only push Jess but also challenge the rest of the group as well. Well, mostly Nick, who views Russell as the epitome of what a real man should be. Jess's new boyfriend has an extra cell phone, carries a pen in his pocket, and owns a sophisticated-looking desk that looks like it would be the perfect place to veto legislation. As Jess falls for Russell, so, too, does Nick.

Once again, though, Russell doesn't quite give Jess what she wants out of a partner—the excitement isn't all there and she's never fully herself around him. Even though Jess isn't *quite* putting two and two together yet, she longs for the kind of push and pull that she gets from her roommate, Nick. As the first season draws to a close, she breaks up with her fancy man, while the rest of the gang face their own forks in the road.

The finale sees Nick yanking his car onto a dusty desert hilltop outside of Los Angeles, after having second thoughts about moving in with Caroline, his on-again, off-again girlfriend. Setting those last scenes far from the comfort of the loft forced the characters to deal with a litany of issues they had with one another and themselves. Jess thinks Nick is settling by going back to his ex-girlfriend. Nick is frustrated that his friends aren't being more supportive of this new chapter in his life. Schmidt, who recently started dating Cece, is threatened by her handsome co-worker. Cece is hurt by Schmidt's distrust of her. And Winston is terrified of the fast-approaching darkness of night.

While the fivesome grappled with their demons, the writers wanted to show how far the characters had come since that pilot episode. By taking them out of the loft and into no-man's-land, they reminded the audience that these people were no longer just roommates. They were all deeply embedded in one another's lives.

To shoot the desert scenes, director Michael Spiller and the cast and crew headed to Red Rock Canyon Park. The landscape, with its colorful, jagged rocks tucked into the Santa Monica Mountains, was a frequent location for Westerns and felt far, far away from their comfy Fox studios. There was a chill in the air that night and the cast filmed deep into the morning, Deschanel wrapped in an old oversized coat because Meriwether wanted Jess to wear one of Nick's beat-up jackets. Spiller remembers questions hanging over them that night—a feeling of unknown. As the season drew to a close, what would tomorrow bring for *New Girl*?

Greenfield was usually so friendly and chatty but he kept to himself before shooting his scene with Simone, which involved an insecure Schmidt breaking Cece's heart by ending their relationship. The actor walked around solo, earphones in, listening to Jeff Buckley's "Last Goodbye." He was in a high-focus mode.

"Okay, this is the last episode of this season," he remembers thinking. "You get a break after this . . . this is it, this is the end . . . you get to bookmark this like a movie and this is your last scene."

Greenfield had put everything he had into that first season. In his spare time, he even took it upon himself to create an online dating video for Schmidt. The footage—which is on YouTube and has impressively high production value—features Greenfield as Schmidt pitching himself as a potential romantic partner. It was shot to look like *The Hills'* opening credits sequence, complete with "Unwritten" by Natasha Bedingfield crooning in the background. Schmidt can be seen cheekily wandering around the streets of Los Angeles, complete with lower thirds that tout his "chill" and "style." "Did you edit this?!" Jake Kasdan asked him when he saw the video. Yes, Greenfield absolutely did.

"I wanted it to work so badly," Greenfield told me. "I didn't want to go back to testing for shows, I wanted to be on a show for a while."

Simone and Greenfield were tired, dusty, and had spent so much time sitting around, waiting to film their breakup scene. Both were dealing with their own share of emotions as Season One came to a close, the uncertainty of a next-season pickup lingering. Simone wondered if she'd ever get an opportunity like this again. Greenfield, she knew, had worked so hard to get to where he was right now. She felt like they both channeled everything they were experiencing into that breakup scene, capturing the feeling of loving something so much that you'd do anything for it.

Back in the edit bay, Welch watched his oversized thirty-eight-minute cut of the finale and didn't want to touch it. There was so much good stuff in the desert, and he loved the idea of luxuriating a little longer as the sun set and the gang sang "Breakfast at Tiffany's" while dancing to an old mixtape of Nick's. "Can we just ask—is there *any way* we could get a longer episode for this one?" he said to Meriwether.

Alas, they couldn't. So much of that fun, loose material Welch hoped to get in there wouldn't see the light of day. Still, as the viewer, you felt a cozy warmth of camaraderie as they drank beer, bundled up in jackets, cocooned in the bubble they had created for themselves as they danced on the edges of adulthood.

Nick doesn't end up moving in with Caroline. Late at night, in a quiet, empty loft with a Nick-sized hole in it, Jess peeks out her window and sees his moving truck down below. The opening notes to Nick's mixtape begin wafting from his room. Her roommate is back and Jess leaves her bedroom, leans against the doorframe, and looks out across the hallway at him, a little smile playing on her lips.

"Welcome back, you clown," she says.

The last moments of the finale end on a warm, euphoric note, with each of the characters in their respective rooms, dancing their hearts out. "This is what we're going out on," Spiller reminded the cast before shooting that scene. "This is what your audience is going to see before the long summer break, waiting for the show to return."

Spiller made sure that music was actually playing as they all danced with joyful abandon. In moments like that, which required actors to completely let go in front of forty or so crew members, the director liked to jump in and dance alongside them, encouraging the cast to shed any remnants of self-consciousness.

Those final minutes of "See Ya" ended up being the perfect *New Girl* bow on a season that had spent much of its time trying to figure out what exactly it was. As the episode came to a close, we were left with a reminder that we'd have a fun, welcoming apartment to return to when summer break was over, where life was never all that bad when you had your friends by your side.

The actors, it turned out, needn't have worried. Fox happily ordered a second season, with the network's entertainment chief sharing in a statement, "Over the past season, *New Girl* has become the hottest new appointment series for young adults."

* * *

Johnson was frequenting poker rooms in the LA suburbs of Inglewood and Commerce when he got some unexpected feedback from a fellow player. "Dude, your character and the main girl, you guys are going to get together, for sure."

"I don't know . . . ," Johnson responded.

"Bullshit, dude. That was the setup from the beginning."

Johnson gleefully texted Meriwether after that exchange. He had met a male fan of the show and, not only that, the guy *cared* about the romance. *New Girl*'s first season was striking a chord with viewers. And it was getting big-time awards love to boot. The show was nominated for five Emmys—including a nod to Deschanel for Outstanding Lead Actress, Greenfield for Outstanding Lead Actor, Kasdan for Outstanding Director of a Comedy Series, and Yanklewitz for Outstanding Casting. Greenfield was on his way to film the comedy *They Came Together* during hiatus when he got news that he'd been nominated. Paul Rudd, his co-star, was one of the first people to congratulate him. He tried to act cool but, in the privacy of his trailer, Greenfield thought to himself, "I can't believe this is happening."

That wasn't all. The writers and actors discovered fan fiction about their characters—*sexy, dirty* fan fiction—that made its way onto the set. One young woman had taken the "Landlord" episode and added a steamy twist to it, penning a very R-rated scene between Nick and Jess. Another story, spanning more than thirteen thousand words, featured Nick and Jess hooking up after the "Wedding" episode, and has since been read more than eighteen thousand times.

Articles popped up on how to dress like the show's heroine, featuring shopping links to her identical bright cardigans, polka-dot tops, and pleated red dresses. A Tumblr account called Dress like New Girl was launched, with IDs to her ensembles, from the green plaid Anthropologie dress she wore in "The 23rd" to that Target owl pajama set in "Raisin's Back."

Wildly enough, thanks to *New Girl*'s blooming popularity and successful marketing campaign, the word *adorkable* had found its way into the dictionary. When Fox Networks Group CEO Peter Rice got wind of the news, he promptly emailed Shannon Ryan, the architect behind the slogan, with the subject header: "Adorkable is a real word now and it's all your fault."

Once, Morris was passing through Hollywood with friends and walked by a rowdy party that could have easily been mistaken as a frat house.

There was an obstacle course set up and people were running through it, drinking and screaming. One of the partygoers recognized Morris and excitedly told him that they were in the middle of playing their version of True American, a drinking game that had been introduced in the first season. "Holy crap," he thought.

Simone found herself getting stopped by young brown-skinned girls who would say to her, "Oh my goodness, you're part of a mainstream American comedy!" Growing up, Simone never saw anyone who looked like her on television. "There was no South Asian on TV who didn't have to have the accent or have to explain how they got here," she told me. Playing Cece made her realize there was a place for her. And clearly, it meant so much to the young women who approached her—and continue to approach her to this day.

Excitement had begun to swirl around these once unknown, struggling actors, now burgeoning stars in their own right. A basketball hoop was set up outside the production office and Michael Budge, the show's art director, let his sons play ball with the guys between takes. Not only was he touched by how kind Morris, Greenfield, and Johnson were during those games but he noticed how *excited* his kids were to hang out with actors from the show. "*Dude!*" they'd say afterward. "Winston just shot hoops with us!"

Was there a reason *New Girl*'s first season was clicking in such a big way?

The series, Baer posited in an interview with *Written By*, was the first post-post-9/11 show. Television had become hardened and cynical after the tragedy, delivering us dark dramas like *24* and *Homeland*. In a world of Carrie Mathisons and Jack Bauers, Jessica Day might have served as a cheerful, polka dot–clad antidote for audiences.

"We were all surprised by how connected people felt to it during the focus group testing," Baer explained. ". . . The comedy in the past ten years prior to our show had an edge to it. It was satirical. There was a cynicism about the comedy. What our show came along at the right time for—this weird alchemy that happened—is that we were willing for the first time to go, '*It's okay to feel again.*' I might be completely boneheaded and wrong but it's the first show that actually tries to emotionally connect on that level."

Baer would catch some internet heat for his suggestion that *New Girl* was the first of its kind to reintroduce joy to the small screen post 9/11—*Parks and Recreation* and *Modern Family* were popular shows that also trafficked in joy and lightness—but the sentiment was right.

The fact was, comedy was finally back, in full swing, on television. So much so that *The New York Times* ran a feature in 2011, the same year that *New Girl* debuted, with the headline, "In a Gloomy Economy, TV Sitcoms Are Making a Comeback." In 2008, only two comedies had landed on the list of top ten most-watched TV shows. Two years prior, there had been zilch. Now, drama and reality TV were being nudged out of their reigning era, where they had been comfortably lounging for the better part of a decade.

With tortoise-like job growth and high unemployment, freshman comedies like *New Girl* soared, while existing sitcoms like *How I Met Your Mother* and *The Big Bang Theory* saw bumps in viewership. "Comedy thrives during economic downturns," Chuck Lorre, the creator of *The Big Bang Theory*, suggested to the *Times*. "You know, if you've had a bad day, laughter is a better remedy than watching a coroner pick shrapnel out of some poor guy's private parts."

No sooner had *New Girl* been picked up for a second season than Michael Budge, the art director, was summoned back to the studio lot to help expand the show's world. Fox had approved building an exact replica of the Griffin on their soundstage, and production designer Michael Whetstone, who took over for Jeff Sage after the pilot, alongside set decorator Jane Shirkes, worked together to meticulously re-create the real-life bar.

They scoured eBay for the exact same English-infantrymen lamps that lined the walls, striking gold when they found one in the United Kingdom, which they had shipped stateside and made multiple copies of. The lamps were cast in resin, and each soldier was hand-painted. A maroon-and-white wallpaper was custom made, along with rouge stained-glass windows. Antique beer draws were brought in, along with kegs, and people could pour themselves an actual beer in their fictional bar.

The edict, delivered by Meriwether and filtered down to every department, was that she wanted *New Girl* to feel like a real world. Budge took that to heart, focusing on bringing reality to the smallest of details, down to using asphalt, a smelly tar-like substance on the bar's wallpaper to give it a smoky, lived-in feel, as if nicotine had seeped into the walls long ago. For an extra boost of reality, the crew shot on location when they could and used the real-life exterior and interior of their production office for Associate Strategies, Schmidt's marketing job.

Similar care was put into the rest of the set. When Whetstone came on board, there were several in-depth meetings that revolved around what, exactly, Jess's closet should look like. Meriwether also had a specific vision for Jess's bedspread, which she requested feature a dark background with brightly colored flowers on one side and vintage material on the other. Shirkes selected Pindler & Pindler fabric, a brown spread covered in entwined botanicals. For an added touch of whimsy, the set decorator created custom pillowcases embroidered with blue-and-red trimming and mini-pom-poms. She hung a Victorian calendar dotted with plants above Jess's desk and decorated the walls with vintage-looking artwork, including a framed needleprint by Kathryn Coyle.

Whetstone consulted with every actor on what they thought their characters would have in their space. Deschanel wanted shadow boxes on her classroom walls. Johnson asked for a photo of folk singer-songwriter Jim Croce to be hung in his bedroom. When Whetstone emailed him to ask why, Johnson swiftly replied, "Beautiful singer. Great mustache." That idea was easier said than done—the production designer couldn't use a photo of a celebrity without getting permission. After a series of phone calls, art department coordinator Jon Bush tracked down Croce's widow, who was running a bar in San Diego. Turns out, she loved *New Girl* and gave her sign-off.

As the writers continued to work to define Schmidt, Winston, and Nick, their rooms would reflect the emergence of their personalities. Schmidt was given the most aspirational room, with a plush-looking headboard and a Calvin Klein bedspread. Winston's space was sports themed. Nick's room would be a haphazard mess, with his desk on cinder blocks and the doors ripped from his closet.

Prop buyers scoured spots Olde Good Things, a ten-thousand-square-foot warehouse in Los Angeles packed with reclaimed architecture. Whetstone thought back to his twenties, when he used to go dumpster diving for home furnishings, driving through the back alleys of Beverly Hills to see what wealthy people were throwing out. The cash-strapped guys, he decided, had also found décor on the street and brought it back to the loft, including random bits and bobs like a string of blue glass grapes.

When Whetstone watched the pilot, he was struck by how definitively *not* LA the show felt. It could have easily been New York or Chicago or any big city, really. (There was a taxicab in the first scene, for goodness sake!) He kept that thought in the back of his head when they looked for locations, avoiding trendy LA locales and going for more classic spots, like the Park Plaza Hotel, an elegant, white stone building from the 1920s, which they used for the episode "The Last Wedding."

Heading into that second season, the acclaim and staggeringly impressive numbers didn't seem to be enough for Fox, who fought to get even more eyes on their early darling of a show. This would mark the first time writer Nick Adams got a peek into how, exactly, the industry worked. Instead of nurturing the series and letting the audience grow organically, he remembers, a Fox executive said, "We need to get more guys watching." Commercials for *New Girl* were run during football season, he remembers, and there were talks of doing a tie-in with a football player. That fixation annoyed Adams. "It's Zooey Deschanel and three cute boys," he grumbled to the other writers. "That's the show!"

Still, the buzz was growing louder and louder. Table reads had become an event. Chairs lined the periphery of the room for executives from the studio, network, and production company to sit and watch the latest episode unfold. Then the room grew more and more packed, with no chairs left for seating and visitors lining the walls. "Who the hell are all these people?" Adams wondered. It was becoming clear that *New Girl* was a hit show—*the* hit show—and all these visitors, whoever they were, wanted a glimpse of its next chapter coming to life.

The Making of True American

And remember, everything you hear in True American is a lie, knock on wood.

—WINSTON BISHOP

It was 2 AM on the Fox lot and *New Girl* writer Luvh Rakhe was stuck. The writers' room had brainstormed an idea for a drinking game called True American, which would be used to introduce Russell into the fold of the loft for the first time. They knew they wanted the game to be something ridiculous, to contrast how adult Jess's new boyfriend was, but the rest of the details were hazy. Now, it was Rakhe's turn to fill in the blanks.

"I don't know what this stupid fucking game is," Rakhe said to Berkley Johnson and Kim Rosenstock, as they headed home for the night. "Can you just type up some shit for it if you don't mind?"

The trio gathered at Rakhe's computer, not even bothering to turn on the lights, and typed away: "They walk on pillows. They turn some stools upside down and use them as boots."

When the scene was brought to set, there were still so many questions to be answered. "What are we doing here?" Greenfield asked Jesse Peretz, who directed the episode. Peretz, embracing the chaos of the moment, started doling out instructions to the actors, telling them to jump on this and scream that.

The cast improvised their own rules as they went, with Deschanel setting the tone by calling out historical references. ("One, two, three, four, JFK, FDR!" "George Washington, cherry tree!") Some lines of dialogue were political and patriotic. Some were from another planet. "*I gotta get to the castle*," Johnson declared, apropos of nothing, as he trudged through the loft with two upturned barstools at his feet. The result, Johnson would later tell *Bustle*, was all of them vomiting words for two hours.

Back in the editing bay, Giselle Murillo, the show's assistant editor, looked at the footage that had been shot, bewildered. Three cameras were trained on all the actors for a scene that was completely unscripted and included one line of action: "Playing political game, lots of political references." Every single take was different. She headed into Welch's editing bay. "I don't know how to script this because there is *so much*," she told him, noting that the actors were saying all these random lines, like, at one point, referencing Susan B. Anthony.

"I know you've cut music videos," Welch responded. "Let's see a music video, girl." He added, "You know this footage better than I do, you've watched all three cameras, you know this—do a pass."

Murillo returned to her desk and got to work. "Make it funny, make it move," she told herself.

One of the keys to editing True American, she realized, was to pluck out lines she found most amusing, like Schmidt's random shout-out to Abu Nazir, the fictional villain from *Homeland*. (She loved the show and they shared the same floor with the *Homeland* writers, so it felt like a fun hat tip.) "This is kind of cool . . . ," Murillo thought as she moved around all the takes in crunch time, not knowing that she was putting together, for the very first time, an iconic fixture of the show.

After "Normal" debuted, *Buzzfeed* declared True American "the next big drinking game," complete with a handbook of made-up rules. A website titled True American Rules went live, with an unofficial step-by-step breakdown. The writers and actors started getting asked how to play the game they'd haphazardly made up one sleep-deprived night and they'd have to explain, over and over, that there really were no rules.

As seasons went on, the writers would start leaning on the game as a crutch, when it was the middle of the night and they were exhausted and wanted to go home. "What if we do True American?" they'd ask each other, before adding, "We'll figure it out tomorrow." The next day came and they were left in the same position as they were the night before, only this time, they realized with dismay, they had to come up with *new* fake rules and moves.

For the *New Girl* fans who would still appreciate some guidance on playing True American themselves, the best road map I can find comes courtesy of Hannah Simone herself. "I think it's just get really drunk and yell a bunch of stuff," she said. "And never forget that the floor is lava."

6

The *New Girl* Lab, Part I

When you're going through a 'Taylor Swift–like range of emotions,' I should come over, right?

—CECE PAREKH

NICK ADAMS WAS ON SET for "Pepperwood," an episode he wrote about a potential murderer in Jess's creative-writing class, when Nate Corddry—who played the suspected killer—approached him.

"Hey, can I ask you something?" Adams remembers Corddry saying.

"Yeah, what's up, man?"

He whispered, "Is this how you guys always work? They're just yelling lines at me."

"This is kind of what we do," Adams responded.

The *New Girl* set was often described by Meriwether as a lab—a place where off-the-cuff comedy was created by the cast in the moment or through a long list of alt jokes, which were additional scripted jokes to the ones written on the page. Meriwether would often pull jokes out of thin air as well, calling out lines from off camera—"Max, say this!" "Okay, now, Jake, you say that back to him!"—and write a scene on the spot.

"Have a billion options," Kasdan told Meriwether, Baer, and Finkel. "Have a billion places to go because you never know where the money is going to come from." Jokes might land perfectly at table reads but, come shooting day, they could fall completely flat. Being armed with new and fresh one-liners on set ensured that, somewhere in that footage, there was the perfect slice of comedy to slot in. It was also a way of covering their backs. As a single-camera comedy without a studio audience, it felt like a guessing game as to what was actually funny.

First assistant director Michael Risoli used to call Jake Kasdan "No-Stone-Unturned Kasdan." The sheer volume of ideas being thrown out on set were copious, and even once they were done getting everything they needed, there was still interest in coming up with more material to shoot. "Should we check with the craft-service people?" Risoli would quip. "Maybe they have an idea?" He himself pitched a joke while they were shooting the episode "Tomatoes," during a long run that involved Cece's Russian roommate Nadia listing everything she loved about America. Risoli suggested she give a shout-out to Tom Brady, who had just won the Super Bowl.

The process for coming up with alt jokes went something like this:

A script would get thrown up on the screen in the writers' room and, fast and furious, the writers pitched multiple versions for every single joke. Some jokes would end up getting a hundred alts and, whether they got a laugh in the room or not, were typed up in a master document. It was important not to be stingy with which jokes were collected—just because it didn't get a reaction in the room didn't mean that the cast couldn't take that line and find humor in a surprising way. Meriwether, Baer, and Finkel would eventually narrow each of those alts down to roughly ten options per joke, which were thrown out to the actors to deliver while shooting.

The writers' room was churning out so many jokes that, for one Secret Santa, Meriwether was gifted a blanket from a writer that was printed in a *New Girl* alt packet, so she could quite literally wrap herself in alts.

There was something more going on with the joke collecting. Meriwether was very confident on set and in the editing room. When it came to the writers' room, though, she found herself shying away from vetoing jokes or picking a favorite. She wanted to create a safe environment where the writers could play and laugh and have fun. Selecting a joke felt like it shut the conversation down and changed the vibe in the room.

"I didn't have the guts to say, 'I want that one in the script,'" Meriwether told me. "The writers' assistant would write everything down, and then at the end of the day, I would just get, like, a massive document with pages of jokes."

She added, "It was hard for me in the room in those early years to kind of be the person saying 'we're doing this, we're not doing that.' As a showrunner, it's your main job. But it was hard for me to get used to doing that because you want to be people's friend. You want to please everybody."

At the time, Meriwether also didn't feel like she had the confidence to know what was going to work or not.

Throughout the week, writers would break up into separate rooms, tasks in hand. In one room, rewrites were being done after a table read. In another, an upcoming episode was being outlined. And in another, writers huddled together and pitched alt jokes. One evening, a group gathered in a dark, windowless room on the Fox lot and stayed there until one in the morning trying to come up with the best jokes about a whale belt that Schmidt was going to wear in an upcoming episode.

Every day, the joke about his belt would get bolded in the script, accompanied by a longer and longer list of alts. All of those jokes, Berkley Johnson told me, could have been wrapped around the circumference of the earth three times. For a useful point of reference: journalist Talib Visram investigated what prime-time TV show had the most jokes per minute in 2014. *New Girl* came in second, with roughly seven jokes a minute, just behind *30 Rock* and right ahead of *Parks and Recreation*.

As they got deeper into the season, the writers would get more and more exhausted. That left room for Sophia Lear, the show's writers' assistant and future staff writer, to step in and start pitching more. Her first joke that made it into an episode was pulled out of a pile of alts by Meriwether. "My boobs are loving this unemployment thing," Jess says as she sips a soft drink out of a glass while lying on the couch. "They don't have to go to boob jail anymore."

For every great joke that made it in, heaps of material never saw the light of day. Early on, writer Kay Cannon shared a story about an old roommate who went through a bad breakup and coped by watching TV all day, drinking, and wearing a top hat. It seemed like the perfect storyline for Nick, and a card that read TOP HAT TIME was plastered at the end of a whiteboard. The writers would continually reference that note card with eager tones, a glimmering sign of hope when things felt rocky. "As soon as we get to Top Hat Time, it's smooth sailing!" they told themselves. Time stretched on and the card lost more and more of its meaning, until finally they asked, "What's Top Hat Time . . . ?"

Excitement similarly grew—and waned—with a pitch involving Winston and his cat, Ferguson. When the writers were huddled in the room, hour after hour, they began to think they had a dynamite idea about Winston building a cat condo. "We can't wait till Liz gets back in the room so we can pitch her on how Winston tries to build a cat condo, this is *it*," the group murmured excitedly. "We've done it."

Meriwether arrived and they began to share the pitch. One sentence in, the writers realized that it wasn't remotely good. Back to the drawing board. (Their idea didn't totally die, though. At one point, Winston does, in fact, allude to a cat hotel he purchased for Ferguson.)

Stories always started from some kind of a real place. Meriwether was inspired by Kasdan's description of the *Freaks and Geeks* writers' room, where everyone pooled their funniest, most humiliating, soul-crushing high school moments to build out episodes and refashion them for their characters. Dig into many stories on *New Girl* and you'll find a kernel of reality. When writer David Feeney was in fifth grade, he once dropped an entire card catalog on the floor and a librarian unleashed hell, forcing him to put each card back one by one as she screamed at him. He had been scared of libraries ever since. Winston, in turn, was terrified of school monitors after being forced to eat a tray full of Tater Tots by a disgruntled lunch lady.

Once, while chatting with one of her co-workers, Lear divulged a dating mishap. "I thought I was texting with one guy and this other guy turned up and his name was Bearclaw. . . ."

"You should pitch that," her co-worker responded. "That's a good story."

"Oh yeah," she thought. "That *is* a good story." Her encounter with Bearclaw became the basis of the episode "Katie," in which Jess accidentally ends up on a date with a strange fellow named Bearclaw (Josh Gad).

In the early days, the writers were in data-collection mode, watching the actors and trying to figure out what material worked best for them. They'd approach Johnson with a dense, highly crafted verbal joke and the actor would respond, "It's a lot of words. What if I just go, 'Come on'?" Baer swiftly learned that Johnson had a knack for taking a joke and condensing it into one burst of emotion, capturing the essence of the comedy without needing any long and winding lead-up.

Early on, the writers learned Simone could really nail a withering one-liner. Morris was so good at delivering non sequiturs, which, *New Girl* writer Kim Rosenstock recalled, resulted in him getting a lot of truly bizarre lines, "often about sex stuff that no one could relate to." Deschanel and Johnson soared when they were allowed to engage in playground-like arguments. One scene, for instance, involved the pair angrily shaking their butts at each other in the episode "Tomatoes." It devolved into something progressively sillier when taken to set, with Deschanel and Johnson deciding to run really fast while arguing over who had the fastest butt.

The actors were encouraged to put their own spins on every script, prompting Johnson and Greenfield to develop a methodology for how they did their scenes together. The first take, they stuck to the original script. The second take, they did a little variation on the script. The third take, as Greenfield put it, they went to "outer space." The fourth take, they would not-so-subtly let the writers know they were done.

In those early seasons, Johnson told me, "We would do five hundred takes of every single coverage. Nobody would stop and the director can't stop, because the writers want it and the writers win. So at a certain point, somebody has to say, 'We're at hour eighteen. . . .' It was like a bunch of coke addicts at a party, we're never going to stop talking, we have to go home and sleep so we can come back tomorrow."

An "outer space" take could look something like Season Six's "Christmas Eve Eve" episode, in which an infuriated Winston discovers that Schmidt refused a package for retired Rear Admiral Jay Garage-a-Roo, not realizing that it's one of Winston's aliases. "You should have known it was me!" Winston declares, and proceeds to rattle off a slew of his other alter egos, all improvised by Morris, including Rik Smits, a former basketball player for the Indiana Pacers, and Pontius Pilate, a Roman governor of Judaea.

Over the course of multiple episodes, Johnson would try again and again to ad-lib a line comparing Schmidt to an "evil Disney prince." It was the first thought he had when he met Greenfield during the audition process ("He looks like a fuckin' evil prince from a Disney movie!" were the exact words that went through Johnson's head. He added, "But, like, the bad one—not the one you end up marrying, the one who's trying to take over the castle.") He diligently improvised that bit to no avail, save for some chuckles that could be heard from the producers.

A natural marriage between the script and the improvised moments emerged, which would result in gems like the Gstaad scene in "Heat Wave." As the gang tries on old ski jackets, Schmidt declares, "Real après-ski vibe. I feel like I'm in Gstaad. Gstaad's all about après-ski."

"Well, it's nice in the summer, too," Winston offers.

"Oh, have you been?" Schmidt asks.

"Have you?"

"Have you?"

"Have you been, is the real question?"

Reagan, their new roommate, steps in then, bored and annoyed. "What does it matter? Just tell the truth. Have you been there? Have you been there?"

"I'm sorry," Winston says to her. "Have *you*?"

The core of that was 100 percent in the script, written by Matt Fusfeld and Alex Cuthbertson. "I think on take four or five it was like, let's open it up," Greenfield recalled. "Neither [me nor Lamorne] know what Gstaad or après-ski is but now we understand the bit and let's go back and forth on it eight more times than we need to and then let Liz figure out what she wants to do in editing."

When Nelson Franklin arrived on the *New Girl* set for the show's second season, he had never improvised on a television show before. The actor, who was cast as Robby, Cece's boyfriend, walked into the Griffin for the episode "Re-launch," and the first person he spotted was Greenfield, shirtless and lathered up in baby oil, texting in his chair. The actor was shooting a scene involving his character celebrating the healing of his broken penis, and later—apropos of nothing—decides to toss fire around the bar.

Greenfield would become Franklin's frequent scene partner and a thoughtful, encouraging presence while on set. The pair of characters end up bonding when Robby and Cece break up, and the two bump into each other when they're both caught spying on Cece at a restaurant.

Franklin was given a hat to wear as his "disguise" during the scene and he made an offhanded joke to Greenfield.

"Max, you know what would be funny? If I said, 'Of course she saw you, you're not wearing a hat.'"

"Oh yeah," Greenfield told him. "You gotta tell the writers that."

"No, no, no. I don't want to step on any toes—"

"Shut the hell up," Greenfield said, taking Franklin by the arm and marching him over to Kasdan, who was directing the episode.

"Listen to this line Nelson just pitched me," Greenfield said, and the actor retold his joke.

"Put it in," Kasdan replied. "That's way funnier."

New Girl would turn out to be a formative gig for Franklin. He was in his early twenties, new to the business, and initially too shy to offer his own ideas on set. But Greenfield, who was so outgoing, would push him. "You say whatever you want, Nelson!" he told him firmly. "You do whatever you want!"

Though he appreciated Greenfield's advice, Franklin never felt like it was his place to initiate bits as a guest star on someone else's show. If another actor took the lead, though, he would happily go as far as they wanted to go. While filming the episode "Halloween," the script called for Schmidt to attempt to head butt Robby, who amiably blocks him. The scene was supposed to end there, but Greenfield just kept at it, pretending to wind up and go in for the head butt, which allowed Franklin to improvise right back, blocking him each time.

"Schmidt!" Franklin, as Robby, said. "You did it again."

"How do you see that coming every time!?!"

"When you wind up, you make, like, a little windup thing—"

Johnson was doing his own share of pitching to Meriwether. Only for him, it was in hopes of finding more interesting layers to his character. In the early days, the structure of most episodes usually involved Jess getting a monologue, Nick responding with a question, and then Schmidt getting a monologue. At every table read, Johnson felt like Deschanel was shining, Greenfield was shining, and he and Morris were setting up all their jokes.

"I didn't know if spiritually I could do seven years of this," Johnson remembers thinking at the time. "Because I'm a maniac and—mind you, if it was a multicam and the hours were short, I would have been fine—but I'm here too many hours, and this is not filling my soul at all."

As Greenfield put it, "Jake is the most talented improviser I've ever worked with. He can improvise as the straight man, he can improvise as the punch-line guy, and he's so fast. When we were in that first season, they needed him to play straight [man] against Zooey a lot of the time."

There were moments, though, that offered glimpses of who Nick would become. The first breakthrough came while shooting the episode "Fancyman Part 1," which involved Nick accompanying Jess to a party at Russell's decadent home. At first, Nick rolls his eyes at all of the pretentious trappings. Then he walks into a beautiful home office and is instantly charmed.

"Jess, when I put my hand on this desk I feel sexually proficient for the first time in my life," Nick declares. He picks up Russell's phone. "I'm President Miller! You're all fired! Bring our boys home."

Looking back, Johnson said, "It was weird and it was really funny and they had a bunch of jokes for me and that was the first time I felt like, 'Well, I'm actually getting funny stuff.'" There were other early moments he loved, too—like when Nick meets a man at the bar who claims to be a future version of himself and becomes a Yoda-like presence in his life. Meriwether, Johnson realized, was really clocking what was working for him and his character and building around that.

"Liz would find where you score and give you opportunities," he explained. "If she's a coach, she's a player's coach. She's going to change her offense for the players, and a lot of people don't know how to do that, a lot of people have what they think is funny and it is your job to hit it. She's just the opposite."

As time went on, Johnson continued to unpack the comedy of Nick Miller. One of the best road maps could be found in the Season Two episode "Models." It starts out simple enough: Schmidt gets Nick a cookie. That little gift results in a much larger discussion about the fact that Nick doesn't do enough sweet gestures for his friend. By the end, a helpless, frustrated Nick tries to remedy the situation by buying Schmidt a cookie, which he has smashed into the shape of the Star of David, in celebration of his Judaism.

When Nick's gesture goes unappreciated, he's at a loss of words, frantically and emotionally blurting out, "You gave me a cookie, I gave you a cookie, you gave me a cookie, gave you cookie, gave me cookie, got you cookie! You gave me cookie, I got you cookie, man! Gave me cookie, got you cookie! We're even! We're even, Schmidt! I mean, what do you want from me?" That scene served as a perfect example of what made Nick's comedy shine. Johnson had discovered that Nick was funny when his character was trying *really* hard but didn't quite have the emotional tools to figure out what was happening.

The cookie scene was performed exactly as scripted. After Johnson and Greenfield finished the take, there were conversations about opening it up for alt jokes and improvisation. Johnson could see that Russ T. Alsobrook, the director of photography, was starting to get mad. "Why would you put your foot through a Picasso?" Alsobrook grumbled under his breath. "It's perfect."

Indeed it was, and on that scene lives.

Across every inch of the show, the cast and crew were bringing scenes to life in their own wonderfully scrappy ways.

Like the time, while filming the episode "Clean Break," the writers learned Sugar Ray Leonard had turned down the cameo they wrote for him, which involved the boxer starring in an infomercial for an appliance called the "Sugar Ray Leonard Crepe Pan." In the bit, he was scripted to look at the pan and say, "It's a knockout!" before giving it a punch. After finding out that Leonard had declined the role, the writers moved quickly. They offered the infomercial to Regis Philbin, who was the father of *New Girl* writer J. J. Philbin. The famed television host said yes and, cherry on top, he still wanted to do the *exact* bit they had written for Leonard, down to punching the pan.

Then there was that one Sunday night, ahead of filming the episode "Valentine's Day," that first assistant director Michael Risoli got a surprise call from Meriwether and executive producer Erin O'Malley. "Could we put a cockfight together for tomorrow?" they asked him. There was a flashback they wanted to do, which would involve Nick drunkenly trying to fight roosters in Mexico.

Risoli went into problem-solving mode. It would probably not be too hard to get roosters. But where would they shoot it so last minute? The scene was scripted to be in some sort of back alley. Their stage, he realized, was actually pretty old and had an antiqueish look to it. Maybe they could just take a small corner, throw some dirt on the ground, and surround Johnson with raucous extras? Within twenty-four hours, he had the rooster, a makeshift pit, and the last-minute scene in the bag. Looking back, he told me, "It was really funny, actually."

* * *

The *New Girl* lab was highly effective at delivering episodes that felt fresh, funny, and real. Creating the magic, though, was becoming increasingly exhausting. For Johnson, the Fox studios had come to feel like it stood still in twilight hours. Much like casinos, there were no clocks and no windows inside their sets, making it easy to lose track of time. They weren't shooting on location at the downtown loft's exterior as much anymore because the occupants of the real-life building were frustrated by big lights being shone into their windows late into the night. Whetstone designed a replica of the building's exterior on the soundstage, along with a coffee shop called Brickfields, building a whole world within the world of the Fox studios.

Hours, hours, and more hours were spent on the Fox lot. Johnson would step inside at 7 AM and when he left, it was dark all over again. "I'm having a nervous breakdown and everyone just keeps putting makeup on my face," he thought to himself.

The day before table reads were often all-nighters, with Meriwether, Finkel, and Baer sleeping in their offices in shifts—grabbing two hours here, two hours there of shut-eye—while the other writers took over. During the show's first season, the whole cast presented Meriwether with blankets. Baer and Finkel gave her a chest of drawers filled with pajamas and slippers.

When O'Malley first met Meriwether, she thought, "Oh, she's one of those brainiacs." The writer was beautiful and brilliant—a little like a mad scientist, she recalled. Her office, it might be said, was her laboratory, located around the corner from the *Simpsons* bungalow, which featured a massive yellow Homer Simpson hand holding a pink donut.

Meriwether spent many of her sleeping hours in that space, her sleeping bag in tow, passing out on her couch as she worked deep into the night. Sometimes, when Risoli knocked on the door to her office and opened it a crack, he wasn't sure if Meriwether was even in there, her stacks of clothes were piled so high he couldn't see past them.

The Fox lot had become a home of sorts to Meriwether. She loved seeing all the stray cats roam the studio lot after nightfall. She got a kick out of the pigeons who would perch on rafters and poop on the sets during scenes, ruining takes. And she got emotional when the security guard didn't ask her for her badge one day, waving her straight through the gates. That made her feel like more than just a number, like he was saying to her, "Hey, you come every day, and you try pretty hard. I see you. You're a person. Come on in."

The writer was hard on herself. Every season, Meriwether would point to an episode she didn't like with a forlorn, "*Ughhh.*" Her ethos was: "It's never right, never good enough until we don't have time to make it better." She cared deeply about every detail of the show, whether it was the length of Schmidt's running shorts or when Jess should wear her signature black-framed glasses. She stepped in when guest star Peter Navy Tuiasosopo, who played Bob the bartender, was dressed in a T-shirt for a scene in "Quick Hardening Caulk" and switched it to a button-down.

O'Malley originally tried to take tasks off Meriwether's plate before discovering how much the writer genuinely *wanted* to weigh in. The producer learned when to show her something, when to narrow the options down, and when to realize that yes, Meriwether would want that ridiculous bow for Jess's hair.

The writers were often racing against the clock to get episodes out. While filming Season Two's "Cabin," Morris and Greenfield shot a scene fifteen minutes away from the Fox lot. By the time the crew arrived on location, just outside a liquor store, there weren't any scripts available to rehearse from. The camera was ready, lights were set up, and time was running out before they needed to start filming. News arrived that the writers were still rewriting the scene. Pages were sent over via email, which the actors read aloud using iPads. Eventually, someone drove over to the parking lot with hard copies.

That same episode found Deschanel, Johnson, Olivia Munn, and David Walton shooting on location in Thousand Oaks, California. The actors were getting their hair and makeup done when a brand-new scene arrived for them to perform outside the cabin. Alec Berg, who directed the episode, remembers the cast looking at the last-minute pages and saying, "How are we supposed to do this?" At one point during filming, Berg saw Meriwether nodding off in the corner. She'd barely slept for days. "Oh, this is not sustainable," he thought.

During the first week of filming the show, Meriwether lost her voice. She ended up going to an ear, nose, and throat doctor to figure out what was going on.

"Have you been drinking a lot of coffee and trying to sound authoritative?" the doctor asked.

"Yes to both of those things," Meriwether responded. For the first time in her life, she was managing a staff of one hundred–plus people, along with walking into rooms that were filled with men and telling them what to do. She had changed her voice in the process, thinking she needed to sound more masculine in order to be taken seriously.

Episode after episode, Meriwether was learning valuable lessons about making television. If the A plot—the central story of the episode—didn't have a deeper emotional component, it wouldn't play the way that it was supposed to. Even B plots needed to have some heft to them, regardless of how silly they were on the page. Take the story of Schmidt mourning Cece's potential breast reduction in "Goldmine." At first, it's a straightforward, superficial desire for his ex-girlfriend to stay just as she is. Then it turns into something else.

Berkley wrote that episode, which saw Schmidt visiting Cece at the hospital during her breast-reduction consultation and asking her to plug in earbuds so he can privately say goodbye to her chest. (He has completely misunderstood the meaning of a consultation.)

"I need to look them in the eyes," he explains, earnestly. "I can't leave without letting them know how much they meant to me."

We can't hear what Schmidt is saying when he bids her breasts farewell, but he makes plenty of confusing hand gestures as a baffled Cece looks on, including several rounds of peekaboo. When she pops one earbud out to find out what in the world he's talking about, she hears his concluding words.

"I guess if I'm being honest, it doesn't matter what size you are," Schmidt says. "I'm always going to love you because you're attached to the most beautiful person in the whole world."

There was that sweet spot: an on-paper broad story paired with a serving of emotional resonance. Berkley felt a special satisfaction as he watched Greenfield perform that whole bit. The actor was only given a general sense of what to do ahead of filming, and he took those directions and ran with them, inventing a multitude of gestures as he went. He had the unique ability to thread the crazy with the sentimental, gracefully sliding from one to the other.

Greenfield would commit *hard*, with full-throated dedication, to any joke he was given. Hand him a monologue that touches on Schmidt's Long Island roots for the episode "LAXmas"? He will do you one better and proceed to improvise an entire run on Long Island, including several repeated references to Billy Joel.

He would also happily follow the ball. When Rob Riggle guest starred as Schmidt's cousin in the episode "Parents," the script called for him to walk Greenfield around in a wheelbarrow as the two competed over who was the manliest. While the shirtless men postured, Riggle improvised yelling out that he could do this "ALL DAY." Greenfield loved it, quickly and gleefully following suit, yelling, "ALL DAY," right back, with increasing levels of volume. (That line, by the way, continues to follow Riggle. When he takes part in golf tournaments and makes a putt, he'll hear people scream, "ALL DAY.")

Or there was that time, while filming the episode "Neighbors," when Berkley offered Greenfield a selection of popular '80s catchphrases to rattle off to his hipster neighbors. Greenfield ran with it, improvising an entire list of additional catchphrases, which went on and on, taking everyone on a long, winding tour of '80s television. Tears of laughter streamed down Berkley's face as he watched from behind the camera. The four young actors who played the neighbors, on the other hand, looked concerned. Berkley got the sense that they feared the shooting day would never end, that Greenfield would keep coming up with new jokes until the world ended.

In the beginning, Schmidt was a comedy reservoir for the writers. The more emotionally driven stories were built around Nick and Jess, and the jokes fell into Schmidt's lap. Greenfield caught on to that dynamic while filming the show's second episode, "Kryptonite." One scene called for him to bounce from various parts of his room, while asking Nick and Jess which part of the space he looked sexiest in. "*This* is the vibe," Greenfield realized. "It's Jake and Zooey walk in, and they're like, 'What's this guy doing?'"

That's how most successful shows begin, Greenfield told me. Take the early days of *The Big Bang Theory*. "You had Johnny Galecki and Kaley Cuoco . . . they're going to ground what's happening a little bit and we're going to see a potential romance build out between the two of them," he said. "But we've also got Jim Parsons, who is going to run a train through this set and we *need* him to because that's what audiences, I think, latch on to first."

Greenfield added, "Who's the character that's really making us laugh here? As you're watching that, you can start to really invest in the other relationship, which ultimately becomes the most important part of the show."

The actor memorably—and quite accidently—struck comedy gold when a script called for his character to say the word *chutney* in an early episode. Greenfield, who grew up in Dobbs Ferry, New York, moved to Los Angeles with a noticeable New York accent. His girlfriend, now wife, Tess Sanchez was a casting director and offered Greenfield some advice. "You're going to audition for a lot of Warner Bros. things," Sanchez said. "You gotta go see a vocal coach."

She was right—he'd go into audition rooms for WB shows like *Gilmore Girls* and get feedback that could be best summed up as: "You're from New York. *No one* on these shows is from New York." Greenfield started seeing a coach, who had him walk around the room while biting a pencil in his mouth. He developed a habit of overenunciating words and announcing every syllable, even the ones that were supposed to stay silent.

Greenfield really didn't know how to say the word *chutney*. He thought it was pronounced "chut-a-ney." When he said it and heard Meriwether laughing, he knew he was onto something. There was no better feeling on that show than making Meriwether laugh.

With the success of "chut-a-ney" under his belt, Greenfield decided to keep the mispronunciations coming. Sometimes he would see a word in the script and think, "I'm *really* going to lay into that one." (See: Jay Cut-tah-ler.) He also, at times, pronounced Nick's name, "N-Y-ICK."

Ahead of working together on the show's second season, director Alec Berg sat down with Meriwether and sang Schmidt's praises. "I think he's my favorite character on television right now," he told her. He loved that Schmidt had such a specific point of view and he was incredibly articulate. In one episode Berg directed, the character went on a rampage against a hutch Jess had brought into the house that was made of pine, which, as he explains, is the wood of "poor people and outhouses." He was opinionated about everything—whether it was Nick's fashion choices or his grudge against a florist. As Meriwether once put it, "Comedy is very high stakes about something that doesn't matter. It's finding a character who cares a lot about things that don't matter to a lot of other people."

From season to season, Schmidt went from someone tiptoeing into the danger zone of one-dimensionality—with his penchant for ripping off his shirt and making gross remarks—to a far more textured, interesting version of himself. The person who would ultimately turn him into a fully formed character would be Cece.

Hard as it is to believe, the pair's long-lasting relationship almost didn't happen. Meriwether had been so determined not to move their dynamic into emotional territory, shutting down any pitches that pushed them in that direction.

"And then Schmidt and Cece . . ." a writer would begin a sentence.

"No," she'd respond.

When the connection between the two became undeniable, Meriwether gave in . . . with a caveat. The pair could *teeter* on the brink of a real relationship in Season Two, only for Schmidt to mess it all up. Cece, determined to have a family, gives up on Schmidt altogether and decides to allow her mom to arrange a marriage for her. She's introduced to Shivrang, someone who seems able to offer her everything Schmidt can't—stability, steadiness, and the potential for a real future.

Pushing the pair even further apart is the introduction of Schmidt's college girlfriend, Elizabeth. When writer J. J. Philbin pitched the idea that Schmidt reunite with a past love, Meriwether was skeptical. Was it too deep into the season to bring in a brand-new love interest? But then she quickly became enamored with the idea of meeting the woman who Schmidt fell in love with before he lost all his weight. She decided that Elizabeth (played by Merritt Wever) would call Schmidt out on his bravado, while bringing out a softer, childlike side of him.

Wever would turn out to be Greenfield's favorite guest star on the series. "There's so much of the show that I look at now and go, 'I don't remember any of this. I don't remember saying this, I'm ninety percent sure none of this was in the script,'" he said. Having Wever there reminded Greenfield of the original objective: stick to the story and really play out what was written. The pair knew full well how invested the audience was in Schmidt and Cece and they worked together to create this new relationship on-screen, digging into their scenes as a team. "How do you play this? How do you make people believe in this story?" they asked themselves.

As Meriwether watched early cuts of Wever and Greenfield together, she thought, "This is good. This is really good for him and for us." The duo's chemistry was palpable enough that audiences might actually root for them. In fact, Meriwether mused, Elizabeth could be making Schmidt a better person than Cece was at the time. Still, unresolved feelings lingered, and the season finale offered the chance to tackle their love triangle . . . plus one *other* love triangle that neither the audience nor Cece ever saw coming.

The idea landed while Meriwether was in the shower. What if there was a *Graduate*-style interruption in the middle of Cece's wedding? Only instead of it being Schmidt breaking up the ceremony, it would be one of Shivrang's ex-girlfriends. That thought in place, Meriwether decided that whoever they cast in the role should be somebody fancy—a fun cameo and wink to fans as she stood up in the crowd to declare her love for Shivrang.

An offer was sent out to none other than Taylor Swift.

When Greenfield, a massive Swift fan, heard rumblings that the singer had been offered the role, he had his doubts she'd say yes. "I wonder who we'll end up with?" he thought. "Because there's no way she'll do it. I mean, can we make an offer to someone more reasonable? Because when she passes two days before we shoot, it gives us a very limited time to find someone."

But lo and behold, it turned out Swift was happy to come on. As the actress got ready for her cameo, she showed costume designer Debra McGuire pictures of her cats on her phone and told Douglass and Glaser that she loved Deschanel's makeup. The makeup artist gave Swift a product that she and Deschanel had become enamored with while working together on *500 Days of Summer*—Benefit's Benetint Rose-Tinted Lip & Cheek Stain—and Swift seemed genuinely excited by the little gift. While on set, she quoted lines from the show.

Morris didn't get the chance to interact with Swift—the majority of his scenes were in the vents—but he checked in with Johnson to see how it went. Turns out, just like her fellow cast members, the singer had been fed multiple alts and delivered them with an impressive amount of ease. "Dude, she nailed every single joke, one take, one take, one take, one take, and it was over," Johnson told Morris.

Greenfield, meanwhile, was psyching himself up to chat with the pop star. "*I'm gonna talk to Swift*," he decided, and approached her while she was behind the monitors. As the pair hung out and discussed her tour,

Greenfield asked if she preferred performing for an intimate audience or an arena. "If you could fill the ocean with people, I'd like to play for them," she replied, in the sweetest way possible.

Alongside Swift, there was one more wedding attendee who was dead set on ruining Cece and Shivrang's wedding. Only this one was furry, four-legged, and packed a mean bite.

The Season Two finale didn't start out with a subplot that heavily featured a badger on the loose. It began as a Rashomon-style story that dove into Nick and Jess's past and examined how the two secretly felt about each other from the start. The writers knew that they wanted the pair to end up trapped in an air duct at the wedding, but they couldn't yet figure out exactly *why* they were up there.

As a placeholder, they discussed the idea of a badger getting stuck in the air duct and Nick and Jess being forced to capture the animal. Every time the pitch came up, they all started to laugh . . . but there was no way that they were *actually* going to do that. Right?

In the midst of outlining the episode, *New Girl* writer J. J. Philbin took the morning off, leaving the room thinking the episode was going to feature the whole Nick and Jess flashback. Later that day, she called her colleague Josh Malmuth to check in.

"How's it going?" Philbin asked.

"Yeah," Malmuth said. "It's about a badger getting lost in the air duct."

As the crew set about finding a badger, landing on one named Digger from the Turtle Bay Exploration Park, the writers were each assigned a scene to script for the episode, with only a small window of time left. "How broad can we go?" they kept asking themselves. A badger falling through the ceiling when Cece got married was, indeed, pretty broad, and they'd need to surround that plot point with stories that had real emotional depth.

Amid the chaos of a loose badger and Winston potentially getting rabies, there was the very real story of Cece, Schmidt, and Elizabeth. Both women were still in love with Schmidt and the writers knew they wanted to end

Season Two on a cliff-hanger, leaving audiences wondering whom he would choose. They worked diligently to get their character to a place where either Elizabeth or Cece could feel like she was an organic, truthful pick.

But here's the thing—they didn't *want* Schmidt to pick anyone. At least, not yet. They believed there would be a joy in watching him squirm before ultimately deciding to secretly date both of them at the same time. Little did they know, that decision would pave the way for one of the most contentious plotlines of the series and an exhausting, frustrating hole to dig themselves out of. In that moment, though, it all felt exciting and different.

Then there was the Nick and Jess of it all.

The audience had watched as the pair struggled to figure out if they should take the leap and turn their friendship into something more, debating whether or not their differences would drive a wedge between them. They had kissed, fought, kissed some more, and kept bumping into obstacles that left them a throwing distance apart. The writers wanted to bring that tension to a head in the season finale, with both Nick and Jess wondering if Nick is just a little too broken to be a good, lasting partner.

Much debate had sprung up in the writers' room over what should happen to the pair at the end of Season Two. There were conversations around the idea of them having sex for the first time and closing the episode with a thirty-second postcoital shot of them in bed. But there was something about that idea that felt tired and too familiar. Instead, it was decided that Nick and Jess would get a whisper of their happy ending, with hints of danger to come.

"Look, I know you think we should call it," Jess says, as she waits outside of the wedding for Nick. "But I don't want to give up on this, even if we don't know what this is. I want to uncall it, please, can we uncall it. Before you say no . . . don't say no."

Nick walks over to her then and goes in for an intensely passionate, insanely good kiss.

There was debate over what song should play as Jess and Nick peel off together into the night. They considered going down the romantic route, which would make those final moments feel cinematic, leaning into the driving-into-the-sunset of it all. Instead, Meriwether settled on the song "I Always Knew" by the Vaccines, which had a frenetic and unsettling edge. There was a sense of inevitability to the song but also a stroke of danger, with lyrics like, "So let's go to bed before you say something real/Let's go to bed before you say how you feel."

Meriwether didn't want the scene to feel like the end of a movie. Instead, she thought of a moment in the film *Rushmore*, when Jason Schwartzman says, "Were you in the shit?"

Jess and Nick were about to be in the shit. All the conflict, she knew, was yet to come.

The *New Girl* Lines They're Proudest to Have Written

"I just want to find somebody, Cece. I really do, so bad that it hurts, from my head to my turnpipe."
—ROB ROSELL

"They said, 'Blaze. you're gonna lose it,' and I said, 'Nah, it's too big.'"
—LAMAR WOODS

"I'm old-fashioned, Coney Island fat strong."
—MATT FUSFELD, WRITTEN WITH ALEX CUTHBERTSON

Schmidt: "Need I remind you that you started a petition to get Enya to play at the Super Bowl halftime show?"
Winston: "You're misrepresenting my petition. Okay? I wanted her to play *on the field* during the fourth quarter."
—ELIOT GLAZER

"Thank you, Ms. Fat Booty, you're the best."
—NICK ADAMS
(He told me, "It's a silly throwaway line, but 'Ms. Fat Booty' is a classic Mos Def song and it makes me smile every time I think about it.")

"I'd say goodbye but that wouldn't be true.
So bad-bye, Reagan. Bad-bye."
—BERKLEY JOHNSON

7

Nick and Jess

I fell in love with Jess the moment
she walked through the door.

—NICK MILLER

BACK IN SEASON ONE, WHEN the writers were struggling with the urgent task of figuring out their show's identity, there was, if you will, an eight-hundred-pound gorilla in the room: Nick and Jess and their intense, undeniable chemistry. Early on, writer Nick Adams pitched that the pair hook up right out of the gate. Realistic about the ways of the world, he knew if Zooey Deschanel moved into an apartment with three single, straight guys, there was no way someone wouldn't try to make a move. Give the audience what they want early, Adams suggested, and then have Nick and Jess realize they made a mistake. The pair could go back to being friends and then slowly but surely build back up the romance.

Meriwether wanted to prolong it. She loved TV couples like Rachel and Ross and Pam and Jim, relationships that were designed with a satisfyingly slow burn, allowing fans to become deeply and intimately invested. The writers kept Nick and Jess away from each other when they could, limiting physical contact between the characters. "Don't do that," Deschanel was told when she'd place a hand on Johnson's arm.

Still, there were plenty of moments in those early seasons when writers gave audiences a taste of the sparks that flickered on the edges. We see Jess pushing Nick to believe in himself in "Injury" because she knows he's capable of so much more. And we see Nick being a source of comfort to Jess when she loses her teaching job in "Re-launch." He's the one who's there to make her laugh through her tears as the pair sit on the hood of her car and say goodbye to her old school. When Adams watched scenes like that unfold, he couldn't help but notice that they got an extra boost of magic from being shot on location. There was just something different about seeing Deschanel and Johnson making eyes at each other late at night on a Los Angeles street.

And then there were the not-so-sweet moments between them, when the two would fight with such heat that, actually, it was pretty damn romantic anyway. Steve Welch, the show's editor, delighted in piecing together scenes when the two were going at it, taking particular pleasure in one stormy moment from "Fluffer," when the pair screamed at each other over why they would never, ever become romantically involved:

"Because you drive me nuts, Miller," Jess screeches. "Because you're always sighing like you're the President of the United States deciding whether we're going to war—"

"I sigh because you sing about EVERYTHING—"

"You're cheap! You're so cheap! You never, ever put money in any tip jars!"

"What are you talking about!? Last week when we went to the coffee shop—"

"You put NICKELS in the tip jar!"

On drives home after work, Deschanel and Johnson would call each other and talk about Nick and Jess. They knew how important their storyline was to the show and wanted to make sure they got it right, musing over classic TV couples like Sam and Diane on *Cheers* and discussing what made those relationships work so well. "What are we trying to do?" they'd ask each other. "We know we have great chemistry, what's our goal?"

Before there could be Jess and Nick, though, there was Jess and Sam. Sam, played by David Walton, enters the show in Season Two as a handsome, charming doctor who starts out as a hookup and blossoms into something much more. When Walton first started playing Sam, the impression he got of his character, he told me, was "a straight shooter who was very horny." As his episodes progressed, Walton was taken aback by how much Sam was transforming on the page. "Wait, I thought this guy was kind of a dick," he mused to himself. To his surprise, Dr. Sam was becoming something of a sweetheart.

Walton theorized that the writers' room wanted to turn Sam and Jess into a loving, stable couple, which would make her secret feelings for Nick even more of an obstacle. If we cared about Sam, the stakes and drama of Nick and Jess sharing an illicit kiss could mount even more.

But *when*, the writers wondered, should that big kiss happen? There was endless debate about the timing of Nick and Jess's first lip-lock, with two staunch camps forming in the room. On one side, there were the writers who thought the characters should *absolutely* hook up. On the other side were the naysayers. *New Girl* writer David Iserson felt strongly it was time to get the two together, at least temporarily. "How long are you going to drag out two people not testing the limits of their relationship?" he thought. "Two people who have so much sexual attraction not kissing each other—it just starts to test the bounds of reality."

As Kasdan saw it, having the kiss meant that there were different relationship beats that could now be explored, outside of the perpetual sexual tension. It was an interesting and compelling question—what *would* the show look like if they hooked up? The writers thought back to Sam and Diane, a storied portrait of a fictional couple, who kissed at the end of the first season. If *Cheers*, a show that was so frequently referenced in the *New Girl* writers' room, did it, so could they.

Iserson did understand where the opposing team was coming from. In classic sitcom wisdom, once the main characters get together, there's a tension release that could hurt the show. It's why, in rom-coms, the couples usually don't kiss until the very end . . . and then the screen promptly fades to black.

Ratings had started to dip for *New Girl*, and the network offered Meriwether a directive. "We need something big," she was told. "We need a thing that's going to draw people in." The writers weren't prepared for Nick and Jess to kiss, nor did they have any immediate plans to make that happen, but it certainly fit Fox's ask.

While mapping out the episode "Cooler," the writers decided to inch their way to the explosive moment, offering up a tease of the kiss during a game of True American. The pair would get locked behind the loft's big blue door and dared to make out. Jess, pretending to be annoyed but secretly not so annoyed, acts businesslike about the whole thing, rolling her eyes and speeding it along.

As the writers worked through the scene, Berkley Johnson found himself doing something uncharacteristic. He wasn't really one to get involved with the show's love stories but offered up a pitch. How about—amid Jess's insistence that they kiss and get it over with—Nick says, "Not like this"? Meriwether looked over at him. "Oh, that's good . . . ," she said, startled that he had offered up such a romantic line.

The filming of the kiss was scheduled for a Friday night, right before Christmas break. The shooting day stretched on and all of the cast members emptied out of the loft set, leaving Deschanel and Johnson by themselves. Most of the crew were in the dark about what was happening—makeup artists Douglass and Glaser, who would usually stockpile breath mints and mouthwash for kissing scenes, weren't told until the very last minute. Fox executives filed in to watch, chairs packed into Nick's room, adding another layer of anxiety. Were they doing the kiss too soon? Would this all be a mistake?

I asked Deschanel if she was feeling the pressure and she responded with a simple, "I knew we were going to make it good." The actress looked at the episode like a musical number. So much of it had been chaos—True American! Nick jumping out the window in a stolen trench coat!—

and then in those final moments, it all slowed down, creating the perfect rhythmic bow.

Max Winkler, who directed the episode, had a hunch that rehearsal and discussion wouldn't be as good as the two just trying it for the first time and seeing how it worked. They did rehearse the movement leading up to the embrace, deciding that, as Jess walks away from Nick he should reach out and pull her back toward him. Meriwether really wanted the grab. Nick doubted himself so much and was never a guy who made big moves—this was a way of showing the audience that, when he kissed Jess, he was really sure of himself. She tried to explain exactly what she was looking for as she discussed the scene with Johnson, who seemed annoyed. "I know how to kiss a woman," he informed her.

The clock approached the thirteenth hour of the day. First assistant director Michael Risoli, whose job it was to keep shooting on schedule, felt himself getting nervous. As he tried to move things along, he noticed everyone was making a big deal about this whole kissing scene. Meriwether caught Risoli checking the clock.

"Okay, what's the problem?" he remembers her asking.

"We have fifteen minutes to get this kiss done," he told her.

Risoli was only half paying attention when Deschanel and Johnson leaned in for their first take. Once they started kissing, he got what all the hubbub was about. "Don't kiss me soft," Deschanel had told Johnson before they started shooting. "You have to grab me." He did just that, pulling her hard and creating a kiss that would live on as quite possibly the best (and hottest?) in TV history. The kind of kiss that you *immediately* rewatch several times . . . and then maybe a few times after that.

When they pulled away, Meriwether, Winkler, and everyone sitting on set clapped. Everything had changed in that split second, Meriwether felt. It was like they ignited the show with something really special.

The ripple effect was immediate.

One day after the episode aired, Winkler got a call from his agent. "This is huge," he was told. The director and Johnson were called into

Fox executive Dana Walden's office and inked a production deal out of it. Berkley, meanwhile, heard from people whom he hadn't spoken to in a long, long time. A friend of a friend reached out for a copy of the script, which the writer of the episode, Rebecca Addelman, signed, to be auctioned off for charity. The Wi-Fi password on the *New Girl* soundstage was changed to *theykissed*.

Meriwether was tasked by *The New York Times* to answer questions from fans about the kiss, which ranged from concerned to endearingly specific.

"Did you tell them how to kiss, like with the small pecks in the end or did they just improvise, like they felt for their characters to be right at that moment?" Newgirlfangirl from Germany wrote in.

"Embarrassingly, I actually did try to tell them how to kiss," Meriwether wrote back. "I walked up to Jake Johnson between takes and said: 'I want you to kind of take her, and then do this—' (I demonstrated by making my fingers kiss each other) 'then wait and do that again, but kind of like this—' (more finger kissing). He just stared at me for a beat, and then, to his credit, nodded and said, 'I think I got it.'"

Then there was the concern. "Why, oh why, did you go down the Jess and Nick road?" Mnoelle from New York wanted to know. "Everyone knew the attraction was always there under the surface, but now that they kissed, it is going to be so awkward."

Meriwether tried to alleviate those fears by pointing out that the kiss had added a spark and focus to the series, reassuring the fan that Nick and Jess wouldn't get an immediate happily ever after. She offered similarly soothing words to a viewer who was worried that Jess and Nick would turn into Ross and Rachel from *Friends*, rife with breakups and make-ups.

"Don't you find, in real life, that kissing leads to more comedic situations, not less?" Meriwether asked in response. "I like awkwardness. *New Girl* thrives on awkwardness. But I hope you keep watching. Don't give up on us yet. We might actually figure it out."

* * *

The kiss set Season Two on an entirely different course. *New Girl* writer David Iserson had been plugging away at his episode "Table 34," which would air right after "Cooler," when he got a phone call an hour or so before his deadline. He needed to rework the episode immediately. The story's skeleton—which featured Cece attending an Indian matchmaking convention—could stay the same, but he'd have to incorporate Nick and Jess's reaction to their kiss.

And then, of course, he needed to deal with Dr. Sam. The writers had come to genuinely love writing for Walton, even if they knew his character wasn't the right fit for Jess. "It was a matter of making him a doctor, making him so tall and handsome and making him so explicitly what she thinks she wants . . . and then it still kind of not feeling right," Iserson explained. "I think that's a very real thing at her life stage, which is just trying to reckon with what you *say* you want and what you really want."

The writer had to build a scene early on in "Table 34" between Sam and Jess, to quickly reinforce to audiences that this wasn't a match. In an early draft, Iserson had Sam wake up in the morning and tell Jess all about his very uncomplicated dreams from the night before, which involved him driving around on a mountain bike. That didn't make it into the episode but in its place was a simple, subtle line of dialogue that said it all.

"Oh, sweet," Sam says, waking up and pulling his phone out. "Ten emails." He holds out his closed palm for Jess to fist-bump. When Walton read his script, he knew exactly what the writers were doing with that line—they were making Sam a tool once more. "The story of that episode is obviously about Jess and Nick and we need the audience to be rooting for them," he told me, quipping, "So, I'm happy to just jump on the fucking grenade by getting psyched on ten emails."

Still, Walton had felt disappointed when he found out that Nick and Jess were going to kiss. "Oh shit," he realized. "I guess this is the end for Dr. Sam." He was sad to say goodbye to the show. (That hallway scene, though, was impressive. Walton watched when it aired and thought to himself, "Oh wow, Jake went with a nice, hard, passionate, real thing.")

By the end of the episode, the writers had broken Sam and Jess up. Sam was gone (for now) and Nick and Jess were left to figure out what in the world to do next.

At first, the friends fight back against their feelings. Still, their sexual tension continues to grow, hitting a wild fever pitch in the episode "Quick Hardening Caulk." Jess's desire for Nick, which she has pushed so far down, climbs as she watches him start to get his life together—applying himself at his job, doing laundry on a more regular basis, and expressing a potential interest in eating salads. By the end of the episode, the two go head-to-head in the loft over their mounting feelings and, in typical Nick and Jess fashion, manage to make a screaming match feel impossibly steamy.

"You're a MESS!" Jess screams at Nick.

"You're *so annoying* with your little shorts," he shouts back.

"Why are you so angry all the time?!"

Lorene Scafaria directed that episode and, ahead of shooting the back-and-forth, she found herself preoccupied by the giant aquarium sitting in the middle of the room. By the end of the scene, Johnson as Nick—in a fit of intense passion—needed to accidentally break the glass box, spilling pools of water all over the floor. Scafaria was anxious that the stunt would accidentally ruin the loft set.

Still, watching Deschanel and Johnson together was electric. There was something about the two of them—it felt like she had scored a front-row seat to an old screwball romantic comedy in the tradition of *It Happened One Night*. A highlight, she remembers, was Johnson pitching his voice higher and higher while the pair sparred back and forth and then suddenly . . . he dropped it low. "Take off your clothes right now," he says, businesslike and still pretty mad. "I mean it, take off your clothes."

To this day, Johnson's decision to make that small voice shift stays with Scafaria. Her heart skips a little when she rewatches it. "Oh my God," she thought. "Yeah, it's fun and games and this is all really funny but he's still a man and she's still a woman. This feels real."

Meriwether's reassurance to concerned fans had been right in moments like that. Nick and Jess stumbling through their new relationship didn't feel like a bubble bursting. If anything, it had made their dynamic all the more compelling.

Twenty-four episodes were allotted for the second season, but network executives had a sudden burst of inspiration. What if a special episode was shoehorned in following a buzzy *American Idol* episode to help kick up ratings? The writers hustled to figure out a grabby hook, deciding that Nick and Jess's first date could be a great option, nudging the pair's relationship one step forward. It was an interesting space to navigate, two people who had hung out countless times suddenly thrust into the romantic formality of sitting across from each other at a fancy restaurant, far away from the comfort of the loft.

Roughly twenty-five ad executives from Ford were on set that day, huddled around the monitor into the early hours of the morning as they shot those date scenes. The company had paid to have their car appear in the episode and wanted to make sure that *New Girl* was correctly portraying their product's new feature—a touchless trunk opener.

Scene directions called for Nick to open and close the trunk as he changed in and out of his fancy clothes. Ford's touchless feature could not have fought the joke more. The whole bit revolved around Nick hastily running back and forth from the restaurant to the car, and waiting for the trunk to open slowed down the whole momentum of the scene.

(As an aside—Ford Fusion would end up becoming a semifrequent sponsor of the show, with the writers and actors doing the very best they could to make the marketing material not sound completely insane. An entire episode was written around Ford in the first season, when Jess is forced to try to model alongside the car after Cece gets too sick to do the job. Meriwether came up with that whole clever concept, embracing the mindset of "If we're going to do product placement, we're really going to lean into it and put it front and center!" It was a whole big production and, after that, *New Girl* tried to keep their ads way shorter.)

Nick and Jess run into Jess's ex Russell during their first date and swiftly find their already fragile romance challenged. Mr. Fancyman offers them two pens and two pieces of paper, saying, "I think you guys don't really know what you are to each other . . . Tell you what. Why don't you write it down? Write down what you think this is." The pair comply, privately scratching out their answers, but are both too scared to show each other what they wrote. They've hit a standstill and, once again, Russell is there to remind us that these characters still have some growing up to do.

One moment finally pushes Nick to drop all of his fears and hang-ups and go all in with Jess. It happens in the following episode, "Virgins," when the gang flashes back on how each of them lost their virginity. Nick recalls almost losing his while on a business trip with his dad (played by Dennis Farina) but being too scared to go through with it. When his dad returns to the hotel that night, the pair have a heart-to-heart.

"You think too much, you think too much about everything," his dad tells him, in that signature gravely Farina voice. ". . . Listen, Nicky, you don't have to do anything that you don't want to do. I just want to make sure that you don't miss out on the things in life that are happening when you're not thinking—because, believe you me, those are the best things in life."

Alec Berg directed that episode. There's an old joke, he told me, that the best piece of directing advice is to point the camera at the actors. In that scene, Berg decided to do just that, getting out of the way of Johnson and Farina as they performed together on that hotel bed, while quietly marveling at how natural their performances were.

"Goddamn, are these guys good," Berg thought.

With his dad's words rattling in his head, Nick is finally ready to have sex with Jess. There was debate about how, exactly, he should do that. Initially, there was a whole back-and-forth of dialogue between the pair before they hook up. But something about that scene just didn't feel right. Berg stepped in with a different idea. "What if we don't do anything?" he asked. "What if she leaves for the night and then we cut to the two of them in bed?"

They decided to find a happy medium, cutting down the dialogue and making the moments before the two have sex brief and urgent. Nick chases after Jess as she gets into the elevator, sweeping her into his arms. "What are you doing?" she asks.

Nick, with more authority and confidence than we've ever seen, replies, "Let's not think about it."

He carries her to the bed and they look down at it, both terrified and excited. The episode ends with the pair postcoital, feeling every breath of emotion. Meriwether made the decision to position a camera above Johnson and Deschanel, asking them to react the way they thought their characters would in that moment. The result, Meriwether would later tell *Entertainment Weekly*, was "a kind of a cool thing that you don't always see on TV: two actors and thirty seconds of silence."

"We wanted it to feel honest and, honestly, *hot*," she added. "What's fun is doing a genuinely sexy romance in a sitcom. That doesn't always happen."

At long last, Jess and Nick became an official couple in Season Three. Ahead of shooting that season, Meriwether took the writers on a retreat to Ojai, a craggy mountain city in California, where they gathered in a rented house and discussed what was to come. "Where should we pick back up in the first episode?" they asked themselves. "Should it be a few months later? How do you make the lack of tension compelling?"

At the time, executive producer Katherine Pope had her eye on the big picture. She knew that there would be a stopping point in Nick and Jess's relationship thanks, in part, to Nick's immaturity. "We can set them on this path because he's not ready for her, he's not ready to be in love," she thought. "He's not ready to commit, he's not ready to be an adult. He doesn't have a wallet." The studio used to ask, "One day, Nick's going to go to law school . . . ?" No, the writers collectively agreed, Nick was not going to go back to law school. But he was going to grow up and—at some point—be fully ready for Jess. Now, though . . . not so much.

So, how should they write this short-lived romance, while respecting the fans *and* still being realistic about how these two characters would be in a relationship? It would prove to be one of the thorniest challenges in the writers' room. There were the episodes that really shone, particularly when Nick and Jess were at odds over something that didn't touch too darkly on their fundamental differences. "Basketsball" was a highlight, with Jess trying desperately to win over Coach, who's returned to the loft, by pretending she likes the Detroit Pistons. This infuriates Nick, a lifelong Bulls fan. We get to see Jess and Nick bump heads—in a fun way!—while exploring their dynamics between other characters in the loft. We're also reminded of Nick's love and deep appreciation for Jess as he counsels Coach on how to relate to her.

"This is how you get in with Jess," he tries to explain. "You know when you're driving in your car and you have a random thought, like . . . 'I wonder if seals are friends'?"

"Yeah," Coach muses. "Or like 'I really want to text right now, but there's a cop behind me . . .'"

"That's not what I mean. I mean more like sweet, kind of emotional stuff. Like, if you combed a gorilla's hair, would it like it? . . . Tell that to her and you get a friend for life."

Episodes got stickier when Nick and Jess clashed in ways that felt too painfully real. The writers tried to play into the pair's differences with the episode "The Box," which follows Jess's discovery that Nick has stacks and stacks of unpaid bills stowed away in a cardboard box. She decides to use the money that his dad left him to pay off the overdue bills, catching Nick's wrath in the process. He strikes back, going into her room and messing around with her stuff, including her "metal toothpicks" (bobby pins) and "beat-up old sacks" (vintage purses), much of which was Johnson's improvisation.

On paper, it seemed like the conflict could make for an entertaining twenty-one-minute exploration of the different ways these two characters live their lives. Highlighting that friction when the pair were friends had been fun, but there was something harsher about that tension now. It wasn't as enjoyable to watch and felt genuinely uncomfortable at times. By the end of the episode, it's clear that Jess is compromising her values by not only allowing Nick to remain behind on his bills but trying to embrace that part of him. There's compromise and then there's settling for something that's not quite right. This felt more like the latter.

The impossible had started to happen. Meriwether was getting Nick-and-Jess fatigue. She was tired of writing them into so many scenes together and feeling restricted in the kinds of stories she could tell within the loft. And there was something else that was nagging her, too.

Nick, she told *Uproxx*'s Alan Sepinwall, was a "fucking idiot" and she loved him for it. Jess, meanwhile, was so lovable to her core. The dynamic between the pair might have worked during the intoxicating will-they, won't-they phase, but now that they were in a relationship? She had her doubts.

"When they were dating, suddenly everything got so much more real," Meriwether said. "It was like, 'Maybe Jess is dating an alcoholic, and it's not funny?'"

The writers had painfully honest conversations about their own romantic relationships. Nearly all of their most heart-wrenching breakups had happened suddenly. If there was a kernel of toxicity in that relationship, it could grow and grow, and then, boom—one horrible moment of truth. Nick and Jess had gotten together in such a sudden, abrupt fashion, with neither of them thinking it through, and Jess was still in a committed relationship with Sam.

What if their relationship ended, as Baer put it, under equally fast and dirty circumstances? The result was "Mars Landing." After a drunken night of playing True American, Jess and Nick wake up hungover and running late for a child's birthday party. Exhausted and cranky, the pair quibble over the fact that Nick hasn't put together the toy they're giving to the birthday boy, as he promised he would.

That argument leads to a larger conversation about what they want from life. Jess has grounded plans for their future: moving back to Portland, raising a family, and placing a high value on education. Nick's thoughts are outlandish and on a different planet, quite literally. He's always thought it would be cool to be a long-haul truck driver and thinks that it could be great if they lived on a spacecraft on the surface of Mars. ("If you don't think there's gonna be space travel in the next twenty years, then you've got your head buried in sand, girlie. It's already basically happening.")

As they go back and forth the conversation hits a wall and then gets real . . . a sad amount of real.

Nick: I'm sorry, but I'm not that guy who's gonna put the toy together. That's just not me. I'm the kind of guy who's gonna leave it in the box.
Jess: I don't want you to be that guy. I want you to be yourself.
Nick: I want you to be yourself.
Jess: Are we . . . ?
Nick: No! I love you!
Jess: Well, I love you, too.
Nick: More than I've ever loved anybody.
Jess: But what if that's the only thing we have in common?

By the end of the episode, Nick and Jess have broken up. In one of the most touching moments of the show, the pair stand in the hallway between their two rooms—the exact same place where they first kissed—and Jess pulls him into her, this time for a long, fierce hug. There was rarely time to build in pauses while editing *New Girl*, but editor Hugh Ross made sure to add a few more beats so the audience could really sit in it for a moment. Nick and Jess might be over as a couple, but their friendship, so loving and impressively strong after weathering a multitude of storms, would remain.

After "Mars Landing" aired, Meriwether's finger hovered over the Twitter button on her phone, where fan reactions to the breakup awaited her. She stopped herself. "I can't do it yet," she decided. Maybe next week.

If writing the breakup episode was hard, writing the episode afterward, in which the pair have to deal with the aftermath of their split, proved to be an equally formidable challenge. How could the writers make it, at least in part, funny? Berkley remembers Alex Cuthbertson piping up with an idea. "What if they have a honey roast?" he asked. The resounding response around the table was . . . what in the world is a honey roast?

"It's a roast, but it's sweet," he explained.

That could be the ticket. As Nick and Jess processed their breakup, there could be humor in the juxtaposition of Winston's triumphant news that he had passed his police exam. Not only that, but they'd have to hide their sad news in order to not pull focus from Winston, who has donned an all-white suit for the occasion and awaits their compliments as he sits atop a prominent chair. (Steven Tsuchida, the episode's director, had Morris try multiple versions of his character's first entrance into the loft, as he reveals his suit and cane. They settled on a take where he declares, with unabashed smugness and glee, "You guys, I am walking on air," and then struggles to shut the door behind him.)

Berkley and Kim Rosenstock, who co-wrote the episode together, stood on set that day and watched the scene unfold. "We're getting fired," Berkley cracked, gazing at the tableau of Winston sitting on his throne and Jess beside him, dutifully dressed as a cat, per Winston's request. "Liz and Brett have seen this, right? It looks like a fever dream."

The scene took them a long time to shoot, making their way through a long list of alts and giving the actors a chance to improv. At one point, Tsuchida approached Johnson, who had been wearing a pair of dark shades throughout the scene. "Are you going to be wearing the glasses the whole time?" he asked. "I think we want to see your eyes."

"I just want to wear these glasses," Johnson responded, and he would end up doing so for the entire duration of that honey roast.

There was still plenty of room to explore the awkwardness of Nick and Jess's breakup throughout the episode, including the first few minutes, which finds the pair try to come to terms with their newly fractured relationship. Johnson and Deschanel dabbled in light, improvised moments throughout, with Johnson nervously riffing about monkeys in the wild and Deschanel elongating the word *faaaaaaantastic* after learning that Nick is—allegedly—feeling totally fine about everything.

The final moments of "Big News" find Nick and Jess in separate rooms mourning their breakups the only way they know how. Jess is lying on the couch, crying and watching *Dirty Dancing*. Nick is in the other room, drowning his sorrows in liquor. Only this time, they're grieving together, with Nick drunk dialing her and the two sweetly consoling each other.

Rosenstock wanted to bookend all the farce with a quiet, more grounded ending. She loved the idea of bringing back *Dirty Dancing*, the very movie that Jess had watched when Nick first came into her life and she was dealing with the pain of another breakup. "In that way, it kind of brings you back to the origin of their friendship," Rosenstock told me. "And now all these years later he's the boyfriend she's breaking up with and he's also still the friend who's listening to her watch the movie and offering her tissues. It's so messy and funny and it felt true to life and to the characters that they would help each other through their breakup from each other."

Before shooting that scene, Tsuchida gave Deschanel and Johnson a note. "Look, you guys still really love each other and care about each other as friends, or even more than friends, just remember that," the director said. He didn't want Johnson to make the exchange a complete joke, reminding him, "Keep that tenderness there, dial that in." They got their take quickly, pausing for a short conversation about how much Jess should cry. Tsuchida and Deschanel settled on the idea that she shouldn't cry full-on tears because there was something more endearing about someone trying to hold back the flood.

When Jess tells Nick she's run out of tissues, he opens his door a crack and shoves a box out to her. "Thanks," she says through sniffles. "No problem," he replies. "That's what I'm here for."

A pause.

Nick: G'night, honey.
Jess: Good night.

With that, the Nick and Jess chapter had finally closed. For now.

An Ode to Bearclaw

My apartment has cable internet now . . . did you get even prettier?

—BEARCLAW

Josh Gad didn't want to do guest-star roles. He told his agent as much, explaining that—unless he loved the series—he wasn't interested.

Then he got a call.

"All right, I know you don't want to get guest-star offers but I have one for you that I think you might like . . . ," his agent began.

"What is it?" Gad asked, skeptical.

"New Girl."

That gave the actor pause. "Ah, shit," he said. He loved *New Girl.* Still, he wasn't quite sure how he would fit into the world of apartment 4D until a script for the episode "Katie" arrived. The character the writers wanted him to play was named Bearclaw, an eccentric beer-delivery guy whom Jess accidentally finds herself on a date with.

Gad immediately called his agent back. "One hundred percent, I'm in. This character is *so bonkers*. The only thing I ask is, if I do this, they just trust me and let me do my thing with it."

And indeed, from the moment Gad opened his mouth on set and "a desperate, loud, almost carnal voice" escaped, he was never once asked to tone it down. Gad kept waiting for someone to tell him that he wasn't playing the character right, that his take wasn't what they had imagined. Those words never came.

Instead, he sat next to Deschanel in Jess's bedroom for their date and nobody called cut, allowing their exchange to stretch on and on, becoming increasingly uncomfortable and bizarre. Topics included anal thermometers and a fetish for ghosts.

Later, they'd shoot in the bar's bathroom, where a heartbroken Bearclaw discovers that Jess has ditched their date to hook up with someone else. Gad improvised dropping to his knees and wailing, "WHAT IS HAPPENING." He also made the decision to start sobbing. It's the perfect *New Girl* scene in so many ways: chaotic, confusing, farcical, and deeply character-specific—because yes, of course, in the midst of it all, we'd find out that Nick has a deep love and appreciation for Bearclaw. ("She's not good enough for you, Bearclaw! None of these people are good enough for you!!")

Gad saw his character as a twelve-year-old who wasn't in control of his emotions and had read the pickup-artist book *The Game*. Bearclaw, he decided, would have a singsongy, overrehearsed way of speaking to women, like he had practiced all his lines in his bathroom mirror ahead of time. The actor loved the challenge of making this person, who could potentially be seen as an asshole, lovable.

If Gad's first episode had been a trust fall for the *New Girl* producers, his second episode, "Walk of Shame," was a trust fall for the actor. When he read the script, he was confused. "Wait, they do a woodland-creature musical . . . ?" he thought. "Have they lost their minds?" It was all so avant-garde. Plus, he wondered . . . did anyone care about seeing his crazy character again?

Gad really respected Meriwether and the writers, though, so if they thought it would work, he was ready to help make it happen. The actor, alongside Deschanel and guest star Justin Long, prerecorded the song ahead of time and gave it their all that day, coming up with dance moves on the fly. Director Christine Gernon sat behind the monitor crying from laughter, delaying calling cut so she could get as much footage as possible of the bizarrely earnest performance. When they were done, Gad thought, "Okay, they know what they're doing. This is insane but, by God, I think it's going to work."

More than ten years and a fleeting two and a quarter appearances on *New Girl* later, the sweet, strange legacy of Bearclaw lives on.

"In my wildest dreams, I never imagined a world in which, and I'm not exaggerating, on a daily basis, based on five minutes of screen time, someone sees me and shouts, '*Bearclaw!*,'" Gad told me.

Somewhere out there, Nick Miller would be very proud.

8

Prince

Finish your pancake. Let's get to work.

—PRINCE

DANA WALDEN, FOX'S CEO, HAD a proposition for Liz Meriwether. What if she stepped in as *New Girl*'s co-showrunner? For the first two seasons, Meriwether had served as the head writer, while Baer and Finkel held the role of showrunner. Walden, who knew the writer was a little afraid of power, sensed Meriwether's hesitation, telling her, "You cannot be prolific unless you're prepared to be a leader."

So, Meriwether stepped up to the plate in Season Three, taking on her newfound duties just as the show hit its stormiest season yet. Yes, that season featured Nick and Jess getting together, presenting the newly minted co-showrunner with the challenges of navigating the definitive end to their biggest will-they, won't-they storyline. But there was also the urgent problem of Schmidt. Or, should we say, Evil Schmidt. The writers found themselves accidentally crafting a polarizing storyline for the beloved character, turning him from an endearing comedy fixture in the loft to a two-timing boyfriend, who—unbeknownst to both of them—is dating Cece and Elizabeth at the same time.

Meriwether's thinking was that Schmidt, who genuinely loved these women, was too weak to make a decision and too scared to hurt either one. Ahead of the show's season premiere, Meriwether defended Schmidt's indiscretions to *The Hollywood Reporter*, saying, "He is not a bad guy—but he can be a bad guy sometimes. Under extreme circumstances, he can do bad things. We all can. This felt like the right kind of mistake for him to make."

Much like she did after Nick and Jess kissed, she offered a plea of confidence to fans. "I hope people will go on the journey with us, because I know it's a little bit different."

The writers had been so excited about diving into the Evil Schmidt storyline. But they quickly realized the fans didn't like it. They really, really didn't like it. Meriwether didn't have the stomach to read the comments and social media posts, so Baer and Finkel would summarize the gist of their complaints. Critics had their thoughts, too, with several raising their eyebrows during the early days of Season Three, including *Entertainment Weekly*'s Lanford Beard, who wrote, "There's a reason that Schmidt's love triangle hasn't been as funny as most Schmidt-uations—it was too real."

When Kasdan was working on *Freaks and Geeks* they had a tenet they tried to follow: Never throw any of the characters under the bus. Nothing should be at their expense. The tricky part here was: How do you do this storyline without making Schmidt the total bad guy?

Meriwether realized that she had started to think of *New Girl* as a cable show, where characters could grow and stretch and evolve in shorter amounts of time. After a long, exhausting day of work, fans didn't want to turn on the TV and see their favorite characters morphing in intense or surprising ways. They wanted to like their sitcom characters, people who had become reliable fictional friends.

It wasn't that Schmidt wouldn't have struggled mightily with choosing between Elizabeth and Cece, and it wasn't that he might not have made the decision to cheat. It was that viewers hadn't signed up for this type of uncomfortable, morally dubious material when they hit play. *New Girl* was a comfort watch. While bumps and tension are necessary for even the best kinds of comfort shows, there's a tricky line when it comes to navigating just *how* much reality audiences want to digest.

Schmidt finally tells Cece he's been cheating on her in the middle of a restaurant, after being forced into a corner by Jess. Something about the scene wasn't working and the actors ended up doing a reshoot, which also wasn't clicking. There were jokes peppered throughout and Greenfield approached Meriwether. "I don't know how to rewrite this," he said. "But you are at your best . . . if you write this scene and it is a real apology and a real breakup and then at the very, very end of it, you find some ridiculous, awkward thing for one of the characters to say."

Greenfield knew that's what was so special about Meriwether's writing. So many television comedies felt the pressure to do jokes, jokes, jokes, and follow a template that was familiar for audiences. "You also have networks that are pushing for that rhythm, and when you go against that rhythm, I think it scares them," Greenfield said. "Liz has such a unique rhythm to her writing, and she can write a full scene where there's not a single joke and then slip one in at the very end and it catches you so off guard—and the buildup to it is so exciting as an actor because you know what's coming."

That's exactly what happened with the breakup scene. It's one of the most painful moments in *New Girl* and crushing, masterfully done performances by Greenfield and Simone. You feel so deeply for Cece and, against your better judgment, find yourself experiencing pangs of empathy for Schmidt, too. Just as Cece leaves and your heart is being wound into a tight, tight knot, Schmidt says, "I'm just realizing I don't have any cash on me. If anyone would be willing to loan me twelve dollars for the valet that would be greatly appreciated." He has tears in his eyes as he says his line, adding to the crescendo of the moment.

Greenfield and Simone were invited to improvise during that scene. "We need you to talk to each other," Kasdan told them. Simone ad-libbed, "I don't even know you anymore," and broke down in tears. Greenfield, she remembers, took it in, his face absorbing all her emotions.

"I know that storyline is not necessarily one that people look toward and go, 'That was the show, they really nailed it on that one,'" Greenfield said, looking back. "But I really love how we dug in and found that scene. It was moments like that when I was so excited by Liz's writing . . . when she really digs into that tone, there's nothing like it."

After leaving Schmidt at the restaurant, Cece tells Elizabeth about the infidelity and she arrives at Schmidt's doorstep later that night, pie in hand, which she presses to his face. "You broke my heart," she says. "Mail me back my mouth guard."

Schmidt's downfall was celebrated by *Vulture*'s Josh Gondelman, who took a victory lap after Cece and Elizabeth discovered he's been cheating on them. "I was tired of watching Schmidt devolve into a total dirtbag while he continued to get everything he wanted," he wrote. "He *deserved* these consequences. Seeing Schmidt with his face disfigured by pastry like a delicious Harvey Dent released the tension that had been building up."

Schmidt, Gondelman added, didn't seem to be coming back from this two-timing storyline. "The Schmidt we knew and (reluctantly) loved is dead, at least for now," he posited.

Gondelman was right. Despite the cheating storyline coming to an end, Evil Schmidt continued his reign, turning his attention to Nick and Jess's relationship, determined to break the pair up. The writers had enjoyed seeing Schmidt at odds with Nick and Jess during the previous season's episode "Parking Spot," which saw him competing with Jess for Nick's favor. Maybe it could be fun to extend that rivalry once more? Alas, it was also a little too bleak.

"Do you think fans appreciate that *New Girl* can get a little dark for a comedy?" *The Hollywood Reporter*'s Mikey O'Connell asked the showrunner amid this season's tone change.

"I hope so," she replied. "Or they'll be like, 'I'm uncomfortable. Make it stop!'"

The writers, Greenfield recalled, decided to put Schmidt on ice for a bit. They moved his character to an apartment down the hall in an effort to regroup.

As the show dealt with the unexpected Schmidt backlash and the fallout from Nick and Jess's romance, a dark cloud hovered around the network's growing frustration over *New Girl*'s slipping ratings.

The sitcom had started out with such massive numbers right out of the gate, but those ratings had started to trickle downward with each passing episode, hitting an all-time low by the time "Fancyman Part 2" aired. "What happened to *New Girl*?" the *New York Times* journalist Bill Carter asked. "The sitcom that exploded at the start of the fall season with bona fide hit ratings has moved into a pattern that is approaching a tailspin."

Carter wasn't faulting Meriwether for the plunge. He pointed out that after the show's first three episodes, Fox removed the series from the air for a month. When it returned, it had lost more than 1.2 million viewers. As ratings continued to dip, there was an added sting: the lead-in shows to *New Girl* weren't pulling in nearly enough fans. *Glee*, once a ratings juggernaut, was losing viewers and had gone on hiatus. In its place was *I Hate My Teenage Daughter*, a short-lived sitcom that struggled to gain an audience, and *Raising Hope*, which also wasn't pulling in big numbers, setting *New Girl* up for even lower numbers when it aired right afterward.

Early on, there had been nominations and critical acclaim. "Dude, I got invited to the Golden Globes!" Johnson remembers excitedly saying. "Dude, that amazing actor just said they watched [the show]!" Overnight, it all just . . . stopped. Johnson watched as the show hemorrhaged numbers and the group of actors who used to give him a "bro handshake" were doing it with other people now. At some point, *New Girl* had become the butt of the joke for comedians at cool parties, who would make cracks like, "Oh, Schmidtty and Nick, what are you up to now?"

The number of viewers watching *New Girl* was calculated by Nielsen ratings. The system—dreaded by so many showrunners—measures how many people are watching a show live. Certain households are chosen to have a box installed inside their television and their data is collected for a final tally on a show's viewership numbers. Every Wednesday morning at 8 AM an email would arrive in Meriwether's inbox with the subject line "FW: Blackberry Fast Nationals—Tuesday [the date]." Sometimes she'd force herself to click and sometimes she couldn't bring herself to, instead waiting to see the responses trickling in, which were either somewhere along the lines of "*Woof* . . ." or "Yes!"

Meriwether wasn't alone in her struggle. Two years into *New Girl*, she joined a roundtable of showrunners for an interview with *The Hollywood Reporter* and was immediately asked about sinking numbers across the board on network television.

"From a ratings standpoint, this has been a tough year for network comedy and I'm curious for your thoughts—to comment on why you think that's the case?" Lacey Rose, a journalist for the outlet, asked.

"Oh my God," Meriwether said softly, before letting out a laugh.

"People are not watching less television, they're watching more television, they're just not watching at the exact time that counts for that stupid number that comes out at eight AM," *Parks and Recreation*'s showrunner Michael Schur replied.

"I've noticed a real trend where people will DVR an entire season of something and then they just sit there and consume it all in one great gulp, which I feel like is a relatively new thing," Matthew Carnahan, *House of Lies*' showrunner, added. (Bingeing before it was called bingeing.)

When Meriwether was in the early *New Girl* days, her friend Beau Willimon—the same one who did a Daffy Duck impression for her postbreakup—shared that he was working on a new show for Netflix called *House of Cards*. "Netflix has shows?" Meriwether asked. She really doubted the idea at the time.

But now the landscape was changing—and changing fast. Johnson was blown away to discover that so many of *New Girl*'s biggest fans didn't even own a television set. They were all watching the show on their phones or getting together in groups to watch on a propped-up iPad. When he caught a set designer panicking about what curtains looked like in a scene, he tried to soothe those nerves with a dose of reality. "I'm telling you, the kids are watching it like this!" he said, holding up his phone. "Just get the story right, get the jokes right."

Amid the many questions swirling around the future of broadcast television, Meriwether was pulled into a meeting with the president of Fox. She was already consistently getting the impression that he was frustrated that *New Girl* wasn't more like *Modern Family*, a ratings juggernaut that seemed to pull in just about everybody. This conversation was uniquely discouraging. He held up a graph, showing her the downward trajectory in viewers since the show premiered. *New Girl*, it seemed, was missing a key demographic: men. It would take a long time to dig herself out of the hole that conversation created. Meriwether was left with the impression that she needed to somehow chase an imaginary forty-five-year-old guy, convincing him to declare, "*New Girl*? I guess I'll give this a try."

New Girl wasn't the only show getting caught in the rabid chase for guy viewers. Across the board, Fox's ratings had dropped in the 18–49 demographic and the network was taking swift action. In 2013, the network debuted two shows aimed at recapturing men—*Dads*, about two video-game developers, and *Brooklyn Nine-Nine*, which followed police officers working at the NYPD's 99th Precinct. As Fox attempted to court this elusive audience, *Time* writer Eliana Dockterman offered a plea in the form of an op-ed, titled "Dear Guys, It's Okay to Watch *New Girl*."

"Here's the big secret: *New Girl*—despite its girly title—isn't actually about girls," she wrote. "It's a show about three guys who happen to have a girl roommate. The show addresses just as many 'male' issues as it does 'female' ones." She faulted the show's marketing campaign, noting, "Watch any early ad for the show and you might think it's a half hour of Deschanel singing all the time."

There was something weirdly taboo going on with *New Girl*'s male viewers. Men would approach Meriwether and try to hedge their love of her show. "You're not going to believe this but . . . ," they'd start their sentences.

"I totally believe it!" she'd shoot back. "You can be a guy and watch this show and enjoy it, that is totally normal."

The writers would sit in their room and brainstorm how to get more guys to watch the show. Meriwether was getting constant phone calls informing her that *New Girl* wasn't hitting all four quadrants of the demographic. The network suggested they tell stories about the roommates going out on the town and just generally serving up more "guy energy." Another directive was for slotting in "locker-room" talk. When things would become emotional between the men—like Schmidt expressing his love for Nick—the network notes back were usually in the neighborhood of "Can we be a little more dude about this?" Or as one unnamed person who worked at the studio said of Nick and Schmidt, "It's a little bit gay."

As Greenfield remembers it, the first one or two takes between Nick and Schmidt were probably played how the network wanted it. "And then it wasn't funny," he said. "We both knew it and it was probably me who was like, 'I'm gonna switch this up.' We would improv on it and it would end up moving in that direction."

At a certain point, Johnson had to let those network notes go in one ear and out the other. There would be a quintessential guy scene—like a directive that Winston, Schmidt, and Nick start wrestling—but, Johnson recalls, because it was Meriwether's show, they taped pillows to themselves and drank sangria. "The network would be like, 'You guys, we've got to get you more masculine.' And then I'd go, 'We're sitting under a table talking about how cute we are.'"

Here was the problem. *New Girl* had become so special, in part, because these guys were *no longer* the alpha types, bent on hooking up with women. They felt emotions deeply and genuinely cared about each other. Schmidt, once the most sexually charged of the loft, was becoming a full-on den mother for the group, and the writers really loved the sweet—and yes, honestly kind of romantic—turn his relationship had taken with

Nick. So much of their dynamic, Johnson would later recount, was the two actors sitting on that couch together at the end of a long working day and Johnson asking the writers, "I tell him he's like a husband to me . . . ?"

Meriwether had gone down a similarly unconventional route with Jess and Cece's relationship. These were two women who were never going to duke it out over a guy's affections—even in a jokey, one-off-episode capacity, contrary to the blueprint laid out by so many other fictional female friendships. The *one* time Jess mistakenly thinks Cece is interested in someone she has a past with—Nick Miller—she grits her teeth and tries to help her friend anyway.

"So much comedy pits women against each other, fighting over a man to find comedy," Simone said. "What was so beautiful about Liz's writing when she writes about women is [that] she tells the truth of female friendships. You can find so much comedy in the sisterhood."

Even when Meriwether was being told to go in the wrong direction by the network, she had to play ball. "It's almost impossible to completely reject it because you're in this pressure cooker, and the network has the ability to cancel the show at any time," she told me. "So you're also, like, well, I have to do whatever I need to do to keep the show on the air."

Amid all the anxiety, there was a reason for hope. Apartment 4D was about to get Coach back in the loft.

It all happened in a surprisingly easy, efficient manner. Wayans Jr. and Johnson were out at a bar while shooting the 2014 action-comedy *Let's Be Cops* when Wayans Jr. got the call that *Happy Endings* was being canceled. ABC had decided to pull the plug on the show he had left *New Girl* for, wrapping up the series after three seasons.

"Come do *New Girl*," Johnson told him when he got off the call.

"Are you sure?" Wayans Jr. asked. "Would Liz want me back?"

"Let me find out," Johnson responded.

He gave Meriwether a ring and the showrunner was happy to have Wayans Jr. return.

The actor would be welcomed to his old room with open arms during his first episode back, Season Three's "Coach," reintroducing him to audiences with the explanation that he had split from his girlfriend and was ready to move back in.

While Meriwether was excited to bring Wayans Jr. back into the fold, there was a nagging question on the horizon. Who, exactly, was Coach? They only had one episode with his character, who was painted as a loud, jocky guy. In the seasons since then, the rest of the characters had evolved so much. Loft dynamics had shifted, too. How would Coach fit into this new world? The writers decided they wanted to lean into Coach's alpha energy, creating someone whom the other guys would find cool and a little intimidating.

In case fans had forgotten just how much apartment 4D had changed since the pilot episode, Coach and his kelly-green athleisure wear offered a jolt of a reminder.

In his first episode back, the gang's old roommate is ready to party. He informs all the guys that they're going to a strip club that night, which immediately causes friction between Nick and Jess who, at the time, are in the infancy of their relationship. As she grapples with Nick's inability to call her his girlfriend, Coach, Schmidt, Nick, and Winston hit the town—exactly what Fox network execs had been asking for all along. Only the bro-y night takes a turn. Aside from Coach, the guys don't really want to be there; they're exhausted and Nick is panicking about how he left things with Jess. As the evening unfolds, we learn that Coach is miserable, too, and hiding the pain of his recent breakup behind bravado.

"We're too old for this whole night," Nick tells Coach. "Life changed, you gotta grow up." Well, Nick concedes, maybe they don't have to *fully* grow up just yet. The foursome end up making a big scene in front of Coach's ex-girlfriend's new boyfriend before running away, terrified. It's a temperature check on the characters as a whole, reminding viewers that they're on the road to growing up, while assuring us that there was still childish fun to be had and a multitude of mistakes to be made.

Initially, the writers dabbled with the idea of Coach getting together with Cece. Fusfeld thought that could be a funny storyline, before promptly realizing that there wasn't enough romantic chemistry. It *did* offer an opportunity to find new shades of what made Wayans Jr., as Coach, funny. Cece knocks Coach off-balance, allowing the audience to see him at his most vulnerable. Some of Coach's strongest moments—from nervously getting drunk during a teacher's retreat to tentatively leaning over to kiss his future girlfriend May for the first time—would come from when he was pushed a little off-center.

"Leave it to an old guy to show how much *New Girl* has grown . . . ," *The Daily Beast*'s Kevin Fallon mused. "Has every creative decision *New Girl*'s made been conventional for a sitcom? No. But nothing the show's done—stretching all the way back to the way it handled Coach's exit in the first place—has been. It's taken his return to remind us that its lack of convention is why *New Girl* remains one of TV's most deceptively exciting shows."

Wayans Jr. was a mellow guy, but when he showed up on set he transformed into his character, arriving game ready, like somebody had just switched on a scoreboard buzzer. As Morris worked to find his character, Wayans Jr. would whisper jokes in his ear when they were trying out bits for a scene. "He's one of the funniest people on the planet and his joke-writing ability is top, top, top," Morris said. "So when he pitches a joke, it's funny. And you use it."

It was amid the resurrection of Good Schmidt, the scramble of figuring out who Coach was, and the ongoing battle for better ratings, that Prince reached out.

The email came out of the blue. It arrived in Deschanel's inbox and read, "Hello, I am the manager for the legendary artist Prince and he wants to be on *New Girl*."

"Am I being pranked?" she thought to herself and forwarded the email to her agent. "Can you vet this? Is this real?" she asked.

Turns out, it was no joke. Prince really did want to guest star on the show. Meriwether knew he was a longtime fan of *New Girl*—he would allegedly watch episodes while on the road—and she had offered him a cameo in "Virgins," playing the rock star Cece loses her virginity to. He turned that one down. (The material, the showrunner suspected, was too racy.) But now, here he was, offering himself up, a beacon of hope in a season that had proved to be so exhaustingly thorny.

Meriwether got to work on a pitch for Prince's team. The idea went as follows: all the characters attend a party at the singer's house and he ends up being the one responsible for Nick and Jess saying "I love you" to each other for the first time. Prince liked the idea of helping Jess share her feelings with Nick, and writers Rob Rosell and Dave Feeney started writing a script. The episode would be slotted after the Super Bowl, a coveted spot with maximum eyeballs. This could be an incredible chance to reinvigorate the audience while introducing new fans to the show.

Rosell and Feeney's story begins with Jess and Cece scoring an invite to Prince's mansion, a joyous event that's thrown to a screeching halt when Nick unexpectedly tells Jess he loves her. Taken aback, Jess pulls out two finger guns and points them at him as the car pulls away toward the party. (This was, perhaps, an homage to Johnson's own love of improvising finger guns on set—nothing made him prouder than getting a finger gun on television.)

Nick, Schmidt, Coach, and Winston manage to sneak into the mansion, with Nick desperately trying to make things right with Jess, who is now fully freaking out. When the two find each other at the party and try to sort through their issues, an unexpected figure appears before them in the garden.

"Hi," he says, taking off his very chic pair of moon-shaped shades. "I'm Prince. So what seems to be the problem?"

The *New Girl* crew rented a mansion in Altadena, scheduling four shooting nights there. The Friday before the singer was set to arrive, a production meeting was held in O'Malley's office for final preparations. First assistant director Michael Risoli was feeling confident about their schedule—they had diligently maneuvered timings so that the cast and crew would have the mandated hours required for both work and rest. They were almost ready to start shooting and sets had been built. This was the most expensive episode of *New Girl* they had ever budgeted.

With those ducks in a row, the most challenging part seemed to be over.

"Okay," Risoli told everybody. "We're ready to do this."

"Okay, good, good," Kasdan, the show's executive producer, said, before turning to O'Malley. "Do we think Prince is actually going to show up?"

Risoli was startled. Why *wouldn't* he show up?

It turned out that Prince was known to back out of obligations last minute if he was unhappy. There had already been an anxiety-producing close call for Meriwether, when he almost quit after discovering that the script featured Jess and Nick saying "I love you" after they returned from his party. That wasn't what he had signed up for. He was there to help make that special moment happen *for* them.

Meriwether managed to wrangle him back in with a script rewrite, but the question mark remained if he might get spooked again. They began discussing what they would do if, come shooting day, he didn't show up. Fred Armisen, who impersonated Prince on *Saturday Night Live*, had done a hilarious job when he subbed in for the star during a table read for the episode. As Risoli remembers it, the group began toying with the idea of him filling in just in case they were ghosted.

So much work had gone into the episode. Prince had very specific, detailed instructions, which everyone—from cast to crew—were carefully trying to follow. Deschanel was doing fittings every night after work, trying to find a look for Jess that the singer liked. They'd send Prince photos, to which he'd reply, "Not that, not that." Finally, Deschanel remembers, Meriwether got a call on set and handed the phone over. It was Prince on the other line.

"I want you to look like Stevie Nicks," he told her.

Oh! Okay. That made sense. A box from a store in Minneapolis that he loved arrived. Inside was a crushed ombre dress with ribbons and feathers, which Jess would wear when she tells Nick she loves him for the first time. Prince also brought his own clothes for Jess to model during a fashion montage in the episode. His petite stature allowed Deschanel to easily slip into each one.

Production designer Michael Whetstone was looped in to discuss what the look and feel of the fake Prince's house would be. "We're going to put you in touch with Prince's people," he was told, and a detailed correspondence sprung up between himself and Theo London, chief of staff, tour manager, and a direct line to Prince. They discussed everything from the location to the furniture that would go inside the mansion. The singer was also heavily involved in what art was hung on his bedroom walls—asking that everything be by an artist he liked named Stella Blu. Drawings of eggs featuring his poetry were created at his request. The singer, Whetstone realized, had taken on the role of showrunning his own episode.

When the first day of shooting arrived, the general feeling hanging over that grand Altadena mansion was exhaustion, nerves, and excitement. Johnson, who normally hated having anything put on his eyes, had begrudgingly agreed to allow Douglass and Glaser to apply eyeliner for a flashback that showed teenage Nick singing "1999." If it was for Prince, fine.

A number of familiar faces were invited to make appearances at the party, including baseball player Clayton Kershaw and supermodel Alessandra Ambrosio. Kris Jenner and Khloé Kardashian were also there, two last-minute additions who Meriwether thought could make for funny appearances in the episode. Schmidt would approach Jenner to ask her how he should build his brand.

When the news reached Prince's team that a Kardashian would be in attendance, the *New Girl* crew was told, in no uncertain terms, that the singer would not show up. As Risoli remembers it, Prince didn't like Kim Kardashian.

Panic set in on set. A decision was made to shoot the scene anyway and not put it in the show. If the *New Girl* crew was asked about it later, they'd plead ignorance. "We can't just tell them 'no,'" Risoli remembers saying. "They'll be insulted."

He approached Jenner.

"Kris, we're going to shoot this really fast, we shoot these things fast, we'll get you in and out of here," he told her. "Your car is going to be waiting for you out there, we'll get you into the car and out."

Risoli remembers Jenner being totally fine with that—she was used to shooting scenes fast on their reality show.

They set up the shot, with cinematographer Russ T. Alsobrook barely lighting the scene. "Max," Risoli said ahead of time, signaling to Greenfield, who had been looped into the whole drama. "Do the fast version." Roughly forty-five minutes later, the scene was done.

"That's it?" Risoli remembers Jenner asking.

"That's it!" he responded. "It was really good."

As soon as the duo walked out the door, all script pages that featured the Kardashian scene were ripped away and thrown in a trash can. Just as the last ones were being tossed out, Prince arrived. They were safe—likely having heart palpitations, but safe. Phones were sealed into baggies, per the singer's request, and it was time to start shooting.

Most of the cast and crew were too shy to talk to the singer. Even Meriwether avoided conversations with him, fearful that she would say the wrong thing. But almost every person I spoke to had their own memorable, deeply odd stories from those long nights spent with Prince.

Among them:

He brought his own Ping-Pong paddle and challenged anyone to a match—most of the crew played him and he beat everyone. Fifty vanilla-scented candles were delivered to his room. When Johnson, as Nick, let out a high-pitched scream at first sight of him, he burst into laughter. He was so committed to creating a party that felt authentically like his own that he sent the *New Girl*'s music department a list of songs that he would actually have playing, including "After the Love Has Gone" by Earth, Wind & Fire and "We're Gettin' Too Close" by the Soul Children.

Many, many people shared that he had a big crush on Simone, which was a significant factor in his decision to do the show. The two had one scene together at the very end of the shoot and, in one of the best and most random moments of the episode, a butterfly follows a furious Prince out of the room after he loses to Cece in Ping-Pong. (Men would frequently try to flirt with Simone, including Kobe Bryant when he stopped by the set one day, director Fred Goss recalled. But the actress just wanted to focus on her work. She'd go home after shooting, sit on her balcony, have a glass of wine, and memorize her lines for the next day.)

It would be Risoli's job as first assistant director to interact with Prince frequently throughout shooting. The singer spoke in a soft whisper and would continually call for Risoli when he had an idea for a scene. "Mike," he said in hushed tones, waving a hand. Risoli hunched down, ear pressed closer, to hear his soft sliver of a voice. "What's the director's name again?" he asked. Risoli responded, "Fred." He pointed to Rosell. "Who's that?"

"Oh, that's Rob, our head writer."

"I have an idea. Can you get me a long lighter?" Prince asked. He had a pitch for the team, which would involve flicking a lighter in a scene when he and Jess are alone in a dark closet together. He thought it would be funnier than using a flashlight, as originally scripted.

A little while later—another whisper of Risoli's name. "Can I talk to you for a second?" Prince said. "For the performance tomorrow . . ."

Risoli immediately tried to quell any concerns that the singer might have. "We're all ready. I've got a crane coming in here. They all signed NDAs. We have extra security . . ." Turns out, that wasn't what Prince was interested in.

"Can you get me a bullhorn?" he asked.

The singer's performance was coming up and he had another prop idea. Risoli tracked down the requested bullhorn, and on that final night of shooting, Prince did something uniquely special. Unprompted and right before he was about to perform his big musical number for the crowd, he pulled out that horn and asked, "Anyone want to fall in love tonight?" The crowd of two hundred extras cheered. Deschanel performed alongside him, and Johnson, Wayans Jr., Greenfield, and Simone were up there with them, dancing their hearts out on a stage bathed in blue lights. In that moment, Greenfield completely forgot about the show and his character and acting. He was just feeling it all, dancing near the legend, a big, wide grin on his face.

Ahead of directing the "Prince" episode, Goss had heard stories about the singer's unreliable tendencies. Once, he was told, Prince was doing a commercial and simply walked offstage in the middle of it. The director had diligently mapped out how he could shoot all his coverage of the singer's performance in three efficient takes—letting Prince know ahead of time exactly what to expect.

"Well," Goss remembers Prince saying, "is that going to be enough?"

"I mean," he responded. "If it has to be, yes. . . ."

"Let's just do it till we get it."

So many of the crew members made the trek to Altadena that night and huddled off camera to watch Prince perform. Associate producer Megan Mascena had been working since 8 AM but there she was, too. After the first take, she remembers, they all looked at each other. "Holy shit, that was *Prince*!" Sometimes, she told me, you plan something to death, but it still doesn't come out the way you hoped. This time, it was perfect.

Risoli headed onstage and called out, "We got it, we got it!" He gave Greenfield and Johnson a big high five and then looked up and saw Prince. The singer was sitting there, with a little smile on his face and his hand held halfway up. He wanted a high five, too.

* * *

If *New Girl* needed a win amid a rocky season, they got it with their "Prince" episode. It pulled in twenty-six million viewers, more than double the pilot, making it the most watched episode of the series. *AV Club*'s Erik Adams declared that "Prince" was one of Season Three's "most consistently hilarious episodes."

"The show has Prince's back the whole way, and the guest star improves a plot that would feel like rote rom-com filler without him," Adams noted. "A figure like Prince could pull focus away from a show's true reason for being, but here he gets to inform a new angle on Nick and Jess's relationship."

The episode served as a morale boost of sorts for Greenfield, who, after three years on *New Girl*, could feel the series losing its blooming popularity. "You're on network television, you don't always feel like you're on the coolest show or you're doing the coolest job," he told *GQ*. "And forever, because he did our show, you can't ever say that our show is uncool or what we did was cheesy in any way. It's like, 'Fuck you, man. Prince did our show.'"

In 2016, two years after the episode aired, Prince died of an accidental drug overdose. Meriwether penned a tribute to the artist in *Vulture*, looking back on that brief time he stepped into their orbit.

"During my worst moments as a writer, I have the feeling of 'flying blind,'" she wrote. "These are the times when I feel I've lost the sense of what I want, when my internal compass is spinning, when I close my eyes and I have no vision. It was clear, in those few weeks that we made something together, that Prince rarely, if ever, lost his vision."

She added, "That wasn't because he was a magical, otherworldly being. It was because he was rigorous, and generous, and he knew how to fight for what he wanted. It was a beautiful, constant fight. It was love."

In that third season, when Prince had come onto the scene, Meriwether had been flying blind. She was grappling with low ratings, angry fans, and unhappy executives. "I think you can sometimes feel when a network has a checklist of problems that they have with your show," she recalled in an interview with *3rd and Fairfax*. "No matter what you do, they're going down that list. For this one season, everything was like, 'There's too much conflict, there's too much conflict.'"

"Well," the writers would say to themselves, "if we take out the conflict, what are we watching?"

The lowest moments were when Meriwether felt like she had lost her internal compass in terms of what the show was and what they were trying to do. It was a scary feeling to have. "Oh my God," she'd think to herself. "I'm the person who has to make the decision right now and I feel so turned around."

If she had been given a choice, Meriwether would have stopped working on the show. But that was the thing about network television—it kept moving. It always, always kept moving. And Meriwether had to keep moving right along with it.

Even when, come the Season Three finale, the writers decided to toss the script out altogether after a table read. The story, which revolved around the gang going to the Baseball Hall of Fame in Cooperstown, New York, completely "bombed," Meriwether remembers. They wrote another version, which was promptly thrown out as well. There was a large focus on the aftermath of Jess and Nick's breakup and it felt like a bummer and way too heavy. The episode just wasn't funny. Looking back, Meriwether told *BuzzFeed News*, the episode was "a culmination of the problem we'd been having all year."

Adding to the pressure was the fact that Meriwether had decided this episode would be her directorial debut. It was a Monday, they'd need to start shooting the following Monday, and there was no script. Erin O'Malley, the show's producer, waited outside the door hoping to get any hint of what to prepare for. By the afternoon, the writers had written the word *cruise* on the whiteboard.

They decided to send the whole gang out on a boat, which would force Nick and Jess to come to terms with their broken romance while trapped at sea. There could be additional shades of humor involving Coach, who is terrified of the ocean, and Schmidt trying to woo Cece back. By the end, they'd all end up accidentally locked in their room together, rescued a few days later—highly manic but reaffirmed as a steady, tight-knit group of friends once again.

When first assistant director Bill Purple found out that the episode would be set on a cruise, he had questions. Namely: "Where are we going to get a cruise ship?" It was Tuesday, shooting was starting on Monday, and they didn't have time to build a set.

O'Malley sprang into action. She knew that the *Queen Mary*, a retired ocean liner, was docked in Long Beach harbor, a spot that was used for tours and weddings. The executive producer hopped on the phone, with no script and no shooting schedule, and asked if the boat would be available for the following week.

"How many days?" she was asked.

"I don't know . . . three?" O'Malley responded.

Fine. Booked. "We have three days on a cruise ship and then we'll go from there," Purple remembers O'Malley saying. There was a low moment when Meriwether wondered if she should just back out of directing her first episode altogether. It was around 10 PM on a Thursday, she still needed to write the new script, and maybe it just wasn't the time to take on this big new role.

She kept moving, though, and come Monday, hundreds of extras piled onto the *Queen Mary*. Meriwether's episode, "Cruise," did manage to explore Nick and Jess's broken relationship but through a far more lighthearted lens. It was less about the two of them and more about the group banding together to help the pair work through the uncomfortable gray area of their friendship.

"Things are really weird," Jess admits, as her friends stage an intervention.

"Agreed," Nick replies.

"But I'm okay with it."

"Me too."

After wrapping the third season, Meriwether, Baer, and Finkel reflected on what was next. The stories, they decided, had gotten too big. Episodes should be simpler and less relationship-focused. "Nobody is really watching this show for the story," Meriwether remembers realizing. "That was a helpful burden that I lifted for myself. This show is about these characters." She wanted to focus on her ensemble and the small, weird moments that made *New Girl* so specifically great. Those moments mattered more than plot to Meriwether and she was going to make them her priority.

This time around, they wanted to embrace Jess being single—it had been so fun in those early days watching her explore dating in Los Angeles. And Meriwether decided to bring Schmidt back to who he once was. There were a multitude of qualities she loved about him and wanted to rediscover, like the fact that he had a take on everything, he always had a plan, and he was so confident, often for no reason.

Underpinning it all was the realization that characters couldn't change too much, too quickly. In the world of sitcoms, people didn't evolve in big, sweeping ways. They shifted in incremental, subtle steps as the show marched on.

Meriwether thought back to the "Wedding" episode, when all the friends took to the dance floor together after a crappy night. It felt like a John Hughes–esque moment, a feeling of us against the world. *That's* where she wanted the show to live. It was time to return to the basics. At long last, they were going back to what *New Girl* did best: telling fun, truthful stories about single friends living in the big city.

Okay, One More Prince Story . . .

This one comes courtesy of *New Girl* editor Hugh Ross. It was around 11 PM at the Season Three wrap party, which took place at the Petersen Automotive Museum. The party was starting to wind down and the actors and producers had left, leaving behind a handful of crew members, who had hung around to chat and drink.

Up the escalator comes Prince. He's decked out in a sparkly top hat and cane and there's a bodyguard beside him with a strobe light so no one could take pictures. The singer had arrived too fashionably late—*New Girl* wrap parties weren't all-night ragers like that, Ross explained. "I felt horrible for him but it was, like, he just didn't get it. If you didn't show up at seven o'clock, you weren't going to hang out with Zooey."

"It was so awful and awkward because he comes up to the floor we were on, and it's just like a hundred behind-the-scenes people," Ross told me. "He just basically does a loop with the entire party following him. He's looking for people who aren't there. When he makes the end of his loop with, like, a Pied Piper of seventy people following him, he gets to the escalator, goes down and leaves."

I'd like to believe that a determined little butterfly followed him out that night, fluttering away on his sparkly shoulder.

9

How Winston Became Winston: an Investigation

Use one of my good ones, the ones that make me look awesome. Like the time I fell asleep in the bathtub.

—WINSTON BISHOP

WITH DAMON WAYANS JR.'S RETURN to the loft in Season Three, Lamorne Morris kept getting asked the same question. Suddenly, so many people wanted to know if he was staying on the show.

"Wait, Damon's coming back," reporters would probe. "Are you leaving?"

"What? Why do I have to leave because another dude's coming back on the show?" he'd respond. "There's room for all of us."

Still, the question kept coming, so much so that on the Golden Globes red carpet, Johnson snapped back at a reporter. "What are you implying?" he said. ". . . Damon did one episode of the show! I think we're a good twenty episodes in with Lamorne. It's safe to say he's a member of this cast."

It was uncomfortably clear what was going on. With one Black actor returning, an assumption was made that the other Black actor on the show would have to leave. In the world of broadcast ensemble shows that primarily, if not entirely, featured all-white casts, having multiple actors of color seemed like a hard concept for some people to grasp.

For a long time, people didn't know Morris's name. Despite being the star of a hit TV series, he kept hearing himself referred to as "the Black dude from that show." He wanted to embrace the joy of finally getting his big break on television after so many years of hitting the pavement in Hollywood, but something just didn't feel quite right. Over the years, he'd try to get booked on a late-night talk show to no avail. "I wanted [it] so bad, just to feel validated a little bit, to be honest," he later told *Vanity Fair*.

When Morris arrived for the second episode, Greenfield remembers Dave Finkel and Brett Baer saying, "Okay, here's the deal, Lamorne. The show is about Zooey moving into this loft. Episode two can't be about Lamorne moving into the loft. We don't know what the character is . . . and just hang on tight."

Behind the scenes, the writers struggled to figure out what to do with Winston. Maybe he could be a jock like Coach? Would it be funny if he got random erections? What *role* did he play in the loft? Before Morris entered the picture, Baer, Finkel, and Meriwether had diligently mapped out who the rest of the characters were, going as far as to write superfluous scenes just to get a sense of the actors' speech patterns.

There wasn't enough time to do any of those extra writing exercises for Winston. As the first season marched on, Morris found himself thinking, "What am I doing here way in the background?" The actor felt like his dialogue was generic and his character as a whole was just filler. Every day, he worried he was going to get fired.

Greenfield would offer him encouragement from the sidelines. When Morris was given a scene that involved Winston spiraling over something, there was his co-star off camera, egging him on. "Keep going," he'd whisper, seeing that there was more Morris could do. "Keep going, just go for it."

Morris had a strong knack for improv and was proving that he could deliver. Which, I suppose, brings us to Theodore K. Mullins. Mullins, who was designed as Winston's alter ego, first appears in the Season One episode "Bully." The character hadn't been fully fleshed out yet and the writers approached Morris for ideas. "Do you have any voices?" they asked.

Morris could do an Eddie Murphy impression, which he rattled off for the first few takes. Then he switched gears and started doing an over-the-top, dramatic voice, which he deemed a cross between a pretentious actor and an old ghost. The writers liked what they were hearing and asked him to reprise Theodore K. Mullins again a few episodes later for "Secrets," in which Winston tries to scare off two women who are fighting over Nick in the loft.

"Go and improvise and don't stop," the episode's director David Wain told Morris. "We're not going to say cut, just go and talk as long as you want."

Morris did just that. He went on and on, and, even when he was sure they must have gotten their take, Wain had him keep going. The director cleared the rest of the cast out and let him continue to riff. That offered Morris the chance to really let go. When everyone else was around, he felt uncomfortable sucking up the air with too much of his own goofing around.

As Morris channeled the cantankerous spirit of Theodore, he got a small, reassuring moment of validation. The crew was laughing from the sidelines.

Winston was originally crafted as a grounded, capable presence in the loft, but that character trait wasn't exactly a fertile breeding ground for jokes. The other guy roommates were so bad at so many things and the idea was that, in contrast, Winston would be the best at *everything*. As they got further into Season One, the writers quickly realized that the fabric of the character just wasn't working.

"What are we doing?" they asked themselves. This was a show about people stumbling through life and it wasn't *fun* to write a character who was actually an adept, well-functioning adult. The revelation posed an interesting question. What if Winston was actually the *worst* at everything?

And also—on top of that—what if he was a little strange . . . ? Berkley remembers watching Morris on set for the episode "Elaine's Big Day," emerging from an air duct after being bitten by a badger. The actor made the choice to walk into the room in such an off-kilter way, kind of like he was drunkenly sashaying, and it caused the writer to think to himself, "*That's* how this guy should be all the time."

The needle for Winston kept moving, creeping closer and closer to who he'd become. It wasn't until they filmed the episode "Re-launch," aka the one when Schmidt's broken penis gets fixed, that Morris finally felt like he landed on something tangible.

Winston didn't have much scripted in that episode, aside from the fact that he loves the fruity cocktails Nick makes for him. As he sipped on a coconut elegantly adorned in cherries, limes, and a white flower, Kasdan, who was directing the episode, yelled out: "More girly!!"

At that point, Morris was stuck in the mode of "I don't want to offend anyone, I don't want to piss anyone off . . . what does *girly* even mean . . . ?" But when a director is yelling at you to do something, he thought, you have to do it. So, Morris really went for it, eyes wide, a big, flirtatious smirk spreading across his face as he says to Nick, "Look at me being so *naughty*."

His performance was a hit that day, offering the actor an important, lasting realization. "*Oh*, so I can go for it," he thought. From there on out, he decided he was going to take big swings when it came to Winston.

What did those swings look like? Sometimes they were comedy moments that had nothing to do with the show but found their way onto set and just magically fit. Between takes, Johnson and Morris used to do a running gag imitating a bit from the sketch troupe GoodNeighborStuff, which involved comedian Kyle Mooney acting superconfident when he wasn't, causing him to trail off into an awkward stutter. Sometimes a *New Girl* director would call action, and the pair, still stuck in their joke, brought that stuttering into a scene. It would become a small but endearing fixture of Winston's speech patterns. Case in point, "LAXmas," when

Winston tries to explain the term *polo horse* before realizing he has no idea what he's talking about.

"It's actually a polio horse," he begins. "Uh, originally they were bred as helper horses for people with polio, but I don't think anything of what I just said was correct, so . . ."

The writers, too, were having small, surprising moments of discovery, one of which occurred as they mused about introducing a pet into the loft. The animal definitely had to be a cat, they decided, because it would need to be able to disappear for long stretches of time and no one would notice. Meriwether had seen a picture of an exotic shorthair tabby and thought it looked amusing, with its sad eyes, pancake-like face, and perpetually inquisitive expression. The writers decided to give Winston a cat named Ferguson and introduced the animal in Season Two, with the thought that he might be a one-off storyline.

Ah, how wrong they'd be.

The writers realized, almost immediately, that Winston being a cat guy was funny. They began to craft more and more stories around the newest member of the loft, discovering that the stranger Winston acted with Ferguson, the better the stories got. Odd details emerged as time went on: Winston and Ferguson take weekly selfies together. Winston gives Ferguson a cell phone to take with him when he leaves the house. Winston and Ferguson like to share plates of pasta together.

As Morris spent more and more time with his furry scene partner, he discovered he was horribly allergic. There were conversations about switching to a different breed, but Ferguson had become such an immediate fan favorite that it felt awkward to suddenly replace him. Morris started taking medication to get through takes with the cat and, at one point, handed his companion off to Simone while filming a scene in the building's hallway. "This is physically impossible for me," he told her.

Second only to the Winston–Ferguson love story would be his unhinged obsession with pranks, another facet of the character that happened in a moment of haphazard pitching.

It was the early days of the show, and Berkley Johnson was meeting with Meriwether to lay out his ideas for the Season Two episode "Neighbors." The story revolved around Jess and Schmidt befriending their much-younger new neighbors, who take a quick liking to Jess and a deep loathing for Schmidt. There needed to be a B plot—the episode's secondary storyline—and Berkley suggested that Nick spend the episode pranking Schmidt, revealing to the audience that he's actually surprisingly good at intricately thought-out, wildly expensive ruses.

"What's Winston's role in the story?" Meriwether asked.

"He's bad at pranks . . . ?" Berkley Johnson responded, which elicited a look from Meriwether that the writer would come to view as "Why are you trying to ruin my show?"

Once that idea landed in the writers' room, though, it began to take shape. Maybe Winston wasn't just bad at pranks but he had no idea what his sweet spot was, fluctuating between the mundane (slipping a blueberry into an unsuspecting person's cereal) to the legitimately dangerous (unleashing a bear in a restaurant). One of the keys to Winston, Berkley realized, was that he took big swings in life. He was the ultimate "Yes, and . . ." person. Whatever stupid thing Schmidt and Nick wanted to do, Winston was in, and he would proceed to one-up them by adding his own even more outlandish ideas.

That prank pitch served as a teachable moment of sorts for Berkley. You could put so much effort into pitches and all the sweat never amounted to anything. And then you could blurt out an idea to keep your boss happy for five more seconds, and it could turn into something that really stuck.

The more eccentric Winston became, the more excited the writers were to pitch ideas for him. Particularly in Season Three, when there was such an exhausting struggle surrounding Nick and Jess's relationship, it was a joy to focus their comedic energy on a character who, with each passing episode, was becoming more and more of an oddball. Wild as his antics could be, Meriwether pushed back when a reporter suggested that the character had become "insane."

"But I don't think he's a totally insane person," she replied. "I think he's both extremes. When he gives advice, it's always the best advice. He's the most reasonable in terms of having a perspective on whatever the other guys are doing, but then he's a complete crazy person in other ways."

If Meriwether needed any reassurance that she was getting Winston right, she got it courtesy of critics who shone a warm, bright light on the surprising turn the character had taken. Journalists were starting to take note of the intriguing shifts that were happening on-screen, with *Entertainment Weekly*'s Lanford Beard expressing particular joy over the Season Three episode "Sister," in which a procrastinating Winston hires Coach to be his trainer in lieu of checking the results of his police exam.

"Also, WINSTON!!!" Beard declared in his recap. "The writers managed to do what has heretofore eluded them by giving him a primary storyline that showed substance beyond a new set of tics. Yet the episode also allowed Lamorne Morris to run wild with his brilliant improv skills—the very ones that have made him my favorite character in season 3 in spite of Winston's flimsy character development. Tuesday's episode inched him a step closer to being fully fleshed-out."

On top of that, Meriwether was getting positive feedback from her father, who had become a fan of Winston after he started wearing bird shirts. When he was done watching that week's episode, Meriwether's dad would check in with her to share an entirely Winston-specific report.

"Dad, there are so many other characters!" Meriwether told him.

"Here's where I felt Winston was really great tonight," he'd reply, undeterred.

* * *

With the exception of Shelby (Kali Hawk), the audience had yet to see Winston experience any kind of real, lasting love. And then he met his police training officer.

Aly, played by *Saturday Night Live* star Nasim Pedrad, didn't start out as a love interest. The writers wanted to give Winston a no-nonsense partner whose tough exterior would bump up amusingly against his goofy tendencies. There was a consensus that getting the two of them together romantically felt way too expected.

What *would* be interesting, though, was if Winston doggedly pursued Aly's friendship to no avail. He attempts to break through her frosty exterior by asking if she wants to grab a beer after work, an idea that gets unequivocally shut down. In classic *New Girl* fashion, though, there needed to be a sprinkling of catch-you-off-guard comedy that took place right before Winston was rejected.

Ahead of shooting, the writers asked Pedrad if she could improvise a bunch of weird noises in the lead-up to saying no. The actress did just that, emitting an extended run of nonsensical sounds that included much clucking, *hmm*ing, and *oooooh*ing. "Okay, that was superfun but probably too crazy and there's no way they'll ever use it," she thought at the time. Lo and behold, there it was in the final cut. That was the thing about *New Girl*, Pedrad discovered. The show could take swings—things that might have seemed too silly on the day of shooting but ended up working seamlessly in the edit.

With Pedrad in the role, the writers began to rethink the moratorium on romance. Fusfeld, who co-wrote one of the pair's early episodes together, "The Right Thing," watched Morris and Pedrad together and found himself doing a 180. They had such a natural rapport together and the pairing just felt right. "Well, I guess we're doing this . . ." he thought.

In that episode, Aly decides to let her guard down with Winston, admitting that she was close friends with her last police partner until he fell in love with her and ruined their relationship. That's why, she explains, she was concerned about becoming buddies with Winston.

"Damn, you're conceited!" he declares in response, proceeding to caution Aly against falling in love with *him*. "'Cause I'm lovable as hell," he informs her. The pair decide to become friends and then Aly, apropos of nothing, chugs her entire beer in one gulp, as a baffled Winston looks on.

It was the beginning of a beautiful friendship and an even more beautiful romance, which would last the duration of the series. To this day, Pedrad remains one of Morris's close friends. Fans, it turns out, want more. People became *really* invested in the pair getting together in real life, so much so that Pedrad and Morris would joke with each other, "We should just date. Why not?"

Pedrad found herself genuinely looking forward to coming to set every day. There was a joy in working with Morris, who was so funny but got such an excitement out of other people scoring in a scene. She also liked the moments when she got to just hang back and watch the core cast riff together. Johnson and Greenfield, in particular, never let anything slide. If another actor said or pronounced something even slightly off, they would pounce on it with an improvised run, poking holes and dissecting everything wrong in a detailed fashion.

Morris was taken by Pedrad. She was one of the greats on *Saturday Night Live* and he wanted to impress her and make her laugh. When he decided to go really big with a scene, she was right there with him, encouraging it. Particularly, Morris remembers, while filming the episode "Mario." In it, Winston is given a pair of glasses that will finally fix his colorblindness. Morris decided to go really over the top for that scene, gasping, shaking, and yelping as he experienced colors for the first time. Picking up a box of cleaning wipes, he asks with great emotion and some tears, "This is purple?!?! I'm touching purple??"

"Oh no," Aly responds, concerned. "Don't cry, baby, don't cry."

Pedrad was there with him throughout that whole run, having his back as he did the silliest stuff.

What was working so well with Aly, Fusfeld realized, was that she wasn't an off-center character. It was a lot of fun writing scenes with Winston and his former flame Bertie (Jessica Chaffin), because both were equal levels of bizarre, but having those two weird characters together didn't feel like the right fit. They needed someone who was grounded but still appreciated all of who Winston was. (Aly, and no one else, is amused by the fact that her boyfriend once fell asleep in a bathtub.) Yes, she *will* sing a romantic song Winston made up for the two of them while they were in a long-distance relationship . . . but she won't sing all the verses and will hang up on him halfway through.

It was also important to the writers that Aly be deeply attracted to Winston, as evidenced by their plethora of sexual encounters and shared fetish for mermaids. As time went on, grounded as Aly might be, we learn about her oddities, too: a secret Japanese-game-show past, a passionate love of DDS (Deep Discount Shopping), and a willingness to participate in over-the-top maternity boudoir photo shoots.

It would only be appropriate that Winston's proposal to Aly took place in an impossibly insane yet wildly romantic fashion, all while Winston is concussed and wearing a bobcat costume. "Operation: Bobcat," which aired in the sixth season, was the first episode that *New Girl* writer Lamar Woods wrote for the show, and what a wonderful doozy to start with.

Woods was feeling green when he stepped onto the Fox lot for his new job. He had worked on one show prior to *New Girl*, a series called *Survivor's Remorse*, and was still finding his sea legs when it came to pitching in a room. The *New Girl* veterans, he discovered, were joke machines. Woods considered himself on the junior varsity team and would nervously take a step back when he pitched jokes that didn't get traction. Sometimes he worried that people hadn't heard him if there was no response, because he had such a soft voice.

"Should I repitch it if no one said anything?" he asked a friend.

"No, they heard you," his friend gently replied.

It wasn't until he was tasked with penning the episode "Operation: Bobcat," which tracks Winston's multistep proposal to Aly, that Woods began to feel confident about his place in the room. He had carefully observed the established writers, who stayed true to what they found funny. Their comedic senses were so deeply specific that he could read any pitch and know immediately which writer was behind it. Woods decided to take that same approach with his script, writing what made him laugh, including a character named Trevlo who sells wedding rings and punctuates his sentences with the phrase *Stay blessed.*

Fusfeld worked with Woods on the episode, and the pair discussed the idea of finagling Jess into the proposal scene. *Or*, if they took it one step further, what if *she* proposed to Aly on Winston's behalf?

"How do we reverse engineer this?" they asked themselves. Working backward, the writers decided that Winston would try to surprise Aly in a dingy bus-station bathroom, dressed as a bobcat, which was meant to reference a private joke that the two shared while on the job. Only Aly is so startled when Winston leaps out in his costume that she kicks him into the air and he slams his head into the wall. (Fusfeld particularly reveled in that moment—he liked seeing just how badass Aly was.) A concussed Winston is forced to hand over his speech to Jess because he's too woozy to deliver it. As she reads out Winston's words, a choir belts out the Elvis Costello song "Alison," an idea pitched by Berkley.

When it came time for the episode to be screened in front of the other writers, Woods discovered, with great joy and relief, that the parts of the script he was proudest of had made it in. He was particularly pleased that they included one of the proposal lines he wrote—"As a young Black man, I never thought I'd feel safe with a police officer"—because it felt so specific to Winston and was so funny coming out of Deschanel's mouth.

After "Operation: Bobcat," Woods found himself feeling more confident when he pitched ideas in the writers' room. Not only had his episode gone over well, but he made it through the entire daunting process—from the writing to the edit bay. "I'm not ruining the show," he thought to himself. "I'm actually doing a good job." Plus, he watched the writers who he admired so much pitch ideas that never made it into the script, let alone the whiteboard, and they didn't let it stop them.

It had been a rocky start, but Winston managed to not only become one of the strongest characters on the show but a full-blown audience favorite, the rare kind of character who elicits a universally warm reaction

The initial design models of apartment 4D created by production designer Jefferson Sage (*Jefferson Sage*)

The *New Girl* living room set as it was in the pilot (*Jefferson Sage*)

The *New Girl* kitchen set featured in the pilot (*Jefferson Sage*)

Jake Johnson and Damon Wayans Jr. joking around offset (*Jorjee Douglass*)

Makeup artist Robin Glaser does Hannah Simone's lashes. (*Jorjee Douglass*)

Zooey Deschanel filming "Cruise" (*Jorjee Douglass*)

Lamorne Morris, Max Greenfield, and Jake Johnson dressed up for a flashback scene (*Robin Glaser*)

(ABOVE) Director and executive producer Erin O'Malley and first assistant director Michael Risoli with the beloved grapes (*Michael Risoli*)

Jake Johnson dressed up for a flashback while filming "Prince" (*Jorjee Douglass*)

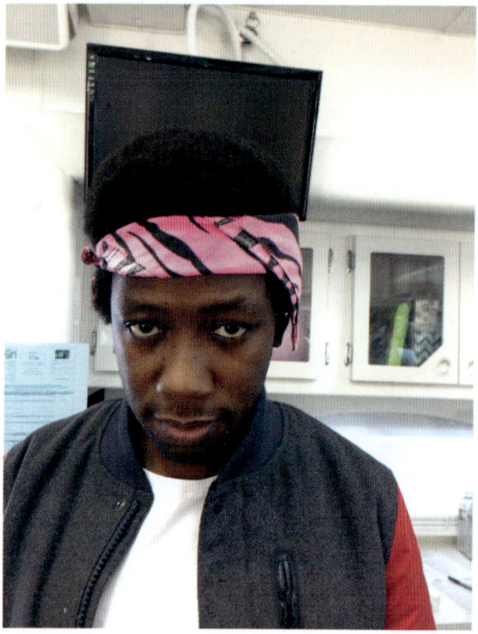

Lamorne Morris dressed up for a flashback while filming "Prince" (*Jorjee Douglass*)

Zooey Deschanel in her Stevie Nicks–inspired outfit for "Prince" (*Jorjee Douglass*)

Damon Wayans Jr. and Max Greenfield between takes of "Birthday" (*Jorjee Douglass*)

(TOP) The *New Girl* production crew building the exterior of the loft on the Fox lot (*Michael Whetstone*)

(ABOVE) Brickfields, the cafe set that was built on the Fox lot as part of the *New Girl* world (*Michael Whetstone*)

Creator Liz Meriwether onset filming *New Girl* (*Jorjee Douglass*)

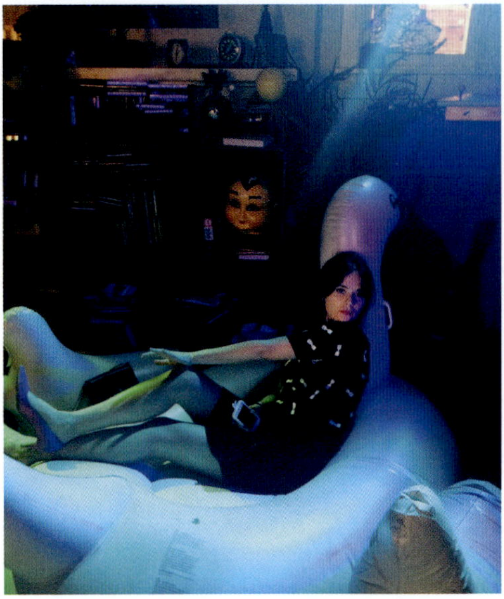

Zooey Deschanel filming "Dice" (*Jorjee Douglass*)

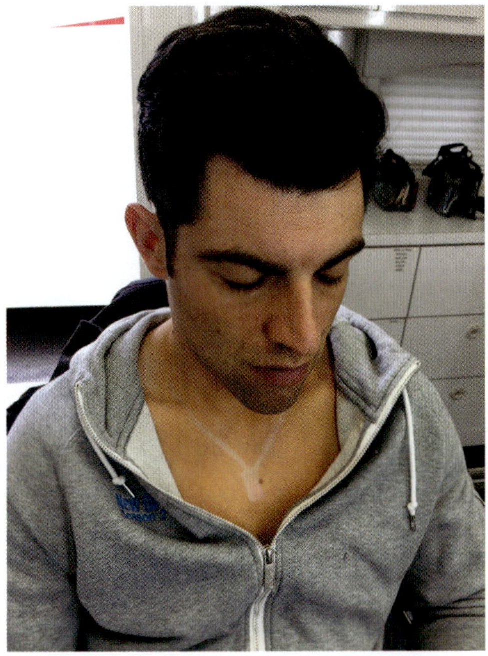

Max Greenfield with Schmidt's infamous flash drive tan line from "Wedding Eve" (*Jorjee Douglass*)

Hannah Simone in the *New Girl* makeup trailer (*Jorjee Douglass*)

Jake Johnson rocking Julius Pepperwood sunglasses in the *New Girl* makeup trailer (*Robin Glaser*)

Zooey Deschanel and Jessica Biel pose together during the filming of "The Last Wedding." (*Jorjee Douglass*)

Celebrating Zooey Deschanel's birthday while filming Season Five of *New Girl* (From left to right: makeup artist Michelle deMilt, hair stylist Jocelyn Mulhern, makeup artist Jorjee Douglass, Zooey Deschanel, hair stylist Nicki Alkire, and makeup artist Robin Glaser) (*Jorjee Douglass*)

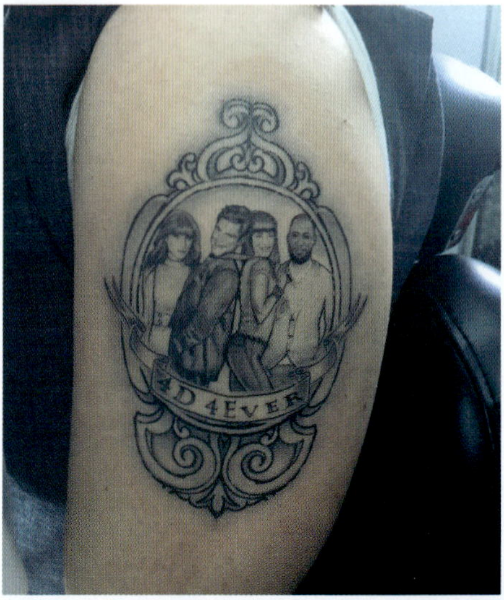

Jake Johnson wears Nick's wedding tattoo while filming "James Wonder." (*Jorjee Douglass*)

Stage	Scenes: 42	INT	**JESS & NICK FUTURE HOME** 3.0 The Gang & Kids play True American in the future	Day	FF1 1 1/8 pgs	1, 2, 3, 4, 5, 7, 12k, 13k, 14k, 15k 8A/11A
CHANGE OVER MAIN CAST TO CURRENT LOOK Mayor's Office						
Stage	Scenes: 49	INT	**OFFICE OF THE MAYOR** 1.5 Mayor Moscato is on the prank with Winston- POP	Day	FB10 2/8 pgs	4, 20 11/12³⁰
LOFT- TRUE AMERICAN						
Stage 1	Scenes: 35	INT	**LOFT- LIVING RM** 1.5 The Gang is assembled for True American	Night	N1 6/8 pgs	1, 2, 3, 4, 5, 100, 101, 102, 103, 104, 105 12³⁰/2P(L)
Stage 1	Scenes: 36	INT	**LOFT- LIVING RM** The Gang leaps from box to box 1.0	Night	N1 2/8 pgs	3, 4, 100, 103 245/345P
Stage 1	Scenes: 37	INT	**LOFT- LIVING RM** .5 Jess & Cece wrapped in bubble wrap suits	Night	N1 2/8 pgs	1, 5, 100, 101, 105 345/415
Stage 1	Scenes: 38	INT	**LOFT- LIVING RM** 1.0 Jess pulls kitchen island wagon, Donnor Party!	Night	N1 1/8 pgs	1, 2, 3, 4, 5, 100, 101 415/515P
Stage 1	Scenes: 39	INT	**LOFT- BEDROOM HALLWAY** Nick & Cece behind blue door, kiss 1.0	Night	N1 3/8 pgs	1, 2, 3, 5 515/615P
Stage 1	Scenes: 41	INT	**LOFT- LIVING RM** Nick leaps over the couch- MORPH .5	Night	N1 2/8 pgs	1, 2, 3, 4, 5, 100, 102 615/645P
EMPTY LOFT						
Stage 1	Scenes: 43	INT	**LOFT- LIVING RM** 1.25 The Gang takes in the empty Loft one last time	Day	D2 3/8 pgs	1, 2, 3, 4, 5 645/8P

End Day # 5 Friday, December 22, 2017 -- Total Pages: 3 6/8

NEW GIRL LOVE FOREVER. THANK YOU!

THE END

(ABOVE) The last table read of *New Girl* (*Michael Risoli*)

The final shooting schedule for the last episode of *New Girl* (*Michael Risoli*) when his name gets brought up in conversations with fans. (Over the past year of writing this book, I can say that sentence with quite some confidence. Almost every time I mention *New Girl* to a friend, Winston comes up and always, *always* a delighted smile follows.)

Perhaps one of the best snapshots of who Winston was to his core can be found in the episode "Goosebumps Walkaway." Schmidt, who is self-conscious about dancing in public, turns to his friend for advice. Winston has his own dance gathering later that day and he's dressed for the occasion, wearing a low-cut gray tank top with the words RECKLESS ABUNDANCE printed on the front. Schmidt is startled to learn that his roommate is planning to wear that ensemble to work and warns him, "You can't go to the station like that! They'll make fun of you."

Winston's response was born during a frantic writing session when Berkley, who wrote the episode, was up against a fast-approaching deadline. Here's what Winston ends up telling a concerned Schmidt:

"When I look into my suggestion box, it is full. People have a lot to say about the way I live my life. But there is only one comment card that I pay attention to. And you know what that card says? It says, 'Great job, Winston. Keep it up.' And you know who filled out that card? Me. You know how I know? Because I recognize my *motherfreakin' handwriting*."

When Morris delivered that speech at the table read, he swapped out *motherfreakin'* for *motherfucking*. It was an oddly profound moment, Berkley remembers, and so perfectly delivered.

That was one of the greatest joys of Winston. Of all the roommates, he became the character least apologetic about who he was, embracing every ounce of his lovable, offbeat self. As a result, we embraced him right back. I'd posit that maybe we could all stand to be a bit more like Winston. Bird shirts, puzzles, alter egos, and all.

When Nick Met Tran

I'm sorry to pull you out of your dance class.
—NICK MILLER

During the early days of *New Girl*, when Jake Johnson was still figuring out what made his character funny, he would text Meriwether pitches for Nick. She'd typically pass on most of them, but every once in a while, she liked one. "That's really funny," she'd text back. "Let me run it by the writers."

Late one night, he sent her an idea involving a brand-new addition to the cast. "What if Nick has a friend at the park who's an old man who does not talk?" he asked. "But Nick thinks they're having a back-and-forth and this guy is one of his best friends?" In that moment, Tran was born.

We first meet Nick's park friend, played by Ralph Ahn, when he shuffles over to a grumpy Nick in the episode "Menzies." Kim Rosenstock wrote that script and, as she got to Tran's first line, she paused. The writer realized she had no idea what Tran would say or what language he spoke. Instead of writing his dialogue, she decided Nick would look into his new friend's eyes and project onto the silence whatever he wanted to hear. Rosenstock had her concerns that the idea was too bonkers or would make Nick seem insane . . . but Johnson brought such a groundedness and sincerity to the scene that—actually—it made complete emotional sense.

While Nick is irked by the stranger at first, he concedes,

"You've got a nice face." Nick proceeds to open up to Tran, showing him how high he can jump, sharing how frustrated he is with his roommates, and admitting that he's afraid of dying. As the pair shot their first scene together, a wonderfully wacky one-sided exchange that would live on as one of the *New Girl* greats, Johnson thought, "This is what I know how to do."

Later that episode, Tran takes Nick to get a water massage. The idea was born from Dave Finkel's own experience getting a Watsu—a type of water massage—during his first anniversary with his wife at Two Bunch Palms, a wellness hotel in Palm Springs. As the couple put their shirts and shoes back on, the masseuse told him, "I had you opened up like a mermaid."

When Finkel shared that story, the writers immediately knew they wanted something like that to happen to one of their characters on the show. Out of everyone in the loft, Nick would hate an experience like that the most . . . so, naturally, it had to happen to him.

The crew filmed the water massage in the basement of a women's spa in Koreatown. For hours and hours, Ahn and Johnson floated around in a hot tub as a Watsu practitioner tried to teach Johnson their craft. The level of discomfort we see on the screen was an accurate representation of what was being felt behind the scenes.

Not only would Tran become a beloved fixture of the *New Girl* universe—he'd go on to appear in seven episodes—but he helped deepen the character of Nick, reminding the audience of his intense capacity to love. Aside from Jess, some of Nick's most passionate platonic romances were with the men in his life (Tran, Schmidt, Russell), a refreshing twist to the typical male sitcom character.

In 2022, Ahn passed away at the age of ninety-five. Johnson paid tribute to his frequent scene partner on Instagram, writing, "RIP. So much fun to work with. He gave so much with literally no lines."

10

The *New Girl* Lab, Part II

Who's talking to you, Depression-era garbage man?
I've been holding that in for two years.
—COACH

***NEW GIRL*'S EDITOR STEVE WELCH** came from the world of *Malcolm in the Middle*, which had a straightforward polish. They didn't do a lot of extra takes and there wasn't enough time to screw around in the editing room. Scripts were superprecise, as were the performances. The philosophy, Welch remembers, was "The writer spent a lot of time working on these words, we made them as perfect as we can, we'll say them exactly as written."

Coming into *New Girl* felt like doing a total 180. Meriwether and the cast she had assembled didn't care about polish. In fact, Meriwether *encouraged* the actors to be imprecise. At first, Welch was thrown by the whole concept. "They're not landing jokes," he thought as he watched the footage coming in. "They keep talking!"

He learned that Meriwether didn't like the typical sitcom rhythm. Instead, she leaned into a jazz approach to comedy, straying away from the usual setup, punch line, setup, punch line. She loved when it felt like the characters were actual human beings talking to each other. Unlike many showrunners, she didn't view her words as precious and, in fact, reveled in being surprised when she watched footage in the editing bay that deviated from the script.

In the beginning, Welch tried to search for the cleanest reading of a line. Then Meriwether would walk in, look at the takes, and say, "I like that one."

"That's the sloppiest line read I've ever heard," Welch responded.

"No, it feels more real."

"Okay," he said. "I think I see what you're talking about."

Meriwether loved when the cast improvised. "A lot of creators bullshit, and they say, 'We want you to improvise,' and they don't . . . when they're in postproduction and they're insecure, they just go back to their script, even if it's not the best take," Johnson told me. "That is not Liz. Liz will choose whatever makes her laugh the hardest in post, she doesn't give a fuck whose idea it was, how it happened, there's no ego in that for Liz—the best moment wins."

With the wealth of material entering the editing suite, there was always an episode and a half, if not two episodes, worth of footage that Welch would need to whittle down into twenty-one minutes. So many bits and weird moments and silly scenes never saw the light of day. "Does this still make sense?" Welch found himself worrying as he trimmed away at footage in the editing room. "Does the emotion hold up? Does the scene still work?"

Welch liked to home in on the story before tackling the comedy of the scene. "Worry about the joke last," he would tell Giselle Murillo, the show's assistant editor. "Cut the story and emotion first." Once they had that blueprint, their attention could turn to the jokes, which were often the toughest part of the equation.

Welch would pick out his favorites and present them to Pope and Meriwether. "Okay, I lined up ten jokes for this blow of the scene," he'd say before pressing play, and then laughing heartily at each one.

He particularly got a kick out of watching footage of Nadia, Cece's eccentric Russian roommate, played with devilish precision by Rebecca Reid. As he sifted through daily takes from Season One's "Tomatoes," Welch wasn't expecting quite so much material of Reid delivering one reason after another for why she loved the United States—from Wilmer Valderrama to ice skating (as she explains: for fun, *not* to save lives). From behind the camera, the writers threw more and more wacky lines at Reid, and Welch delighted in watching Greenfield trying to keep a straight face as he sat opposite her.

Murillo loved seeing the dailies of Johnson and Rob Reiner, who played Jess's dad. Much of their exchanges weren't scripted—or went well past what was scripted—and it was always enjoyable to watch footage of the two going back and forth with each other. (In one particularly memorable scene, Reiner, in character, informs Nick that his zombie novel is actually a direct rip-off of *Twilight*.)

The director, who died tragically in December 2025, was a beloved fixture onset. He appeared in eleven episodes of *New Girl*, and made his debut in Season 2's "Parents," alongside Jamie Lee Curtis as Jess's mom. "That was very exciting to have them both show up, and both be incredibly kind, generous, and fun to work with," Jesse Peretz, who directed "Parents," said. "Even though they're iconic actors, and Rob Reiner is an iconic director, they were happy to be there. They never made it feel like, 'Oh, we're above this,' and they recognized that it was exciting for all of us to be in their presence." During lulls, Peretz and Reiner talked politics. "Just getting to have incredibly long, in-depth, nerdy conversations about politics with Rob Reiner was incredibly satisfying," Peretz said.

Unscripted moments—like the ones Reiner offered with Johnson—were gems in the editing room.

Moments like that were gems in the editing room. "You know what we're missing in this episode?" Baer remembers the group saying on one occasion. "A little bit of that kind of loose, fun stuff."

"Oh yeah, I have a couple of moments of it," Welch said. "We should dig that out and use that stuff." Then they went fishing for some of those off-the-script moments that gave *New Girl* that extra boost of unexpected comedic magic.

Often they were bits that had little or nothing to do with the story itself. In a completely improvised exchange between Winston and Nick filmed during the episode "Walk of Shame," the pair discover that Coach and Schmidt have secretly uninvited them to a fancy gathering. This realization prompts Nick to declare, "Those damn lousy serpents."

"*Ssssss*," Winston hisses, coyly wiggling his fingers in front of him.

"How do you do it so smooth?" Nick asks, trying to mimic the slick hiss. "It's just—exhale." Winston tries to explain. After a few failed attempts, Nick gives up. "I just can't do it," he says, resigned. "I don't even care about it."

Or there was that time Johnson improvised telling Simone that he doesn't like her shirt in the episode "Operation: Bobcat," insisting that she put some sparkles on for Valentine's Day. "Sparkles are *IN*," he declares with great conviction. "Sparkles are *INNNNN*."

Integral to the story? No. Funny and unique slice-of-life moments? Absolutely. That's where the comedy lived, Meriwether had discovered. In the middle of a high-stakes moment, somebody says, apropos of nothing, "But wait a second, I hate your backpack."

Greenfield, multiple crew members observed, had the toughest task when it came to comedy bits. Often his character was supposed to speak in a wordy stream of consciousness, and Greenfield needed to authentically allow those monologue-like stanzas to tumble out of his mouth. He wasn't a character of expediency, he was a character who was going to describe, in great detail, why Winston was absolutely *terrible* at puzzles while getting progressively more and more agitated about it.

Greenfield, alongside Deschanel, was frequently asked to take the lead on the show's "cold opens," which are the first few minutes before the credit sequence. The actors were tasked with neatly setting up the episode, offering exposition that would help preview multiple storylines at once. Deschanel remembers the difficulty of having to sell those scenes naturally, which often involved bursting into the loft and declaring that it was the first day of school, Coach was starting a new job, her parents were in town, and other statements that aren't natural in day-to-day conversation but a necessary evil in storytelling.

As the core cast grew from four to five to six, with Wayans Jr. back in the loft and Simone becoming a core cast member, the editors would navigate the delicate balance of giving each actor their time to shine in those big group scenes. "How do we balance them all?" Murillo would ask herself. "Do we give them jokes? Do we take jokes out? We want to keep this person alive and not forget about them." Sometimes she would try to find reaction shots of a character to insert, with the caveat that they needed to be genuinely good ones, not obligatory cutaways. Deschanel was always a helpful one to cut to—she did perplexed so well.

Episodes like Season Four's "Background Check" somehow managed, within a tight time frame, to allow every character to shine—all while expertly interconnecting stories together. Over the course of a chaotic twenty-one minutes, Winston attempts to pass his police background check conducted by Sergeant "The Fish" Dorado (Cleo King), and Jess mistakenly thinks she has a bag of meth in her room that will cause Winston to flunk out of the police academy. Nick tries—very unsuccessfully—to distract the sergeant while singing "Landslide" and sweating profusely. Cece and Schmidt, who are helping Jess hide the "meth," butt heads over a guy she's dating. And Coach, poor, poor Coach, is forced to try to find a child named Duquan, after claiming Winston volunteers for the Boys & Girls Club.

"It's such a sweet episode, actually," Lorene Scafaria, who directed "Background Check," told me. "All of them are trying to do right by Winston." She was taken by one of the final scenes, when Winston explains to Jess that she should have asked for his advice about the drug situation from the get-go—that she underestimates him and he could have *helped* her. "Those are those amazing, grounded moments . . . in the middle of this absolute mess of chaos . . . I love those little moments that feel so real," Scafaria said.

Throughout the course of filming an episode, cinematographer Russ T. Alsobrook used a technique called cross-coverage, which featured two cameras set up on either side of the room, capturing the actions and reactions of the performers in real time. They discovered this was absolutely necessary after the first season, when the actors would offer up great improvisations and the camera missed reaction shots from the rest of the cast members. Those unspoken moments—the downturn of Johnson's mouth, the bemusement in Cece's eyes—was what Meriwether loved most. "The things that I think are the funniest are the weird moments that are small and maybe not even a punch line," she said. "Just, like, a look or an awkward way of getting up from a chair."

The technique meant that the cast could never phone it in. "In a normal single-camera comedy, one person is actually acting and the other person is off camera reading lines," Welch told *The Ringer*. "And they're acting with each other, they're trying to help each other out, but they're not performing at a hundred percent. The nice thing with cross-coverage is both actors have to be performing at a hundred percent because they're both on camera. And so you get a much more natural interplay between the two of them."

There wasn't a lot of time to breathe within the tight constraints of an episode, but Welch would build in even the smallest of pauses. He loved the comedic back-and-forths from decades past, like Walter and Hildy in *His Girl Friday*, and carefully spliced in occasional moments of quiet between that vintage rat-a-tat.

While the show was airing, *AV Club*'s Emily St. James penned a love letter to Welch's editing chops, spotlighting his work in "Cooler"—not when Nick and Jess kiss . . . but when Nick and Jess *almost* kiss. Deeming *New Girl* the "best edited comedy on television" at the time, St. James pointed to the scene of the pair behind that blue door, when they nearly lock lips but can't quite get there. It's filled with strategic pauses to build up the tension and you can feel the weighty awkwardness as the pair start and stop leaning into each other.

"Without that breathing space, this is just another wacky scene in an episode full of them, the final kiss doesn't play, and the season's most important story arc is a flop from the start," St. James wrote. "*New Girl* succeeded so well in season two because it understood that just as much power could come from a pause as from barreling forward."

Editing a typical sitcom for network television often involves sucking out as much air as possible in service of meeting a strict runtime. That *New Girl* could take that breath or splice in an irrelevant, off-the-cuff moment made it feel different. Those extra split seconds meant something to the cast, too. When Deschanel watched a cut of the episode "Keaton," she was delighted to discover that they kept a small bit of improv she had done—mispronouncing the word *Batmobile*—knowing full well that, by slotting it in, the editor had to sacrifice other footage.

The same could be said about an extra-long bit that happened while filming "Return to Sender." It was a small scene—Winston is offended that Dr. Sam won't wear the bird shirt he gave him and starts to back away, making prolonged eye contact with the doctor as he goes. It was one of those comedic runs that was born on set, Walton told me, and he was so sure it wouldn't make it into the cut. In true *New Girl* fashion, it did, and every time you think the camera will cut away from Winston, as he slithers away, it just . . . doesn't.

That was the thing about the show, Walton remembers. The actors had to be open to a slower tempo on set to collect those bits of comedic moments that might make it into a cut. There was permission for plenty of failure, too. Improvising something really funny that also worked within the framework of the episode was tricky, and nine times out of ten, the footage was unusable.

The longest cut clocked in at a whopping forty minutes. It was Season Two's "Chicago," and editor Hugh Ross's first episode of *New Girl*. Oh, what a *surreal* one to start with.

The initial idea was pitched by writer David Iserson, who had once attended an Elvis Presley–themed funeral. He loaned that memory to "Chicago," which would revolve around Nick's dad dying and the whole gang returning to his childhood home for a service that features an Elvis impersonator.

If you go back and rewatch the episode, you'll be struck by how distinctly not *New Girl* it looks and feels. There's an independent movie–like quality to the way it was shot, with shaky camera movements and a frantic undercurrent to it all, set far away from the Sandra Bullock romantic-comedy world of crisp, polished brightness. They filmed in Pasadena, a quiet city outside of Los Angeles, which was transformed into wintery Chicago for the occasion. Fake snow was piled on the ground, which kept melting under the baking California sun. You really get the sense that Kasdan, the director of the episode, was trying something different and—as interesting a leap as it was—this would be the first and last time the show deviated from its classic visual template.

Bill Burr and Nick Kroll guest starred as Nick's relatives, and the two comedians, alongside Johnson, clicked into improv mode, doling out joke after joke and bit after bit, much of which Ross was forced to leave on the cutting room floor for the sake of time. (Bill Burr wasn't well known at the time and first assistant director Bill Purple found himself thinking, "Who is this guy? He's so funny.")

All hell breaks loose during Nick's dad's funeral, when the Elvis impersonator gets drunk and can't perform. Jess swoops in to try to save the day, donning his costume and performing "In the Ghetto" to the group of mourners. When Jess initially dressed up as Elvis, it wasn't immediately funny, Purple recalls. But Deschanel took it and found the humor, adding little touches like replicating the Elvis deep knee bend but making sure that it was off by just a little bit. Purple, who would go on to direct several episodes of the show, was taken by Deschanel's ability to tackle Lucille Ball–esque physical comedy. She had such a good command of her space and knew how to control her body to the best comedic effect. Nothing outlandish, à la Jim Carrey, but subtle movements, down to the way she'd push the hair off her face.

There was a line in that episode that really stayed with Ross. "I have your back, no matter how stupid it gets," Jess tells Nick, after their long, emotionally taxing visit to Chicago, which includes Schmidt sticking his head in the casket. That was how the editor would end up feeling about *New Girl*. "That really is sort of the theme of the whole show," he told me.

"In production, in the writing, it just went off the rails and got so weird at times you just learned to adapt, you had to figure it out."

After table reads, Finkel recalled, he'd feel a wave of *everything*. "You're like, 'Oh my God, that was weird and exciting and horrible. Every emotion just rolls off you," the writer told *Uproxx*'s Alan Sepinwall, who visited the Fox lot during the writing of "Tinfinity" to get a sense of how an episode was made. When a script wasn't working, the writers would delve into a bizarre mathematical equation which involved reverse engineering an entire story to figure out which pieces worked, which didn't, and what plus what told the perfect comedic and emotionally resonant story, which stayed true to both the show and the characters.

The original plot of "Tinfinity" revolved around Jess, who was in a weird in-between space with Nick after their kiss and wanted to rebound with a cute professional football player, Jax McTavish (Steve Howey). That story, in and of itself, created a problem. Fictitious celebrities can feel corny on-screen, and immediately rip audiences out of the story. The writers entered problem-solving mode. Maybe if Nick was impressed by Jax, it would add an extra layer of authenticity to the character? Also, it could up the stakes for Nick! Not only does his crush have a rebound, but it's a guy who's a cool professional athlete.

Also, though, the writers asked themselves, why was Jax hanging out with the group in the first place . . . ? More problem-solving ensued. Maybe Winston is looking after him as part of a promotion at his job at the radio station? But—do the viewers care about Winston's job? If they scrap that angle, though, what is Winston's role in the story? These were the questions that would keep the *New Girl* writers up until the wee hours of the night. They ultimately decided that the interesting tension would come from Winston, in awe of Jax, desperately wanting his friendship and feeling scorned when his idol would rather hang out with Jess.

The original script had Jax walking in on Jess while she was using a porta-potty at Nick and Schmidt's ten-year-anniversary party. Philbin pitched the idea of that awkward moment prompting Jess to say, as an homage to the iconic Julia Roberts line in *Notting Hill*, "I'm just a girl standing in front of a guy who saw her poop." By the time the final script was ready, the poop storyline had been thrown out the window but a piece of it remained. Nick would purchase a horrendous, broken-down porta-potty for the party, allowing for the line, "I'm a small-business owner."

From script to stage, there was a relentlessness to the way *New Girl* turned out episodes. As Philbin put it to journalist Joy Press, there was a feeling of "having been in 'Nam together" during those early years in the writers' room. While shooting the show's first Thanksgiving episode, the cast and crew ended up working around the clock, filming from Sunday night until Monday morning in a Best Buy parking lot. That episode had been particularly hard to crack, with Finkel and Baer spending forty-eight hours in the conference room of the InterContinental Hotel, trying to figure out how to make the script work. They set their alarms for ten-minute catnaps and Finkel laid down on the table, using his computer bag as a pillow.

"The Landlord" turned into another delirious late-nighter, with Baer and a few of the other writers working through the night on the episode. At around 6:20 AM, as they tried to crack the big ménage-à-trois scene, Baer was so tired he started hallucinating. It was near Halloween and there were a bunch of little pumpkins on the writers'-room table that suddenly appeared very fond of him. In a moment of lonely desperation, Baer swept the tiny gourds into a warm embrace and declared out loud, "I'll always have my pumpkin patch."

Deschanel remembers being particularly jealous of the *Modern Family* cast, who shared their studio lot and always seemed to get out of work early. It was demoralizing for the ensemble, Meriwether remembers, because they'd perform so many pages of extra material, much of which would end up on the cutting-room floor because of time constraints.

By the end of the third season, Meriwether thought she might get fired. Dana Walden, who was running the studio at the time, called her in for a meeting and the tone was serious. "You need to change the way the show is run," she was told. After that, Meriwether went on a listening tour. She talked to the actors, the writers, the crew, and the editors. "How can we make this better?" she wanted to know.

Meriwether, Baer, and Finkel had been prone to throwing out joke after joke from behind the monitor for the cast to deliver, which could make some cast members feel like they were just puppeting lines. "We don't want you to scream jokes," the actors told Meriwether. "I was like, 'fair enough,'" the showrunner recalled.

Looking back, Meriwether told me, everyone was so tired. "The hours were insane, and I just didn't know how to do the job," she said. "I didn't realize it at the time, but it's a lot like parenting in that you never know what you're doing. You always feel like you're failing but you have to constantly be coming up with new plans and then immediately be ready to throw those plans out of the window and come up with a new plan."

They'd continue to work twelve-hour days, but the eighty-hour work week was gone. Shooting scripts had to be twenty-seven pages long. An agreement was made that the alts brought to the set would be whittled down to three to four per joke, and not every joke was given an alt. The actors also wanted to reserve the right not to deliver an alt joke if they didn't want to.

Meriwether decided to find a moment or scene in every episode that she loved and hang on to it, no matter how small it was. She stopped sleeping in her office.

As her characters were growing up in their own ways, so, too, was Meriwether. After so many years of Craigslist sublets, the showrunner had purchased a three-bedroom, mid-century ranch house in West Hollywood. When she first moved in, all she had were clothes and some mugs that she brought over in her Honda. She hired an LA designer to decorate her home, which featured an airy kitchen with turquoise-washed walls and an all-white furniture set in her sunny backyard.

There were her own touches as well, like a statue of an alligator and a fake Mona Lisa in a garish gold frame hanging in the powder room. "Try not to use *quirky* too many times in this story, okay?" Meriwether told the *Elle* journalist who came by for a house tour, as she adjusted her framed painting of a unicorn beside a rainbow.

* * *

Life was evolving behind the scenes of *New Girl*, and you didn't have to squint all that hard to feel the shift on-screen. Season Four marked a definitive tone change, with the show getting an irresistible boost of effortlessly fun, fresh, and easily digestible storytelling.

Best of all, Jess started dating again.

With the help of Schmidt as her bossy guru, she hits the town, knocking into immediate roadblocks on the dating apps and briefly dating an annoying guy with a micropenis. She finally gets a suitable love interest in the form of Ryan, a British teacher who fulfills all her Victorian-esque, *Downton Abbey* fantasies. (And he owns spools of yarn to boot!) As the writers mulled over the character of Ryan, they knew he needed to be leaps and bounds different from her previous relationship. "Who would be the person you would date after Nick?" they asked themselves, ultimately deciding he needed to be perfect and very charming.

Ryan would end up being played by Julian Morris, who landed the role after a series of auditions and a chemistry read with Deschanel. The scene they read together, which would end up getting cut from the episode, involved Ryan and Jess conducting a science experiment that results in a volcano explosion. Julian wanted a prop for his audition, so he headed into a nearby kitchen and fished out a piece of cardboard that he fashioned as a makeshift volcano. When he landed the role of Ryan, the actor had never done a comedy before. "How does this work?" he thought to himself. "What if I can't help but laugh? Am I *allowed* to laugh?"

He didn't get much sleep before his first day of work. As he stood behind the door, waiting for his cue to enter the classroom for Ryan's first introduction to Jess, he found himself nervously thinking, "Wow, this is it, this is really it."

Julian walked into the room and saw Deschanel. She had a beautiful smile on her face and he felt himself instinctively starting to smile, too. As an actor, it was his job to act out a romance, something he'd certainly done in other projects. But with Deschanel, the chemistry felt real. He was only supposed to be in a small handful of episodes but his run kept getting extended, with Jess and Ryan going from will-they, won't-they colleagues to something much more.

As Julian found himself entering into unfamiliar territory of alt lines and whip-fast improv, one of his co-stars offered him a piece of advice. "Hey, if you want some funny alts, ask Damon." Everybody in the cast, Julian discovered, would turn to Wayans Jr. for comedy ideas, so the actor diligently did the same, taking his script over to him during the school scenes and asking for guidance on how to make the scene even funnier.

Ryan and Jess finally kiss in the episode "Teachers," with some unexpected assistance from Coach. As Jess struggles with her attraction to her employee during a staff retreat, Coach is dealing with his own fears of becoming a sex-ed teacher, which results in him getting very drunk and trying to do a cannonball into the pool. Ryan, being Ryan, heroically jumps in and saves him, lifting him out of the water *Baywatch*-style. Jess realizes—despite her best efforts—she can't fight her crush any longer.

The next beat finds Ryan and Jess sitting on the hotel-room floor, with Coach passed out on the bed. There wasn't anything scripted for the pair as the scene opens, and discussions sprung up over how to open the shot in a romantic way. Julian had always enjoyed blowing into wine bottles and listening to the tiny whistling sound they made, so the actor suggested the pair blow into minibottles of hooch. Shows don't typically let their actors choreograph their own scenes, but there he and Deschanel were, scrappily building something together on the fly. The whistling noise made them both laugh, creating a small, genuine moment between the two as the scene opened.

When they kiss at the end of the episode, it felt earned. Yes, you're pulling for Nick and Jess, but *New Girl* had the unique ability to make you root for guest stars, casting people whom you wanted to keep seeing on your screen. Finkel realized as soon as their lips locked that there was actually something special between Jess and Ryan that the writers needed to explore.

Of course, the duo couldn't wander into the sunset too quickly. Jess, panicked about crossing boundaries with her employee, tries to shut down the romance. The pair butt heads about their simmering attraction during the following episode, "Thanksgiving IV," in which every member of the loft must bring a date for someone else in celebration of Thanksgiving. (Not that it needs to be said, but this was orchestrated by Schmidt.)

Meriwether had been unhappy with the way their previous Thanksgiving episode turned out. "Thanksgiving III" involved the gang celebrating in a forest, Nick setting a bear trap, and Jess getting giardia after eating a rotten fish. Coming up with fresh holiday-themed episodes was getting increasingly hard, but this year, there was a feeling of focused purpose. Meriwether wanted to make Ryan and Jess official. She wanted to introduce Nick to Tran's granddaughter Kai (Greta Lee). And, at long last, she wanted to set Cece and Schmidt back on the path to reconciliation. This would be the episode that solidified just how wonderfully close their friendship had become, with Cece rejecting the cute guy Schmidt set her up with, so she could spend the evening playing a board game with her pal.

Ryan's story ends abruptly, a few episodes later, with his decision to take a job as headmaster at a prep school in England. In truth, Julian was already committed to another series—the Amazon show *Hand of God*—and he filmed his *New Girl* arc right up until the last day he had to contractually go and shoot his next project. Morris recalls the writers having to figure out a quick way to explain his absence, which led to the episode "Oregon," where Jess leans on her friends as she mourns their crumbling relationship.

Late at night, after breaking up with Ryan via voicemail, Jess takes everybody to Crush Pond, a tucked-away pool of water she and Cece used to go to when Jess wanted one of her crushes to like her back. The routine was simple—all she had to do was say their name, throw a rock into the pond, and they'd love her forever.

The group all pick up rocks to throw in the pond in solidarity with Jess, despite the fact that Coach doesn't totally understand what's going on.

"Uh, I'm gonna say 'Detroit Pistons,'" he mumbles to Nick.

"You're not getting it, man."

"What—what is it?"

"You got to say, like, a lady's name."

In that moment, we're reminded that, above all else, good, reliable friendship was the main course this season, taking the show right back to where it started. Critics rejoiced in *New Girl*'s return to form. *Vulture* writer Jenny Jaffe began her review wishing the previous season had been some sort of fever dream, where Jess wakes up from a terrible nightmare of everything that had unfolded in the year before. Much to her chagrin, that didn't happen, but much to her delight, the fourth season was proving to be a welcome invitation back to apartment 4D.

"By the end of this episode, it really felt like a new leaf was being turned over," Jaffe wrote. "There was some Jess and Nick catharsis, but it didn't feel forced. No major snafus were made in Schmidt's pursuit of Cece. It was funny, light, and ended with a cheerful hang-out scene. Oh, and Jess finally got a new phone case. Happy days are here again."

Despite the fact that romantic entanglements had been placed on the back burner, the writers weren't totally shelving Nick and Jess's love story. As the season drew to a close, fans were offered a reassuring wink of what was to come.

It all started with an off-topic pitch about a cup. The *New Girl* writers would go on retreats ahead of each season, taking time to pitch out possible story ideas together. During one of these gatherings, Alex Cuthbertson and Matt Fusfeld suggested that everyone in the loft streamline their collection of mugs, which would lead to a flashback episode about the origin stories behind each one. While Meriwether liked the idea, she kept pushing it back and back until, one day, the room realized that they could use those mugs as a storytelling device for Nick and Jess.

In the final episode of Season Four, "Clean Break," it's revealed that the pair used to have a "sex mug" that they would leave out in the entryway whenever one of them was feeling—to use a Jess term—twirly. Turns out, Jess had left the mug out recently, which forces the two to come face-to-face with their potentially unresolved feelings.

While at first Nick refuses to acknowledge that he might still have sex mug–like emotions for Jess, they eventually have a frank conversation about their relationship as it stands.

"Do you really think I haven't thought about putting the mug out?" he asks.

"I don't know, Nick, you said it. What's past is past. Clean break."

"*Think* about my living conditions for the past year. I live across the hall from my *beautiful* ex-girlfriend. And your living conditions—you live across the hall from your *beautiful* ex-boyfriend. Two true beauties."

"Just admit it, Miller! You're thinking about putting the mug down right now!"

"No. Admit that you want me to be thinking about it."

As the pair look at each other and that familiar heat starts to rise, they're abruptly interrupted. But the door is left open, more than just a crack, for something more.

That same episode, the gang bids farewell to Coach. Wayans Jr. had decided not to renew his contract with *New Girl* and packed his bags one final time, with the door left open for return appearances. He decides to accompany his girlfriend, May (Meaghan Rath), to New York City, where she's landed a new job, and initially refuses to get sentimental about this chapter of his life closing. He adamantly declares that he's packing only the essentials from the loft, which causes friction between himself and a sentimental Winston, who would really like Coach to bring the crepe pan they once purchased together.

Coach's tough facade starts to crumble throughout the episode, and he ultimately decides to pack the pan, along with a few more nonessential items—like Jess's mystery novels, Nick's largely unused workout CD, and the loft's remote control. "It smells like all our fingers," Wayans Jr. adlibbed, a moment that remains one of *New Girl* writer Kim Rosenstock's favorites in the series.

The audience says goodbye to Coach—and Wayans Jr.—at the very end of "Clean Break," as he heads to the airport with May to start their new life together. It's a genuinely moving moment, packed with emotion (Wayans Jr.'s voice cracking when he tells his friends he loves them never gets old) and great one-liners ("Coach," Schmidt says, "I used to wish you were uglier. I don't wish that anymore. I only wish you the best.")

As much as she felt like she could have happily kept going with Coach, there was some relief for Meriwether when the cast shrunk by one. Now she had fewer characters left to serve and more time to flesh out what was happening with each actor. "Okay," she could now think to herself. "There's an A story and a B story, and there's only two characters in each story."

Amid Wayans Jr.'s departure, a major plot point for Simone and Greenfield hung in the wings.

Part of the unintended joy in Schmidt and Cece's fractured romance was watching Schmidt slowly but surely earn back Cece's trust. The two form a genuine friendship in Season Four, and we get to bask in that dynamic for a while, sitting in small, sweet moments like the pair hanging out in the airport together, eating fast food and totally at ease in "LAXmas," or that time Schmidt takes it upon himself to—very bossily—tutor Cece for her GED test. ("Where are your flash cards? Do you not have one single flash card? There's maraschino goo everywhere! You don't have a flash card? I'm taking over.")

Still, lingering feelings remain, and we watch as Cece begins to pine after Schmidt who, with his steady, stalwart friendship, has managed to prove he's worth another chance. Who knew all it would take was a five-dollar bill, a trip to the top of Mount Shasta, and an unhinged phone call from Winston to finally bring those two together?

11

Schmidt and Cece—Together at Last

Girl, will you marry me?

—SCHMIDT

IN THE EARLY DAYS OF *New Girl*, the writers were surprised by just how well the pairing of Schmidt and Cece was working. Meriwether first noticed sparks while they were filming Season One's "Thanksgiving" episode, which involved a flirtatious Cece teasing a horrified Schmidt by sticking her hands in a bowl of mashed potatoes. A few episodes later, when Schmidt gifts Cece a rancid-smelling perfume and she wears it anyway, Meriwether knew the pair had to hook up. If *she* had been Cece, she would have hooked up with him.

Behind the scenes, Simone and Greenfield were developing their own warm connection. One late night during Season One, while sitting in the corner of the loft set waiting for their cue, Simone asked Greenfield all the questions she had been too shy to ask everyone else—like how the set worked and what, exactly, it meant to get the back nine episodes picked up. She didn't want anyone to know how new to the business she was, but Greenfield was so kind as he answered everything, the two whispering so they wouldn't disrupt filming. "I think that's really how chemistry builds," Simone told me. "It's those real-life friendship, trusting moments as we kind of guided each other through it."

New Girl writer David Iserson likened Cece and Schmidt to Monica and Chandler on *Friends*. The *Friends* writers hadn't initially conceived those characters as a potential couple but, when the two shared a surprising hookup, suddenly—it felt right. Cece and Schmidt made just as little sense on paper, and yet there was chemistry between them. It begged the question: Why not at least try and see what they'd be like romantically?

The pair briefly upgraded their status from hookup buddies to something deeper at the end of Season One thanks, in no small part, to Schmidt breaking his penis. The inspiration for that storyline came courtesy of Meriwether, whose two friends had, at one point, broken and sprained their penises. (The writers Wikipedia'ed it, and reverse cowgirl is supposedly the most dangerous sex position.)

As Schmidt lies immobilized in the hospital, the pair realize that, hookups aside, there's something bigger and more emotional there. "I like you," Cece tells Schmidt, with all the naked, vulnerable earnestness of a teen telling another teen for the first time about their crush. "I can't always just say how I feel, it's just . . . whatever, Schmidt."

"You like me?" he asks. "You like my personality?"

"I was surprised, too," she says, smiling.

They'd get pulled apart and brought back together and pulled apart again over the next few years, while both explored what they needed and wanted from a partner. As the show approached the middle of the fourth season, there was one last romantic relationship that stood between the two of them. And what a formidable match she'd be.

For so long, Schmidt had been attracted to women like his hypercritical mom, who showered him in negative feedback and left him huffing and puffing to earn their approval. Councilwoman Fawn Moscato, with her penchant for finely tuned insults, fit that bill and then some.

Her name came courtesy of Berkley, who would pass the long hours in the writers' room coming up with preposterous monikers for characters and seeing which ones he could sneak by Meriwether. He was responsible for J. Cronkite Valley-Forge, Schmidt's boss, and retired Rear Admiral Jay Garage-a-roo, one of Winston's aliases. (That was actually a joint effort with *New Girl* writer Dave Feeney, who called his garage garage-a-roo.)

Many of Berkley's names were inspired by the spam emails that arrived in his inbox. He had gotten junk mail from someone named Moscato and liked the idea of using a dessert wine for Schmidt's new love interest.

When Zoe Lister-Jones was cast as Fawn and read the script for her first episode, "Shark," she was struck by how deeply specific the character was. Her cadence, her directness, her ability to cut people down, and her pure domination of Schmidt made Lister-Jones think to herself, "I get this woman and I love this woman." The classic Fawn Moscato voice, studded with authority and sharp, sultry edges, was born as she scanned through those initial pages and played with her dialogue ahead of shooting. It came out of her mouth quite naturally, something, she told me, that could either be interpreted as exciting or scary. (Her personal favorite Fawn line: "I firmly believe that power emanates from the vagina. So why block it?")

As they began to develop the character, Berkley decided that Fawn was someone who always felt like there was somewhere else she'd rather be. The character's ethos within the world of apartment 4D was "I'm so busy, I can't believe I'm spending time with these idiots." When Berkley watched Lister-Jones in action on set, she felt like a version of Katharine Hepburn, paired with a tenor that consistently sounded like she was in the middle of delivering a keynote speech.

Lister-Jones came from theater, where the script was considered king and you didn't stray from the written word. Entering *New Girl* was a different kind of ball game. She was invited to step outside the pages, while navigating the delicate balance of staying on story and not slipping *too* far from the script. While shooting a scene in the loft for the episode "Par

5," Fawn and Cece butt heads over their shared love of Schmidt, which prompted Lister-Jones to improvise the line "What's her name? Cecil? What is your name?"

"You'll learn it, don't worry," Simone ad-libbed right back.

True to form, the love affair between Fawn and Schmidt wraps up just as briskly and efficiently as it started. The couple end on a—shall we say?—unusual note, with Fawn, in an attempt to try to save her political career after an upskirt photo, forcing Schmidt to go to a lingerie store to buy underwear with her in front of the press. It's an undoubtedly silly turned surprisingly emotional moment as the pair realize they don't have a future together amid the chaos of lacy panties being thrown about.

There was a joy for Lister-Jones in that scene. Fawn had been such an arch character throughout filming and this was a chance to play the grounded reality of the breakup. As the pair look at each other one last time, the actress felt a wave of gratitude for Greenfield. He had been such a reliable safety net throughout it all, making her feel comfortable to play around while shooting their scenes, with the knowledge that he'd always be there to catch her.

Hot on the heels of the Fawn breakup, the writers knew they wanted to end the season with Cece and Schmidt getting back together. "He should propose immediately," Fusfeld said, as they worked out those final episodes. "Let's subvert that bullshit. We don't need to string this out any longer. He needs to propose to her right away."

There was something so daunting about that prospect, though. How could they make the proposal feel as special as possible? It needed to be grand and romantic, to do justice to these two people who had come so far and were finally in the right emotional place to be with each other. At first, there were conversations around Cece—so crushed by Schmidt's relationship with Fawn—deciding to embark on a solo hiking expedition. Schmidt would break up with Fawn and then chase Cece up that mountain in the second-to-last episode of the season. The finale would see him proposing to her.

As they brainstormed what that proposal might look like, Greenfield offered his own pitch to Meriwether. What if, when Schmidt finds out that Cece loves him, he pulls up a playlist on his phone that's called In Case Cece Ever Says I Love You, and it's just "Chandelier" by Sia, which he promptly dances to around the loft. Meriwether liked the idea and they even tried it out, but in the end, the showrunner thought it was a little too abstract.

The writers decided to keep the storyline simple. Winston calls Cece and tells her that Schmidt and Fawn have broken up. ("It's your girl Winston, aka Winnie the Bish, aka aka aka Brown Lightning. Schmidt dropped Fawn like a bad habit, okay, so ain't nobody riding shotgun.") In the last moments of "Clean Break," Schmidt opens the door to the apartment and sees Cece, back from climbing Mount Shasta, ready to finally tell him how she feels. As the two gear up to lay all their cards on the table, we flash back to the very first time they met. The two stand in the entryway of the loft together and Schmidt declares—with firm conviction—"Girl, I'mma marry you."

"Jar." Cece responds, unimpressed. When Simone found out about that flashback, she was touched. "I rooted for these couples on the show," she told me. "Nothing was inevitable, you don't know how the story would go. The fact that they found their way back to each other, the fact that it felt known and destined from the second he saw her and they gave us that moment—it was so beautiful."

Back in the present day, Cece, dusty and roughed up after climbing down a mountain, admits she still loves him. There were conversations beforehand about just how much mud and grime Cece would be covered in. Should there be sticks in her hair? How *much* should they lean into the fact that she tumbled down this mountain? Ultimately, they decided that they didn't need to make a big joke out of it. This was the height of a romantic moment between Cece and Schmidt and some of the dirt was rubbed off to avoid distraction.

The big scene was originally scripted to happen in front of the rest of the cast, which gave Greenfield pause. The actor rarely emailed Meriwether but he did so before they shot this episode. "I just read the script," he wrote to her. "I know how to play this but in order for me to do this . . . [the guys] can't be there. They're going to make fun of me. They're going to make noises."

By that point, Morris, Johnson, Wayans Jr., and Greenfield had had their share of romantic moments on the show. "Whenever we would do them or whenever we had to be serious on the show and the guys were all around each other, it would get really bad and it was very unprofessional," Greenfield recalled.

He knew how much this scene was going to mean to the people who loved the show and he didn't want to work against his co-stars as they filmed the moment. "I'm *begging* you, please, get them away," Greenfield told Meriwether.

He suggested moving everyone else into the kitchen, so he could film his scene with Simone separately in the entryway of the loft.

Later, Johnson asked Greenfield, "Did you tell Liz to put us around the corner?"

When Greenfield confirmed, Johnson responded, "I get that, man. I get that."

The scene hits its crescendo as Schmidt finally takes a vulnerable, full-throated leap with Cece. "I know this might seem crazy and probably a little bit impulsive, but it's not. Not for me," he says. "I've known since the minute that I met you . . ."

"Oh my God . . ."

"Cecelia Parekh . . ."

"Oh, God, you're going to say something stupid, aren't you?"

"Girl, will you marry me?"

There's a rule in comedy that you're not supposed to cover your face, Simone told me. The audience wants to see the performers' reaction. But Simone couldn't help but put her hands in front of her mouth when Greenfield, as Schmidt, proposed. That little gasp was a genuine reaction to how heartfelt he was playing the scene. She remembers laughing and crying in that moment and feeling so *happy* for these characters. It was the very same feeling she'd experience seasons later, when Schmidt tells Cece she's pregnant.

As the episode—and the season—drew to a close, the occupants of apartment 4D prepared to step into brand-new life chapters. Schmidt and Cece were officially together and about to plan their wedding. Coach was off to New York City. Nick and Jess realized there might be more to come for them. Winston was finding himself in a profession he loved.

Of course, in true *New Girl* fashion, things couldn't stay copacetic for too long. Deschanel was heading on her maternity leave, and they'd need to introduce a new roommate to the loft. Welcome to apartment 4D, Reagan Lucas. Utilities are *not* included.

12

No Girl

Bring your A game, okay? Any previous injuries that I need to know about? Bring something to numb your mouth. Oh. Look. The sweater was in my hand the whole time.

—REAGAN LUCAS

SETH YANKLEWITZ, *NEW GIRL*'S CASTING director, had been trying to get Megan Fox on the show for years. There was a real-life quirkiness to the actress that made him think she would fit perfectly within their oddball world. He had, after all, seen her wear cat ears to a table read.

The answer was always no or she was unavailable or she simply didn't want to do TV. And then, magically, right when they needed her the most, Yanklewitz got a yes. With the show losing Deschanel for six episodes during her maternity leave, the writers decided to write a storyline that involved Jess being sequestered for jury duty, partially because they were tickled by the idea of her being a foreperson. (Hint: she's bossy and takes a hard line when it comes to bathroom breaks.) There was an empty room that needed to be filled and Meriwether had a clear vision of who would be the best subletter. What if, she posited, a confident, tough-talking woman entered the loft and added a fresh dynamic to a group of otherwise neurotic occupants?

"She's, like, a pharmaceutical rep," one writer suggested, as they delved deeper into the idea. "She always has a wheelie suitcase full of Cooch Balls and pens." That helped cement this character, whom they named Reagan and decided would be hot, sarcastic, and never suffered fools. She was someone who was used to being a lone wolf out on the road . . . not surrounded by a group of old friends with a whole bunch of emotional baggage. The time had come, Meriwether decided, for someone to "call them on all their shit."

It felt important that Reagan was someone who was markedly different from Jess. Kasdan had worked with Fox on the dramedy *Friends with Kids* and threw her name into the ring. She was tough and cool and could definitely pull off Reagan's ability to put everyone in their place with a steely one-liner. Fox had made a name for herself starring in the Michael Bay blockbuster film *Transformers*, along with the dark comedy *Jennifer's Body*, about a teen girl turned flesh-eating monster. She also had a small role in the Judd Apatow comedy *This Is 40*, and her comedic chops caught Meriwether's eye.

Getting to write for Fox's Reagan would turn out to be the ultimate thrill for *New Girl* writer Eliot Glazer. Here was this beautifully sweet, goofy show and, as he recalls, in walks a "hot vampire lady," injecting sass and a bone-dry sense of humor into the world. "I was excited because it was a tonal challenge to bring her in as the sort of dark horse," he told me. Glazer was so gleeful about Fox being there that he was teased about having a crush on her. "I'm gay," the writer told me. "But, yeah, I really did and I do and I was so thrilled that I got to write for her."

Part of the fun of Reagan was her ability to cut characters to their core in an unexpectedly whispery, silky voice. ("You have a cat, don't you?" she asks Winston softly, eyeing him up and down. "How did you know?" he replies. "It's very obvious . . . ," she says, walking away.) The actress was tough on herself when it came to her jokes, which were often one-liners with effortless punch. If she didn't feel like she had quite nailed a line, she would tell O'Malley, "I need to go again, I didn't get it."

The actress's arrival caused some critics to sit up with a jolt. *The Atlantic*'s David Sims wrote a piece on the "power of sitcom shakeup," applauding the show's writing staff for taking a leap by introducing a new central character and breaking from the network-TV status quo of sticking to the nuclear group. After all, *New Girl*, he suggested, thrived on unpredictability.

"[Reagan] laid bare just how comfortable the *New Girl* gang had gotten in recent years, and Meriwether was clearly delighted to start pulling that situation apart," Sims said. "She was like a new viewer tuning into the show, initially savaging it with withering criticism, but then slowly coming around to its charms."

With Jess's warm ability to bring the gang together gone, Cece attempts to step up and fill in. For the first time, we see a major Cece and Winston storyline, with the former trying to help the latter deal with his elusive girlfriend Cassie, who's ghosting him. Turns out, Cece has zero idea how to calm an increasingly panicked Winston. As he demands tea and sympathy, she offers him uniquely terrible advice.

"I'm going to need you to nurture me!" Winston declares, sipping from a teacup and maniacally riding an exercise bike.

"All right! I can do that part," she promises, offering, "Maybe this breakup isn't such a bad thing. Now you can stop wasting your life and find someone more realistic. Someone who's in your league because you don't want to die alone so you kind of have to settle and lower your standards and find someone who's in your lane . . . someone a little older, dumpier . . ."

When her attempts at mollycoddling don't work, Cece decides to let Winston take the lead.

Through gritted teeth, she agrees to enact a revenge plot against Cassie after discovering that she's been cheating on Winston. The plot involves telling Cassie that Winston died, which on paper sounds *rough* . . . but Simone and Morris not only managed to make it work but also, dare I say, wrangled a way-too-big prank into something charming? The scene would mark the second Cece and Winston mess-around recorded in *New Girl* history. The first, which happened one season prior, featured the pair convincing Schmidt and Coach that they were up for a modeling gig—and resulted in the pair having to pay $1,887 to feature Schmidt on a billboard for "Korean-Jewish interrelations."

It had been a long time coming for Simone and Morris to put their real-life friendship into action on-screen. The pair shared a double trailer since day one and had become close friends, developing a brother-sister rapport that included—as we would later see on-screen—calling each other "babe" back and forth and finger snaps and points. In a rare move for sitcom stars who spend hours (and hours and hours) together every week, the two also hung out on the weekends. When they started getting paired together more and more on *New Girl*, Simone remembers, it felt easy.

Once, seasons ago, Cece asked what her "pogo stick" was—the thing that everyone made fun of when she left the room. "None," Schmidt told her. "All we talk about is how hot you are." We finally get to see Cece's pogo sticks in Season Five, which includes being an absolute slob around the house, setting up a delightfully antagonist relationship between her and Nick. As the seasons went on, that mutual annoyance would steadily grow between the pair. Details of their frenemy status began to emerge, like the fact that Nick has inexplicably never saved Cece's number in his phone and tells Schmidt he views her as "an average worker, uneducated but kind, wears shoes, boyish, never really talked to her."

The weirder Cece got, the writers realized, the better she got.

As for Reagan? She begrudgingly allows herself to become, at least tangentially, a part of the loft, along with an immediate romantic fixation for Nick. After several episodes of struggling to have a basic conversation with her, Nick lets his guard down and the pair share their first kiss in the episode "Heat Wave." The crew so rarely shot on location at the downtown loft anymore but they all trekked to Traction Avenue on a Friday night to film that moment. O'Malley and Johnson were eating their craft-service meals ahead of shooting when the director checked in with him.

"Hey, how are you?" she asked.

"We got the kiss tonight," he told O'Malley, before teasingly reassuring her, "I got this, I got this."

The director could tell Johnson and Fox knew this was a big scene, not just for their characters but for the show itself. The audience needed to see Nick share a loving moment with someone besides Jess and—not only that—genuinely root for the two characters, even if it was despite themselves. As O'Malley mapped out the kiss in her mind, she decided it should feel romantic and sweet. Even though the audience knew Reagan was not who Nick was going to end up with, in that moment, and for many moments after, they were what the other needed.

The kiss happens in the final few minutes of the episode, after the pair cause a blackout in their building and are forced to evacuate. Plunked on the edge of the curb together, Reagan eye-rollingly tells Nick that he clearly has a crush on her. After much protesting, he finally gives in.

"You're a grown man," Reagan says. "I just think you should be able to say it."

"You dick," Nick responds with a resigned laugh. "Fine, I have a crush on you."

"Isn't that better?" she says, cocking her head. "Now we can put it behind us, move on, it doesn't have to be weird."

"No—I, obviously, I know it's not going to be a problem, Reagan. I don't have any illusion that you're gonna go for a guy like me. I am a total mess. I understand that. I mean, you're beautiful, and you're smart, and you're mean . . . but in a hot way. And you have the mind of an electrician, which is so confusingly hot, because that is not, like, a sexy—"

Reagan leans forward and kisses him then. On the leaderboard of *New Girl* kisses, this one was high, high up there. It was short, genuinely pretty smoldering, and after pulling away, Reagan stands up and looks down at Nick with a playful smirk, gesturing for him to join her and the rest of their roommates.

O'Malley didn't like the idea of leaving the end of the episode that way. "They're just going to stand up and walk away?" she thought. "That's going to look stupid." So she created a fake crane shot. Tracks were laid down and the dolly was held back, so that we were left with a bird's-eye shot of the fivesome together. Life was going on as usual around them, but a private spark of excitement between Nick and Reagan glinted on the surface.

As soon as the two pair up, Jess returns home from jury duty, ready to reclaim her room. It would be the first time Deschanel and Fox shared the screen together, and all network eyes were on the set, wanting to make sure that the episode—dubbed "Goosebumps Walkaway"—was a special one.

It was important to the writers that Jess be supportive of Nick's love life, full stop. Her return would not mark infighting or jealousy, which was a relief to Fox, who didn't want to see Jess and Reagan butting heads over a guy. The actress felt fairly confident that fans weren't rooting for her character in that matchup, anyway. She *did*, however, think it could be interesting to examine Jess's inner turmoil as she watches her ex-boyfriend dive into a romance with someone else.

Despite a firm commitment to the women not fighting over Nick, there was a chance to set up, in real time, just how different Reagan and Jess were. Early on in "Goosebumps Walkaway," we learn that Jess has screen-printed matching bright-orange T-shirts for everyone in the loft, which all of her roommates gamely wear for her.

"Where's Reagan? Probably putting on her shirt still," Jess says, to which Schmidt informs her, "Yeah, Reagan's not exactly the matching-tee type." That line of dialogue felt like the tidy equivalent to Julia, Nick's ex-girlfriend, not being a "dessert person."

As Reagan gets ready to say goodbye to apartment 4D, Nick tries to figure out the best line to deliver when he bids her farewell. He dubs those final words a "goose-bumps walkaway," which, in his approximation, is "the line that the guy says to the girl in the movie that gives her goose bumps and then he walks away forever."

It would grant him, as he says in a pleased whisper, *immortality*.

Berkley Johnson, who wrote the episode, was having a hard time wrapping his head around the crux of the script until he came up with the idea of a goose-bumps walkaway. He loved the idea of Nick believing there was the perfect farewell line he could deliver to Reagan. There was an aspect of Berkley's own personality that thought that way, too—the idea that he could rise above everything for just a few seconds and say the right thing, righting all past wrongs.

The writer came up with version after version of what Nick's goose-bumps walkaway could be, writing down a slew of unaired jokes that included "Reagan, from where I'm sitting, 'adios' is just shook up 'I soda'" and "Wherever the fridge of life takes you, just remember Nick Miller was a damn good magnet."

The writer ended up settling on the turn of phrase "sayonara, Sammy" for Nick's big moment, which is delivered to a perplexed Reagan. Later, she calls from the airport and says the line right back to him, in lieu of sharing all the things she wants to say: that she's crazy about him, she cares about him, and she'll miss him. As she stands up, we see that Reagan, the coolest of the cool, is wearing that very loud screen-printed orange shirt Jess made for her. Maybe she is a little bit of a dessert person, after all.

* * *

"Reagan" marked one hundred episodes of *New Girl*. The cast and crew packed inside the loft set to celebrate, and furniture was pushed out of the way to make room for a four-tier cake with bright-yellow frosting, daisies, and a glittery blue 100 sign decorating the top. Rows of champagne lined the table and a big mural featuring snapshots of the cast and crew was plastered on the loft's blue sliding door.

"Sure, anyone can count the number of episodes," Meriwether told the crowd, as she stood up to deliver a speech. "But when I close my eyes and

Adele is blasting and I'm naked-sob crying, this is the stuff that I see." She gestured around her and continued:

> I see the moment when I first heard Zooey Deschanel reading the part of Jess in a room in the creepiest building of the Fox lot and everyone just freezing with joy because we realized this whole show was going to work.
>
> I see Lamorne's original audition, when he showed up in a blond wig and cutoff jean shorts until Seth Yanklewitz asked him to "try one without the wig."
>
> I see Jake Johnson and I at a weird office on Hollywood Boulevard working on his audition for the pilot and him asking me, "How smart is this character supposed to be?"
>
> I see the poor guy who read for the part of Schmidt after Max Greenfield and how bad I felt for him because all of our minds had just been blown and none of us were listening to anything he was saying.
>
> I see Hannah Simone teaching me a very important lesson about men when I asked her to call Prince to get him to do the show, and she told me that the best way to get him to do it was if she didn't call him. Honestly, it's changed my life.

Meriwether's voice cracked as she brought up Pope.

Finally, I see Katherine Pope, looking gorgeous in all black, sitting across from me at our first meeting at Hugo's in Santa Monica, telling me she believed in me. And I see her telling me that again and again over the years, in both the moments of great joy and the Sunday-night reshoots that make me want to get in my car and reinvent myself in Mexico.

As Morris walked the blue carpet that night to commemorate the milestone event, he spoke to an *Entertainment Weekly* reporter and expressed just how meaningful the moment was to him. At one hundred episodes, it felt like they had finally joined the ranks of so many television greats.

"It means that people love it. It's developed a fanbase. Hopefully it will stick around for a while," he shared. "I grew up watching shows like *Martin*, *Friends*, *The Fresh Prince of Bel-Air*, and *The Cosby Show*. That's something that seems unattainable, but now here we are in that same realm, especially in an age where digital has taken over, so I feel great about it. One hundred episodes is amazing."

Five seasons deep, the show was both far, far away from where it started and, in some ways, ready to get back to the basics. Which meant that it was time, at long last, for the writers to reopen the Nick-and-Jess discussion. The pair would be set on the slow trajectory back to each other . . . but not *just* yet. First, Dr. Sam, again.

David Walton was standing outside of Easton Gym in Los Angeles when he got a surprise call from Meriwether. "Hey," she said. "We want to bring you back, we've got some fun stuff coming up. Are you available?"

The answer was yes, with a quick follow-up question: How many episodes would he be appearing in? Meriwether estimated at least six. "Oh shit," Walton thought. "Okay, this is gonna be a nice, juicy storyline again."

And indeed, the actor discovered, there was plenty of new and surprising material for him to play with. Since he had last left Dr. Sam, the character had gone on a surprising journey, becoming a heavily bearded, prayer bead–wearing hippie who lost track of who he was following the heartbreak of Jess and Nick's kiss. In preparation for the new version of Sam, Walton immediately set about growing out a beard. When he arrived to set, the makeup artists examined his facial hair.

"All right, we're going to put something fake on you," they told him. (It was fair enough—Walton hadn't realized that his beard would grow out quite so oily.) Douglass and Glaser hooked him up with a very dry, roughly eighteen-inch fake beard, and it was off to the races for Dr. Sam once more.

After a rocky start that involved a smashed chocolate cake and an unfortunate run-in at a car wash, Jess and Dr. Sam dive back into a relationship. While the pair had their fair share of heat and sweetness, they still clearly lack the je ne sais quoi to go the distance. The writers planted their biggest clue that the two weren't right for each other courtesy of Winston in the episode "Return to Sender." Offended that Sam isn't properly enthused about a bird shirt he gifted him, Winston muses that Jess's boyfriend might not be a good fit for her.

"Cece, you want to know what I think?" he asks.

"Mmm, not really," Cece replies.

"I think there are people who get bird shirts, and there are people who don't. Jessica Day needs to be with a bird-shirt person."

On the eve of Schmidt and Cece's wedding, Jess finds an engagement ring and assumes that Sam is going to propose. The little velvet box throws cold water on their burgeoning relationship when she realizes that she's not feeling what she's *supposed* to feel when she thinks about marrying him.

Turns out, Sam wasn't trying to propose to Jess. Just as she's mid telling him she can't accept his ring, he reveals that he wants to break up. The pair bid a final, deflated farewell in the hallway leading to the apartment. Just as Sam steps into the elevator, he has one final question to ask.

"Just out of curiosity, Jess, why couldn't you marry me?"

"Oh, I don't know."

"Come on, Jess. You know."

"No, I don't."

"Yes, you do. I mean, I know."

"What—what is it?"

"It's Nick."

Sam delivers his final line just as the elevator door closes. Trent O'Donnell, who directed the episode, didn't want that moment, significant though it was, to feel melodramatic. It was important to him that Walton deliver the words with ease and not play the scene at all emotionally, allowing the dialogue to do the heavy lifting.

Walton was on the same page. "I think I just didn't want to fuck it up," he said, looking back. "Those moments are built by the writers, and really your job is to be very simple and just talk to the person and say it like you mean it." As the actor offered up that final word, he felt like he was living out a scene from one of his favorite '80s movies. The elevator door dramatically closing at the right moment, the whole emotional setup, the delivery—it all felt really cool.

One episode later, on the back of Jess's realization that she might still love Nick, Cece and Schmidt get married. There had been a bevy of issues leading up to this wedding. Jess unknowingly makes out with Schmidt's dad. Cece's mom doesn't approve of Schmidt and refuses to RSVP. Cece drunkenly buys a horrendous wedding dress she can't return. (That, in and of itself, was a real-life challenge. While in the editing bay, Meriwether looked at Simone in Cece's ugly wedding dress and realized "She makes it look good." They had to digitally add blinking lights to the gown to make it look worse.)

When it came time for the wedding, Schmidt is nowhere to be found. He's on a plane to Oregon in hopes of convincing Cece's mom to attend their wedding. In an unexpected twist on the classic sitcom wedding, Cece and Schmidt end up having their reception while he's still stuck on the plane, making do by FaceTiming throughout.

When Baer first pitched the idea of Schmidt missing the wedding, which he had planned with such fiercely obsessive detail, Meriwether's initial instinct was an immediate no. It felt like the whole episode would be too sad. But the more they talked about it, the more exciting the prospect became. It would be a gratifying chance to show Schmidt's character development, that he's surprisingly okay with the snafu and has made peace with not getting the trappings of a fabulous wedding. At the end of the day, he's just so happy to get to marry the love of his life.

When O'Malley got the assignment to direct the wedding episode, she knew it needed to be filmed on location and she knew it needed to be somewhere special. "We've got to find a really fucking cool, beautiful place to honor Schmidt and Cece getting married," she remembers saying.

They picked Cielo Farms in Malibu, a Tuscan-inspired estate with sweeping views of the Santa Monica Mountains.

In the midst of the sweet oddity of the nuptials—Schmidt and Cece make out via FaceTime, Winston gets nude in a photo booth—Jess looks on as Nick and Reagan dance together. Nick's feelings are still going strong for their former subletter and it's clear that she feels the same. The pair laugh together on the dance floor, looking every bit the magnetic movie-star couple. It's then that Jess admits to Cece that no, she's not, in fact, over Nick.

O'Malley wanted to shoot that big, important moment at the property's barn, images dancing in her mind of decorating the lofty ceilings with twinkle lights. There wasn't enough money to shoot the scene on location, though, so they had to settle for rebuilding the barn on a stage. In the script, it was written that Jess never actually says the words *I still love him* but rather communicates the feeling with a look.

On the day of shooting, O'Malley and Meriwether gathered together for a quick debrief. "You know what?" O'Malley said. "Just thinking about network notes, you never know if somebody will interpret it or not, I should probably get Zooey verbalizing it so we have it in the edit."

O'Malley approached Deschanel.

"Hey, listen, I want to get a take where you say it, just in case."

The actress looked at her. "No," she said.

"Yeah, yeah, I know," the director quickly responded. "I won't cut it in but we need to have it in our back pocket, God forbid—"

Deschanel stood firm. "I think I can do it with my performance," she said. "I think you should depend on my performance to do it."

O'Malley shot the scene with just a look and, as promised, Deschanel's sheepish, sad smile spoke volumes. Adding to the weight of the moment is Simone's performance, as she touches Jess's arm right after. "I know, honey," she tells her. "You don't have to say it."

Schmidt and Cece finally tie the knot in person at the very end of the episode, after Schmidt arrives home late at night, exhausted from his travel adventures. When O'Malley got to those pages in the script, all it read was "Then they come home and they get married in the loft." The director headed into Meriwether's office, armed with questions. "What do you want, though?" she asked. "What's our story? What are we saying is happening?"

"I don't know," O'Malley remembers Meriwether musing. "I guess we're seeing that they all got it together and Jess brought flowers home and they set up the wedding in the living room."

In O'Malley's head, she decided that the gang had shoved the loft's furniture into Winston and Nick's bedroom and set up folding chairs they had stolen from the venue. She wanted it to be the prettiest wedding that could possibly be pulled off in apartment 4D. Strings of paper hearts were cut up and tied together. Bouquets of flowers filled the room. Lanterns flickered and black-and-white photos of Cece and Schmidt adorned the wall.

In honor of the traditional red used in Indian weddings, O'Malley covered the space in red rose petals. Costume designer Debra McGuire added red trimming to Cece's gold veil and outfitted the bridal party with the same hue, red ties for the groomsmen and a red dress for Jess.

If you think of the wedding the way that O'Malley planned it, with the whole gang coming together to scrappily transform the living room into this beautiful space as a surprise to Schmidt, it makes it all the more moving and Greenfield's reaction all the more touching.

The script called for Schmidt to smash his douchebag jar at the end of the ceremony, putting a clean end to the character we met many moons ago in the pilot. There wasn't really a natural way for Greenfield to cross the soundstage to grab the jar, so they finagled the scene, having Johnson be the one to hand it to him, a knowing smile on his face.

Back in the editing bay, Murillo—who had graduated from assistant editor to editor—sifted through the takes and was struck by how stunning it all looked. She decided to cut the scene the way she would have done when she edited music videos, putting their most beautiful footage forward. The reaction shots are everything in that scene—Schmidt looking at Cece as she walks down the aisle, Cece biting her lip, almost shyly, as she looks back at him.

O'Malley settled on the song "Still" by the Swedish singer and songwriter Seinabo Sey to underscore the big moment. It felt fitting to her that the couple, who had had so many stops and starts in their relationship, were finally reaching a place where they could stand still together. "Take a breath," she told them. "You guys are finally here and it was all worth it."

While Cece and Schmidt are celebrating their love, the heartbreak of Nick and Jess reaches a boiling point. As the episode comes to a close, Nick tells Jess that he and Reagan have made it official—they're going to finally dive into a serious relationship together. He seems startled, wondering what in the world Reagan is thinking, wanting to be with him. Jess explodes then. "Stop it, Nick!" she says, raising her voice. "I'm tired of you being the only person who doesn't see how incredible you are."

It was late at night when they filmed that scene and everyone was out-of-their-mind tired as O'Malley called action. The director was nervous about nailing the exchange, which would require weaving together such a complex web of emotions. There had been a lot of discussion ahead of time about how exactly to play it—Jess needed to show that she was completely in love with Nick but cared about him enough to help him find his confidence to fully be with Reagan.

Much like when Jess reveals her true feelings to Cece, Deschanel captured exactly what they needed, her eyes betraying the hurt and frustration she feels hearing Nick put himself down. There's resignation, too, knowing that she needs to say the magical words that will help Nick fully take that leap with Reagan.

O'Malley got her take, in all its aching glory. And she was so proud of it that she put it in her directing reel.

The Anatomy of the Popcorn Scene

You know, 'cause of the daily wear and tear
and oil and grease just cooking in there.
—NICK MILLER

Let's take a brief moment to talk about the popcorn scene. If you need a refresher, it takes place in Season Four's "Spiderhunt" and involves a mix-up between Jess, Cece, and Nick.

The setup goes as follows:

Cece keeps bugging Nick about getting a popcorn machine for the bar. Through a series of multiple misunderstandings, Jess thinks Cece has developed a crush on Nick and ends up confronting Nick about her friend's feelings. From there comes a back-and-forth conversation in which Jess thinks they're talking about Cece's vagina and Nick thinks they're talking about a popcorn machine. I am aware this sounds insane on paper.

For days, a group of the writers sequestered themselves in a room, trying to crack the code of "Spiderhunt." Berkley Johnson was tasked with writing it as a bottle episode, which means a budget-friendly episode that takes place in one setting with the core cast. He constructed a story that lent itself to multiple two-person scenes—always easier, faster, and far less exhausting than those big group ones.

Berkley crouched down on the floor as he mapped out the episode, scribbling notes onto a whiteboard. He had a kernel of an idea that the characters could get tangled up into some sort of misunderstanding but couldn't quite figure out what that would look like. As time ticked by, the writer could feel himself getting frustrated that no one was pitching anything except Matt Fusfeld, who seemed fixated on popcorn machines. Again and again, he brought up popcorn machines. "Maybe there's an argument about a popcorn machine?" he'd call out from the couch.

Fusfeld kept spitballing ideas. "It's not this but—what if there's a popcorn machine and, I don't know, Jess thinks Nick is talking about Cece's vagina?" Berkley remembers the writer saying, before quickly reiterating, "But not that! But that *kind* of thing . . ."

"What are you talking about?" Berkley Johnson asked, perplexed.

Despite nobody quite understanding the idea, they stuck it on the board as a placeholder until they could figure out what the real misunderstanding would be. It remained there until the bitter end, when there wasn't any time left to come up with an alternative.

"I guess we'll just try this?" the writers said to each other.

By that point, Berkley could actually feel himself getting genuinely excited about writing this madcap scene. Much like the badger moment from Season One, some of the best, most memorable moments from *New Girl* were placeholders that didn't seem like they could possibly be something . . . until they were.

The result is an exchange that, at the time of writing this, currently has 1.3 million views on YouTube. Berkley remains simultaneously proud and ashamed of the popcorn scene to this day.

13

Sayonara, Sammy, Part I

Beanbag chair! Winston, you remembered!
—CECE PAREKH

IN LIEU OF MEETING HIS new co-workers in the writers' room on his first day of work, Eliot Glazer was sent on what could be described, perhaps, as a more terrifying prospect: the group writers' retreat. All of the *New Girl* writers descended on the impossibly quaint village of Solvang, California, its main street lined with Danish-style architecture and bakeries filled with powdered donuts. Glazer found himself driving to a rented estate, unsure of what to expect, homework in hand filled with ideas for Season Six.

The writers gathered in a hot, un-air-conditioned room for a "blue-sky" session, which was a free-for-all pitch meeting where ideas about stories and characters could fly freely. They discussed Nick and Jess and the pair's journey back together. Conversations would always go off the rails, in the best way possible, when it came to Winston and what could be dreamed up for him, from the crazy to the romantic, with Aly as his love interest.

As Glazer began to dip his toes into writing for the fivesome, he found himself keying in on Jess. He loved characters who were bright, sprightly, well-meaning, and sweet, who could say the silliest things that made them sound so lovingly naïve. He also felt a quick kinship to Schmidt. As a fellow overachieving Jewish boy from New York, channeling that character didn't feel like much of a stretch.

Some arcs were already set in place as the writers mapped out the forthcoming season. The audience would return to the show and discover that Jess is still privately pining for Nick, while a surprising new love interest reemerges from years past. The time, of course, had come for the return of Robby.

Nelson Franklin got a call from his agent with an ask. "Hey, are you in town for the next eight weeks?" Johnson had landed a role in the new Tom Cruise movie and would need to miss several days of shooting. The writers wanted someone else to fill out the core cast and had an idea involving Robby coming back for a larger arc as Jess's significant other.

This was thrilling news. Not only was Franklin being called back for the show, but he'd just landed the most significant storyline he'd ever been given on a TV series. Plus, he had never been asked to play the boyfriend of the star of the show. He was quickly folded into the chaos of the loft and, within a few episodes, had a mold taken of his mouth so that bloody, broken teeth could be designed for the episode "Ready," in which Jess drops a barbell on him as they share their first kiss.

Franklin also fielded a question asking if he played any musical instruments, to which the actor responded, "Certainly not." The next thing he knew a script had arrived which called for him to belt out the song "Africa" by Toto in a romantic duet with Deschanel, all while playing the guitar. There was also a script that had him playing the *Seinfeld* theme on the bass.

Feeling stressed, he called one of his friends, a session musician, and told him, "You've got to come over and teach me how to play A) the *Seinfeld* theme and B) 'Africa' by Toto." Turns out, the *Seinfeld* theme song was performed on a keyboard and not a string bass, so his friend took on the challenge of making the arrangement work on a totally different instrument. After two weeks of practicing, Franklin gave his best effort on both, working hard to get the chords right as he accompanied Deschanel on "Africa," while knowing full well that his voice was probably going to get dubbed over.

Franklin was joined by Megan Fox as a frequent presence in the loft, both becoming fixtures in the everyday lives of apartment 4D. The pair shared the screen for the first time in the episode "Christmas Eve Eve," in which the gang surprises Jess with a festive performance by Darlene Love as Reagan tosses glittery pieces of paper from their roof in lieu of snow. It was the night after Donald Trump won the 2016 election, and Franklin remembers a gloominess hanging over the set. When action was called, they put on a cheery facade, singing, dancing, and laughing as scripted. Between takes, there were tears.

At one point, the actors were lined up on the street and Franklin was placed next to Fox. He greeted her with a "hey," and she looked at him but didn't respond. Instead, he remembers her turning to Johnson and asking, "Is this guy supposed to be here?" Franklin suspected she thought he was a background actor.

"Yeah!" Johnson responded. "That's Robby, he plays Robby."

Fox turned back around to him and asked how long he had been doing the show.

"Six years," he replied flatly, which caused Johnson to crack up. The actor later reached out to give Franklin a big hug. "That was classic," Franklin remembers Johnson saying. "That was a great moment."

* * *

If the sixth season of *New Girl* felt rushed, stacked with breakups and make-ups and major life milestones, that's because it was. For the first time in its entire run of the series, Meriwether, Baer, and Finkel weren't entirely sure if they were going to be picked up for another season. A steady ratings decline had left viewership hovering between roughly one to two million per episode, and the network was being coy as to whether or not they planned to give the show another season.

Those numbers weren't telling the whole story. Morris noticed that the viewers who loved the show were holding tight. Despite dipping ratings, people still wanted to line up to take photos with him in crowded rooms and quote lines from episodes that had just aired. He decided that those were the people he was performing for every week. The fans who, come Tuesday night, were tuning in to catch the next episode of their show. There was still a devoted fan base out there—a foreshadowing, in the best possible way, of what was to come.

But for now: What had happened to *New Girl*, once Fox's darling of a hit, now relegated to the rocky waters of potential cancellation? "I think it was just a financial thing," Johnson told me. "We weren't getting good numbers and we weren't cheap anymore."

On top of that, as *Vulture*'s Jesse David Fox put it when he examined the show's legacy, "Cable shows happened. Streaming shows happened. Network shifted to higher concepts, the explicitly political, REBOOTS. A tweener like *New Girl*—smart in its comedy, humble in its scope—felt like seeing someone in skinny jeans today: Regardless of execution, the Zeitgeist had moved on. Sites like this one didn't cover it as much, even if writers like this one still watched it religiously."

While broadcast shows *The Big Bang Theory* and *NCIS* still had a firm grip on their viewership, it was cable shows like *The Walking Dead* and behemoth streamers like *Game of Thrones* and newcomer *Stranger Things* that were drumming up audience frenzy and watercooler talk. The days of *Vanity Fair* writers debating the latest episode of *New Girl* felt like a quaint whisper of the past.

With questions hanging in the air over the show's fate, the writers needed to tie up loose ends fast, while faced with the awkward task of not tying them up *too* tightly in case there was another season. "Guys, we can't fuck up this show, we've come too far," Meriwether remembers saying. "If this is the last season, we have to get Nick and Jess together." Of course, that posed the question of, if the pair did get together, what in the world would they do if there was a next season . . . ? But okay, they'd deal with that when the time came.

As the writers mulled over this looming, potentially final season, their attention turned to Nick. He was the last member of the loft still struggling with finding his professional identity, and a decision was made to give him a surprising career victory.

Early on in the show, Nick declared that he was a writer. The idea of Nick saying he was a writer but not actually *being* one had felt so right for the character. After some nudging, he finally attempts to write his first novel, drunkenly heading to the zoo for inspiration and trying to channel his inner Hemingway. He ends up churning out a book on zombies that includes a word jumble, thirty-eight misspellings of the word *rhythm*, and not much else of note.

That wasn't the end, though. After a false start, Baer realized it would be funny to turn a screw and reveal to their viewers that Nick *is* talented. Their first thought was that Nick's book should be a graphic novel called *The Pepperwood Chronicles*, featuring his alter ego Julius Pepperwood, and would end up spawning a comic book–loving audience.

Someone threw out an alternate suggestion. What if his hard-boiled detective story connects exclusively with teen girls? The idea that Nick could get to the heart of what a fourteen-year-old girl was thinking and feeling cracked the writers' room up. On top of that, they decided Nick had assumed his readers were "blue-collar nautical workers on the coastline of Maine"—and must begrudgingly come to the conclusion that he's written a delicious romance for young women discovering their true selves.

Nick's success as a writer raised another question. If his work got published, how would that impact the ways he'd grow and change as a character? And what, if anything, did it all mean for his relationship with Jess? Both were in separate relationships at the time and, should this be the final season, it felt critical that those romances be untangled before the show ended.

"Nick and Jess have both started to have some personal successes and have firm footing, and I think the move for us has always been, we wanted them to be better people before they were ready for each other," Baer explained to *AV Club* at the time. "Are they completely ready for each other? I can't answer that, but I do think they have better footing than they did three years ago, for sure."

Deschanel had other ideas. If this was going to be the final season, she wanted a more ambiguous ending for Nick and Jess. She fought for a *Graduate*-style closing shot of the pair, with both coming together in delirium until reality hit them, leaving the audience with an unspoken feeling that the characters might not have made the right decision. The network didn't go for that, preferring a more satisfyingly concrete conclusion for the two.

Okay, fine. But now—how were the writers going to break up Nick and Reagan and Jess and Robby in an organic way, while leaving *just* enough time for Nick and Jess to get back together by the last episode?

"What if Robby and Jess are cousins?" one writer jokingly pitched during one of those night writing sessions.

Much like the badger joke from seasons ago, it was so ridiculous but also made the punch-drunk room laugh. Maybe the writers *could* get a little weird and broad with the pair's breakup. They didn't feel like they needed to be quite as precious with Robby and Jess as they'd need to be with Nick and Reagan. As fun and warm as Robby was, the relationship never felt like it could go the distance.

Franklin knew he was only going to be on the show for six episodes. With his final bow coming up, he found himself wondering how the show would choose to say goodbye to his character. When he got the script and discovered that Jess and Robby were third cousins, he felt a wave of satisfaction. "'This is perfect,'" he thought. "This way nobody's feelings are hurt. It's out of the characters' hands, nobody could say that they should have stayed together."

As you'd expect, the scene where the pair discover they are related, while trapped in a rain-soaked cave, no less, is head-scratchingly silly. The episode can be forgiven, though, because of its strong B plot, which features Winston freaking out over meeting Aly's parents. (In an ad-libbed run, Morris practices on Nick, leaning in for a cheek kiss and saying, "Not today, honey! We're going in for the real thing!" Johnson improvised crossing his hands over his body in response, a bit that Morris continues to do to this day.)

Untangling Reagan and Nick would turn out to be a more complicated creative conversation. Writer Lamar Woods quietly threaded a warning sign in his episode "Operation: Bobcat," planting a scene that featured Reagan sending Nick a chain for Valentine's Day, which couldn't have been less of a compatible present for him. They kept the warning signs coming—Nick doesn't share his book with Reagan, Reagan gets a secret apartment—as the relationship quickly starts to crumble.

As much as she loved Nick and Jess, O'Malley found herself starting to pull for Reagan and Nick. While directing the episode "Misery," she watched as the duo fought over Reagan's inability to open up and share her life updates with Nick. It's bigger than that, though, Nick says. Why don't they have nicknames for each other? Why isn't he at his best sexually with her? Why does she still have an apartment when they're supposed to be living together?

Reagan, exhausted, tells Nick, "I'm so tired. Can you just write it all down and I'll fill it out and I'll get it back to you?"

We see the clear cracks in the relationship then. Nick wants something from Reagan that she can't give, as much as she cares about him. From behind the camera, O'Malley found herself actively not wanting the pair to break up. She loved Nick and Jess together, but there was something special between Nick and Reagan, too. She was rooting for them.

The writers ultimately broke Nick and Reagan up in the episode "San

Diego," which featured Nick, too cowardly to end the relationship, ditching Reagan on a train. As a viewer, it felt like Nick had come way too far to do something quite so thoughtless. To make matters worse, he proceeds to hide in the closet later in the episode, before he and Reagan ultimately say goodbye to each other. The Nick who trapped himself in a photo booth in Season One's "Wedding" had returned in a disappointing way.

O'Malley watched with admiration as Fox tackled that breakup scene. Despite Nick's immaturity, the director could still feel the love and resigned wistfulness in Reagan's voice as she says, "Bye, Nick," from outside that closet door. "She really, really understood the nuance of how conflicted Reagan was in that moment," O'Malley told me. "How she couldn't help Nick, but she cared about him."

Network executives had told Baer, Finkel, and Meriwether to prepare a final episode that would work whether the show was canceled or not. They'd need to write a finale that could serve as both a gateway to Season Seven and a final bow on the entire series. And so, the writers wrapped the characters' stories as best as they could. Winston reaches out to his estranged father, with encouragement from Aly. (That phone call features, perhaps, one of the best lines of the entire series: "I have a cat, he's not ready to have a relationship with you so don't try to force it on him.") A publisher is interested in acquiring *The Pepperwood Chronicles*. And in the last moments of the episode, Cece discovers she's pregnant. Well, actually, everybody else finds out she's pregnant before she does, and a game of phone tag ensues. Such was the Baer and Finkel philosophy, Fusfeld remembers. It couldn't just be that Cece was pregnant, everyone else in the loft needed to be involved somehow.

Nick realizes that he's still in love with Jess while sitting in the lobby of his potential book publisher, as Schmidt gently but firmly guides him toward the epiphany. "Nick, you have been in love with this girl from the moment you opened the door and you first laid eyes on her," he tells him. "I have never seen you look at anyone else like that in my entire life. Except maybe, on a few occasions, me."

In classic romantic-comedy fashion, Nick rushes home to tell Jess how he feels just as she's running back to the loft to tell him she still has feelings for him. The pair keep missing each other, with Jess racing up to the loft, Nick trying to find her downstairs, and them finally coming together in the elevator. (Meriwether had a particular fondness for elevator scenes. It reminded her of the theater, with the curtain opening and closing.)

The rest of the shots would take place in the loft building's staircase, which had yet to be established in the series. O'Malley decided the location needed to feature a wide set of stairs, settling on a twenty-story building on the Fox lot, which would allow them to shoot Deschanel huffing and puffing her way to the fourth floor.

Before they filmed those final moments of the episode, O'Malley offered some words of reassurance to Deschanel and Johnson. "I'm going to shoot a bunch of pieces, you're going to feel like, 'Erin, why am I running up the stairs again?'" she told them. "You just have to trust me, I'm going to piece it all together in a montage to a song."

At long last, Nick and Jess find each other.

"Hey, Miller," Jess says with a slow smile. "Hey," he says back, and steps inside the elevator, the pair facing forward with shy excitement. The doors closes, there's a beat, and when the elevator reopens again, Nick and Jess are pressed together, passionately kissing. We are reminded, yet again, that no other sitcom TV couple has ever and will ever kiss quite so well.

As they filmed those last moments in the loft, Meriwether and O'Malley watched them unfold from behind a tiny monitor, making extra sure the camera wasn't catching Deschanel's pregnant belly. Meriwether had stopped coming to set quite so much by that point, and having her there in that moment felt extra special.

When O'Malley and Meriwether felt like they got their take, they turned to look at each other. "I guess that's it," O'Malley said. They called it a wrap, walking away without knowing if it was the last time they'd return to apartment 4D.

Back at the edit bay, the director set her cut of the scene to "XO" by

Beyoncé. A massive fan of the singer, O'Malley was delighted to finally get to include one of her songs in the show. Plus, it played so perfectly as the backdrop for their reunion. Meriwether, it turned out, wasn't sold. She argued that the song was going to feel dated by the time the episode aired and they needed something that was newer and fresher for this pivotal—potentially very last—moment.

Lorde's funky, colorful "Green Light" was nudged onto the table. The song had just been released off her second studio album and delivered all the pulsating, endorphin-packed urgency that the kissing scene demanded. Buying the rights would be costly, but the big check felt worth it. It was a musical moment that served as a sequel of sorts to the Vaccines' "I Always Knew" playing at the end of Season Two. There was that same edge and same electricity, only without the inevitable feeling that Nick and Jess were heading into the eye of the storm. This time, they were getting their happy ending.

As the sixth season drew to a close, the production team wasn't instructed to tear down their sets or empty their offices, which offered some shred of hope. When episodes began to air, the cast, Meriwether, Finkel, and Baer kept getting asked the same question. Was this it for *New Girl*? Was the show done? Their responses ran the gamut from resigned to hopeful.

"Fox won't tell us [whether the show will be renewed]," Johnson told *The Daily Beast*. "But we shot a finale where, if this was the end, the core fan base would be OK." The outlet received similarly ambiguous answers when they reached out to Meriwether for comment: "I genuinely don't know! Fingers crossed," she said. In response, a Fox representative told the reporter, "While no announcement has been made on the series returning for a 7th season, the network and studio are currently in discussions."

There was one piece of information no one was telling the press. Behind the scenes, a determined campaign was being waged to get that final chapter made. "This is going away unless we fight," Johnson remembers Meriwether saying.

CEOs Dana Walden and Gary Newman were still on the fence, so Johnson sent an email to the duo, putting in one final pitch. "I don't think you gave us enough time to finish the show the right way," he wrote. "And I would really appreciate—and I think the fans would appreciate—a final goodbye to these characters."

Deschanel sent an email, too. She didn't want to beg to come back but she did let Walden and Newman know that she would love to give *New Girl* a proper send-off, to go into the season knowing that it was the last.

Newman and Walton heard what everybody had to say, and they had questions of their own.

"Where do you go from here?" the executives asked Meriwether. It was, in a way, the same kind of question one might ask about a high-school show that broaches into the college years. *New Girl* was built on the foundation of young people stumbling through their lives together. What stories were left to tell about this group of friends who, by all accounts, had reached full adulthood?

Meriwether met Kasdan, Baer, and Finkel at Hugo's, a West Hollywood eatery, ordered a plate of eggs, and quickly began sketching out a pitch. The prospect of the show being canceled, without a proper ending, haunted Meriwether. She was determined to get on the phone with Walden and Newman and secure them a final stretch of episodes.

The writers felt like there was still so much to explore. What if Schmidt turned out to be a helicopter parent? What if Winston got promoted and became a detective? How could they mine Nick's new success as a writer? How could they play with Nick and Jess's relationship now that they were unquestionably a couple?

After a hasty breakfast, the foursome felt like they had come up with enough enticing ideas and headed over to Meriwether's house for the big phone call. She pitched her heart out that day, spinning a big-picture vision for what the final chapter of *New Girl* could be. This was a show that started out about four single roommates sharing an apartment. Now the audience would get the chance to see the group navigating new terrains together: parenting, pregnancy, marriage, and long-term relationships.

O'Malley was in her backyard when she got a call from Meriwether with an update. "They're getting on an airplane in New York and they're going to tell me what they think when they land in LA," she said.

The next phone call arrived with a jolt of news. Meriwether had gotten a yes—but with a twist. They could do eight episodes to finish the show up and that would be the end.

Finkel felt a little shortchanged by that. "I wish we would have been able to do at least, like, twelve or thirteen more to dig into some other stuff," he'd later say. But here they were.

News reached the press that *New Girl* was getting a truncated season on a Sunday, a mere twenty-four hours before Fox's big presentation to advertisers. At the time, *Vanity Fair*'s Katey Rich wrote, "An eight-episode sendoff gives Fox the opportunity to pay some proper attention to its one-time favorite child." The series hadn't gotten the same online chatter or promotion that long-running shows like *The Office* or *Girls* had received as they took their final bows, the journalist noted, concluding that *New Girl* deserved better.

As the writers gathered together for their last season, Baer offered some perspective. He walked over to the whiteboard in the writers' room and began jotting down a list of shows and tabulating how many episodes each had, including *Cheers*, which was revered by so many of them. *New Girl* was right there along with the greats, racking up more than a hundred episodes. "Oh wow," Berkley thought as he looked at the board. "We've done a lot." There was something heartening about seeing those numbers. It was easy to forget how much they had accomplished.

As they began their last pitch session, one last mission stood between themselves and the finish line: End this show and end it well. There were only a handful of episodes to see these characters off and the writers needed to be fast and efficient with their storytelling. What is the best way to wrap this up for the fans? What's the best way to wrap this up for the characters?

Ahead of shooting Season Seven, Finkel took part in a Television Critics Association panel and shared that there was one weighty question to answer. "The whole show was built on this idea, on characters that were broken, and we needed to see at the end of this story: Are they going to fix each other? Are they going to be okay? Is it going to work out?" he told the audience.

The answer, he decided, was already there. "I think we can say . . . yes."

With a fierce, rejuvenated dedication to getting this final season right, the cast and crew headed back to set for one final mess-around.

14

Sayonara, Sammy, Part II

You and your dang old aliases.
You have a new alias every day, Winston!
—SCHMIDT

"I CAN'T BELIEVE HOW LONG I've been doing this," Berkley Johnson mused as Season Six took its final bow.

He was the only staff writer who had been there since the beginning, save for Meriwether, Finkel, and Baer. The completion anxiety in him said that—should there be another season—he needed to stay until the very end. "I've devoted so much of my life, time, and stomach lining, I want to at least be there to help smother the pillow over it," he thought. When he got the call that *New Girl* would be returning for a truncated run, it felt right. The idea of doing a whole other full season felt like too much at that point. (If you asked him to do it now, though, it would be different. "I would get to work on a fifty-episode season tomorrow," he told me.)

It was a disorienting feeling going back to work. The *New Girl* world that had once had such a sprawling presence on the Fox lot, its expansive sets occupying Stages 17 and 18, was gone. The sets had all been boxed up, shipped, and crammed into a much smaller soundstage at Occidental Studios, a space that was mostly used for commercials and music videos.

For the first time, the show about roommates was no longer about roommates at all. Nick and Jess were the only characters left in the loft, while Aly and Winston and Cece and Schmidt had moved on and into their own homes. Still, a decision was made that the characters would show up at one another's homes unannounced, reinforcing the idea that these were still codependent relationships. Meriwether wanted to maintain the sense that this was a group of friends who were, by all accounts, *too* good friends.

The writers' task was a delicate one—build new adult lives for their characters while also paying a proper, nostalgic homage to the show as it once was. Old episodes were pulled up to jog their memories as they double-checked which characters said what in different scenes. While watching footage from years past, Meriwether, who was seven months pregnant at the time and already feeling emotional, started crying.

Markers were whipped out to ink a final wish list on a whiteboard. The writers marked down everything they wanted to see in those last eight episodes, from their favorite recurring bits to actors they'd love to see return.

Over the summer, Meriwether called Greenfield and asked him if he could grow a mustache for the first episode back. The actor grew a beard and shaved a goatee, texting a photo of himself to Meriwether. "How about a goatee?" he asked. Meriwether wrote back, "Please don't ever send this to me again." That facial hair, he told me, was disgusting and so awful.

When he returned to set, his mustache was promptly shaved off by Nick, who hates it. (Berkley made sure that moment was underscored with the Sheriff song "When I'm With You," adding an extra layer of sincerity to the scene.)

As the writers mapped out episodes, the conversation turned to Winston and his pranks. They were in agreement that there needed to be one last Prank Sinatra moment to close out the series. As the group pitched thoughts on what that big—undoubtedly *way too big*—ruse might be, Berkley Johnson threw out an idea. What if Nick and Jess get an eviction notice only to discover in the very last episode it had all been a prank courtesy of their former roommate?

Berkley, who was a fan of word puzzles, came up with the name "Engram Pattersky" as the real-estate company kicking them out, which, unscrambled, read "My Greatest Prank." The writers' room loved that idea. It would be an elegant way of sending Nick and Jess onto the next chapter of their lives, while allowing the cast to bid one fine farewell to the loft. Maybe if the audience saw that the couple was moving on with their lives, it wouldn't feel like quite such a heartache to say goodbye to these characters, hitting that perfect *New Girl* sweet spot of sad and funny.

The writers turned their attention to the sixth member of the loft. "What happened to Ferguson?" they wondered, contemplating what Winston's cat had been up to in the roughly three and a half years since we had last seen him. They decided he had probably passed away . . . and then all eyes turned to writer Noah Garfinkel. On a routine basis, Garfinkel had jokingly pitched the idea of Ferguson getting killed off. It had become such an ongoing bit that, come the holidays, Meriwether, Baer, and Finkel gave out mugs that featured Garfinkel on one side and a poorly Photoshopped image of a piano falling on Ferguson on the other.

"Noah . . . ," Meriwether said. In honor of his ongoing Ferguson-death bit, Garfinkel was assigned the cat's memorial episode, putting a final nail in the beloved pet's coffin.

"Where the Road Goes" begins, quite fittingly, with an Enya song, a callback to Winston's deep love for the singer. The episode was an ambitious one and went far beyond Ferguson's memorial, which was an intricately planned affair that featured speeches, song, and an interpretive dance. Garfinkel set about tackling Winston's grief and Jess's fear that she accidentally killed Ferguson, all the while exploring Nick and Coach's argument over a loan and Schmidt's terror that Cece will move on too quickly after *his* death.

It would also be a great opportunity to bring back beloved guest stars—along with hiring the same a cappella group who sang "Alison" during Winston's proposal. They returned to perform "Cat World," a play on "Mad World," at the funeral.

As broad a concept as it was, the writers wanted the episode to feel as real as possible, tracking Winston's mourning of a cat who, as Finkel put it to *IndieWire*, was his "only legitimate relationship [for a while]." It felt fitting for Winston to bid a last farewell to his furry son, just as he's getting ready to welcome a child with Aly.

Ahead of shooting "Where the Road Goes," David Walton was asked to come back for a cameo. It was a quick and easy yes for Walton, who returned to the set for the first time in more than a year. In his brief appearance, Sam wears a cat shirt in honor of Ferguson. Much to Sam's dismay, Winston informs him that, actually, he's more into fish shirts now. "I'm trying so hard, man," he replies.

Looking back, Walton found it strange that he wasn't in a scene with any of his regular acting partners. There was also the larger question of why Jess's ex would have even chosen to go to Winston's cat's funeral in the first place. "The scene was me and Lamorne, who I barely knew, so that was strange in an absurdist, kind of cool way," he said.

The episode was stuffed with so many gratifying, deeply specific character moments—like a perplexed Coach realizing that he'd been allotted twenty minutes to discuss a cat onstage. It's both a funny and quiet reminder of how good and loyal this friend group is. If Winston wants them to pay a comically long tribute to Ferguson in front of a large group of people, of course they'll do it.

Meriwether, Baer, and Finkel had promised the network a new, more adult version of *New Girl*, and they were delivering. Nick, Johnson noticed when he returned to set, had been given a watch to wear. His clothes were tighter and more expensive. He wasn't allowed to wear flip-flops in scenes anymore. Production designer Michael Whetstone, meanwhile, took on the task of turning apartment 4D into a more grown-up space. They decided that they'd change about 35 to 40 percent of the décor, getting rid of the mismatched dining-room chairs and buying a more sophisticated-looking table.

Meriwether wasn't able to take a look at the new set until Friday, three days before shooting began. When she walked in, Whetstone remembers, she said, "We've got to go further. It doesn't look different enough."

With only the weekend left, Whetstone and set decorator Jane Shirkes foraged through stores where they knew décor would be in stock, looking for pieces at Lawson-Fenning, which sold higher-end antiques, and HD Buttercup, a Culver City spot filled with contemporary and modern designs. Nick would get his own home office this season, modeled almost entirely after Russell's office, save for a few details like the framed Jim Croce photo and a blown-up cover page of *The Pepperwood Chronicles*.

To add another adult spin, two pint-sized additions joined the core group. Meriwether went about the strange process of casting young twins for the role of Ruth, Cece and Schmidt's daughter, with Simone and Greenfield coming in to read lines with their potential co-star. Some of the toddlers looked absolutely miserable. Meriwether would find herself asking those kids if they actually wanted to be there and, when the answer was no, she'd reply, "Well, then you should leave and go play."

Six-year-old twins Rhiannon and Danielle Rockoff ended up landing the role, taking turns playing Ruth on-screen. The kids would turn out to be a formidable adversary for Nick, with neither taking an initial shine to the other. (As Nick puts it to Ruth, "Before you, I was [Schmidt's] baby girl.") Within the first few episodes, the twins had already drawn a hard line when it came to the number of alts they'd perform. "I'm not doing any more jokes," one of them said.

Adding kids into storylines shifted the *New Girl* universe. "It felt a little bit like a different show, not in a bad way," Greenfield said. "There were moments where we were like, 'We're shooting *Three Men and a Baby*.'" It had been the least kid-friendly environment for six years, Greenfield remembers, and all of a sudden there were two children on set. For the first time, the parents on the writing staff were able to let loose on their experiences, sharing stories about how being a parent hadn't necessarily improved their personal development.

When it came to Nick and Jess, their road to engagement would be at the center of a tight eight-episode arc. There was a delicate balance of keeping the fans interested in their story while emphasizing that the audience was not going to be jerked around—these two were in it for the long haul.

Meriwether didn't want to end the series with Nick and Jess getting married, though. This was an ensemble show through and through and to do so would suggest otherwise. Instead, the pair would wed in the second to last episode, "The Curse of the Pirate Bride," which opens with Jess slipping and scratching her cornea, forcing her to wear an eye patch for the nuptials. Her accident was based on Meriwether's own experience scratching her eye two days before her wedding to Alex Cuthbertson, a writer and producer on *New Girl.* She had to don a black patch purchased from a drugstore the day before, an unfortunate but amusing experience that prompted her to think, "Well, this is an episode."

Jess and Nick wind up getting married in a hospital hallway when Aly suddenly goes into labor and the whole gang rushes to be with her. Look closely as Jess walks down the aisle: You'll see editor Steve Welch there, playing the keyboard. Welch had decided to exit the show for the seventh season—he loved the job so much but was feeling way too burned out by that point. He returned to the set to offer a little hat tip to that sleepless night, many moons earlier, when he plunked out a piano tune in the editing bay for the episode "Injured."

It was at that moment, as they shot their wedding scene in the hospital, that the reality of what was happening hit Johnson. "Oh, this is all ending in less than eight days," he realized. "This is a goodbye. This is our goodbye to each other. We've been building to this and we got it."

Simone was having her own moments of epiphany. In the midst of shooting, she realized that she was someone who would much rather be broken up with over text than hear the bad news face-to-face. If *New Girl* had been unceremoniously canceled after their sixth season—the equivalent of a breakup text—she could have been a little angry. But the network had granted them these last episodes and now she had to sit with the pain of saying goodbye. She kept tabulating lasts: This was the last day shooting with Jamie Lee Curtis, this was the last day shooting with Rob Reiner, this was the last time filming outside the loft. "It wasn't just goodbye," Simone later said. "It was a million goodbyes."

In the midst of shooting, Greenfield popped over to the writers' room. He knew they were doing Secret Santa, which had become a wildly elaborate tradition among the staff. As *New Girl* writer Eliot Glazer described it, the gift exchange was so high stakes, so high pressure, and the closest he'd ever gotten to a fraternity rush. For reference: Dave Finkel was once gifted a paintball gun and a Billy Joel impersonator whom he could spray-paint all over because he hated the singer's music.

For the final year, J. J. Philbin was Meriwether's Secret Santa. Greenfield watched as Meriwether opened up her present, pulling out large, hand-stitched dolls, each one a character from *New Girl*. As it began to dawn on her what the dolls were, Meriwether declared, "I'm going to sleep with all of these!" The joke was so funny, Greenfield recalled, because it was unquestionably true. In that moment the actor realized 1) Meriwether was actually probably going to put the dolls in her bed, and 2) these characters meant so much to her.

"She *cared so much*," he said. "I think it's what makes any show so meaningful to people—without somebody who cares that much behind every decision, I just don't think it's the same."

When it came to the finale, Meriwether decided she wanted to keep the episode contained to the core fivesome. "The simple episodes, the ones where everyone was just kind of stuck together in the loft, those were my favorites," she told *The Hollywood Reporter* at the time. "I wanted a finale that felt like our show, simple and small and about our people in this space. That's what it's always been."

As they packed up the loft, the group would go through old relics, all their memories laid out on a table. Embedded in that scene was a treasure trove of Easter eggs for the fans who had stuck with them through it all—the ones who could *immediately* clock Schmidt's horribly disfigured penis cast from a mile away.

One late night, Meriwether found herself sitting in the loft, sifting through boxes of all those old props. There were so many of them—that soft-pink MISS DAY'S JAM-BOREE T-shirt, a copy of *Business, Man* magazine, which winkingly featured first assistant director Michael Risoli on the cover. She held each item up and tried to remember which episode they came from. There was something so funny about sifting through every crazy relic from the show, and sad, too.

For one last time, the writers decided to give Nick and Schmidt a flashback scene. Makeup artist Matthew Mungle came out of semiretirement to put Greenfield in his fat suit again, and the two actors sat in a nearly empty loft, taking the audience back to the very first day that they moved into apartment 4D. The script had the pair dreamily looking toward the future, talking about what was to come with their lives.

"I don't know," Schmidt muses. "I meet a nice lady. She wants to have a baby with me."

"What does she look like?" Nick asks.

Greenfield went off script then, and described Nick to a T, down to his orangish-reddish hoodie. The actors laughed, the crew laughed, and Johnson thought, "Another garbage, throwaway moment." Much to his delight, that little exchange would make it into the final cut. Yes, Jess was Nick's big TV romance. But for Johnson, Schmidt legitimately felt like Nick's other on-screen romance. He had performed more scenes sitting next to Greenfield, talking about how he felt about him, than Deschanel.

And there was one more romantic scene between them left to come.

In classic *New Girl* fashion, Nick and Schmidt shared an unexpectedly emotional moment that involves Nick slathering lotion on his feet for the first time, after neglecting bottles and bottles that had been lovingly given to him by Schmidt. When O'Malley, the director of the episode, read that scene, she didn't get it.

"How is that funny?" she wondered. "How's that going to work?"

Johnson, she remembers, also thought it was ridiculous. But—such was the magic of the actor—he figured it out and sold the scene, as Nick delights in how creamy the moisturizer is, realizing for the first time that his feet can be used as "more than just weapons."

While packing up the rest of the loft, the gang decides to play one final game of True American. Lamar Woods hadn't been a part of the show when the game was played, and he found himself feeling genuinely intimidated when it came time to pitch dialogue for that scene. It was such an iconic staple of the series and he wanted to make sure he contributed as best as he could.

"How do I pitch on this?" he asked one of the writers beforehand.

"Just say anything," they reassured him. It was then that Woods realized that, really, True American was completely random. There was no strategy, no intricate rules. "Spaceships!" he called out amid the flurry of word salad. "Marshmallows!"

Using the last minutes of the finale to play a game of True American felt like such a fitting way to capture *New Girl*'s spirit. But Meriwether wanted more. She wanted the audience to know that, even when the show faded to black and the characters moved on, their deeply woven bonds would remain.

"How do we show that they stay friends even without living together?" the writers found themselves asking. They settled on the idea of a flash-forward, which would slip into the future and offer a glimpse of everyone together, leaping from sofa to sofa, playing True American with juice boxes alongside all their future kids.

New Girl didn't typically do any fancy camerawork, but when O'Malley got the final script and read the flash-forward scene, she knew she wanted to try something different. "What if I do a real, real low-angle shot?" she pitched Meriwether. "You literally see Jake leap and then I cut to this kid leaping into a future living room?"

Meriwether was sold and the director designed the shot as she imagined it, shooting from apartment 4D into what was to come. It was a reassuring wink to the audience that there was so much life left to live for this group of friends.

In the last minutes of the episode, the gang discovers that the eviction notice was all a giant fake-out courtesy of Prank Sinatra himself. As they head downstairs with all their belongings, Winston unveils a massive photo of his face on the back of the moving truck, alongside the word GOTCHA!.

The prank doesn't register at first.

"Did you pay the rental fee?" Schmidt asks, confused. "Winston, that's just nice."

Nope. Turns out Winston had put a great deal of blood, sweat, and money into his finest, grandest work yet, bolstered by several blasts from the past, including Sadie (June Diane Raphael), Principal Foster (Curtis Armstrong), and Lorenzo the Biology Teacher (Brian Posehn). Zoe Lister-Jones joined in on the ruse as well, slipping into Fawn Moscato's power suit one last time. The actress felt a weird sense of pride when she saw the plaque on her character's desk: MAYOR FAWN MOSCATO. After so much hard work, networking, antigang krumping initiatives, and one pantygate scandal, the politician had worked her way to the top.

Our last glimpse of the fivesome takes place in front of the loft, as they drive away in the moving truck.

"So was the prank too small?" Winston's voice can be heard when the truck starts to pull away. "You know I've been guilty of that in the past—"

"Too big, man," Schmidt tells him. "Way too big."

"I don't know," Jess says, softly. "I think it was just right." The camera pulls out then, leaving us with a bird's-eye view of the truck crawling away from the loft. Russ T. Alsobrook, the director of photography, used a telephoto lens to compress the vehicle in the background, giving the feeling that the friends were driving off into the distance together.

Satisfying as it was, that wasn't the final scene filmed of *New Girl*.

Risoli made sure to schedule the very last scene at the loft, with everybody together in the empty apartment, looking around one final time at the space where they'd grown up. Inked at the bottom of the call sheet, he wrote, "NEW GIRL LOVE FOREVER. THANK YOU!"

They shot that scene late into the night, rolling until 2:30 in the morning. The writers went off to have drinks and then, feeling nostalgic, returned to set to watch the last moments unfold from behind the camera. When Meriwether looked at the empty loft and her characters standing together on a packing box, she could feel herself getting emotional. It was such a fitting image of what the show was—five people clinging to each other to survive the world.

After the first take, O'Malley called out, "Let's go again!" A few more takes in, she declared, "Cut!"

O'Malley turned to Kasdan, Meriwether, Baer, and Finkel. "Got it?" she asked.

Kasdan offered a thumbs-up. Meriwether gave her a little shrug. "All right, we got it," she told the cast and crew. "That's a wrap."

* * *

The time had come, at long last, to tear down the sets. Simone found herself walking around the empty bar and loft sets, bidding farewell to the space. She had a realization that you don't get that often in life—to be able to say a real goodbye.

O'Malley took out her camera to document every piece of their set being buckled up and taken away, snapping photos as they removed the barstools from the loft kitchen. She and Whetstone had developed relationships with the owners of multiple film locations around town and they reached out to see if anyone wanted pieces of the set before they were gutted. Both hated the idea of arbitrarily throwing anything away. The only people who showed any interest were the owners of Willow Studios, who decided they wanted the bar set. Whetstone and O'Malley sold it to them for a dollar. The studio space is about two thirds the size of the bar and many of the set pieces are missing—multiple members of the *New*

Girl crew took home those funny jockey lamps—but the Griffin lives on to this day, somewhere in a downtown Los Angeles warehouse.

When it came to props, a respectful war was afoot between the cast and crew. O'Malley really wanted the 3D watermelon painting in Jess's room. Turns out, that was the only keepsake Deschanel asked for. The director snagged one of the douchebag jars and the bar cart from the loft instead. Morris grabbed some of Winston's bird shirts. Johnson took all of Nick's pants.

Everybody wanted the blue grapes. For a few seconds producer Megan Mascena thought they were hers. Then she lost them to Meriwether, who would be the final keeper of the glass fruit. The showrunner also took home a copy of *The Pepperwood Chronicles*, with Nick Miller's thick tome finding a home on her bookshelf alongside Toni Morrison's *Sula* and Jack London's *Martin Eden*. In the words of Schmidt, no notes.

The loft set was about to get tossed in the trash when Whetstone noticed with a start that the 4D sign was still on the door. He stood there and thought, "*No one* took the 4D?" So he grabbed it and brought it home with him. The production designer has it to this day and he's been meaning to frame the prop in a shadow box, just like the ones Deschanel wanted for Jess's classroom.

Oftentimes, big shows got major TV spots when their series was ending. The whole *Friends* cast was joined by Oprah for a final big interview. The *Cheers* cast went on *The Tonight Show with Jay Leno*. The *New Girl* cast wasn't getting invited on any of those big talk shows. There was the usual press run for the cast, and then . . . that was it. A relatively quiet wave of a goodbye, without much fanfare, far away from the Fox lot where they once started. That quietness extended to Season Seven's premiere, too. Only two million people tuned in to watch "About Three Years Later."

While doing press for those last eight episodes, Meriwether was asked by *The Hollywood Reporter* how she wanted *New Girl* to be remembered. "Part of me just wants people to remember it," she said with a laugh. "I feel bad when I hear about a show from the past and don't remember it."

She was happy, though, that so much had changed in the world of television since Jessica Day first stepped into that Los Angeles apartment. At the time, there was a massive flurry of press around women making TV shows. These days, female writers and showrunners didn't garner breathless, wide-eyed headlines. And Meriwether was pleased to see there were more complicated women gracing the small screen—and oddball women, too! Jess was in good company.

Still, several questions remained. What would *New Girl*'s legacy be in the days, months, and years to come? How would they be remembered? *Would* they be remembered?

Little did Meriwether, the cast, and crew know, the end of apartment 4D was really just the beginning.

15

Where the Road Goes

I look forward to a lifetime of joy, growth, and constant mispronunciation of common words.

—CECE PAREKH

IN 2020, A DEADLY PANDEMIC snaked across the globe. As people looked for glimmers of hope during dark and scary times, comfort television took on a whole new meaning. Suddenly, the TV shows we invited into our homes had to work overtime to offer up an extra boost of warmth, safety, and entertainment. Amid the loneliness of lockdown, the characters who populated those shows needed to feel like our closest friends, keeping us company through it all.

It's no wonder, then, that viewers flocked to apartment 4D.

Netflix subscribers watched 14.54 billion minutes of *New Girl* that year. Loving tributes unspooled all over the internet, with *Entertainment Weekly* declaring the series a "perfect quarantine comfort binge." *GQ*'s Jason Diamond celebrated Nick and Schmidt's unapologetically loving friendship. *The Guardian*'s Shaad D'Souza suggested that the show, which he felt got funnier and smarter with time, was best when binged.

"Against all odds, I've watched *New Girl* in its entirety multiple times over the past few years," he wrote. "Slightly more acidic than basic comfort food like *Friends*, and not as conceptually dense as, say, *Arrested Development*, it strikes a good balance between smart and undemanding. It might strike as ephemera, but *New Girl* has surprising staying power."

Multiple rewatches led fans to realize that, quite inexplicably, the word *bear*—or an indirect reference to a bear—had made its way into almost every episode of the show. These shout-outs range from the obvious ("This tastes like the inside of a bear, and that is a compliment, my friend") to the subtle (a photograph of a bear can be frequently spotted on the loft's fridge).

If there was ever a time for viewers to discover or rediscover *New Girl*, it was during a global lockdown. The world Meriwether created was a bright, safe, fun space populated with characters whom you genuinely wanted to spend time with. The jokes were refreshingly unexpected. The romance was good . . . really, *really* good. But perhaps more important, the friendships were even better, the kinds of aspirational bonds that we all wish we had during the best and worst moments of our lives.

Few TV shows have earned the illustrious honor of getting friendship right, while sprinkling in just the right amount of fairy dust on top. But *New Girl* did it over and over again, in both the big, sweeping gestures—à la the gang buying Schmidt a trendy, oddly shaped chair to cheer him up—and the smaller, more intimate moments, like Jess and Cece lacing hands while watching *Clueless* and eating cake together.

The show had found its way back into the collective hearts of viewers when life was at its weariest. And, interestingly enough, years later—here it's stayed.

There is, perhaps, no better proof of just how much this show has lived on with fans than peeking into the day-to-day lives of *New Girl* guest stars. Despite lengthy IMDb pages, these actors continue to get singled out for their roles on the show, no matter how brief they may have been.

Suddenly, David Walton found himself getting stopped on the streets of his hometown in Maine, always with the same question. "Are you Dr. Sam?!" ("And I'm just, like, barely in the show," Walton told me.) People still come over to Sonequa Martin-Green, who played Winston's prank-happy ex-girlfriend, to inform her, "You just got Rhonda'ed!" ("I've shared more laughs than I can count with people all over the world over that crazy, hilarious woman," she wrote me via email.) Nasim Pedrad has been approached at train stations in foreign countries by fans who barely spoke English but were able to communicate with her that they loved *New Girl.*

Zoe Lister-Jones remembers being startled when she heard someone call out "Fawn!" as she was walking through the streets of New York City. "*Wait, what?*" she thought to herself. She had no idea that the show was resonating in such a big way with fans.

The same day of our interview, Justin Long had already gotten one "Hey, Genzlinger!" from a stranger. He also gets called "the Genz!" It always makes him smile. There was a point where he was kicking around a spin-off idea with Hannah Simone, which would have involved Genzlinger and Cece being roommates, and they even took it to Meriwether for her thoughts. Nothing came of it but, man, do I have *so* many questions about what that show would have looked like.

When Wayans Jr. does stand-up, he allots the first five to ten minutes to answering *New Girl* questions. It just makes it easier that way—when he wasn't mentioning the show, people would yell references out from the crowd. The comedian didn't know quite how huge the series had become. It was now *Friends*-level famous, he realized.

Once, after asking who in the audience was the biggest *New Girl* fan, a woman raised her hand and revealed an enormous tattoo of Jake Johnson on the back of her leg, which looked like it had taken several days to get done. Wayans Jr. had her onstage and took photos of himself with the ink.

As Greenfield put it, he feels a jolt of energy anytime someone sees him and calls out "TWENTY-NINE" or whatever Schmidt-ism they choose. "My experience with *New Girl*, and what's been so wonderful about it and so incredible about the fans of the show, is that they continue to love it and will love it forever. I am so grateful for that reaction to it," he said. "And the show was *cool*, so we were loved on this cool show that fucking

Prince was on, and Taylor Swift." He added with warm emphasis, "Yeah, I'll take that—remember me as Schmidt for-fucking-ever."

New Girl's resurgence is heartening for someone like Nelson Franklin, who relished working on classic network comedies like *The Office*, *New Girl*, and *Veep*. The golden age of network TV, he told me, is over in favor of streaming. "There's less opportunities for people to experiment with funny shows," he explained. "That used to be the philosophy—make a bunch of pilots, all kinds of different pilots, and we'll see which one is funniest. That experimentation, that discovery process, is gone."

When people started getting back into *New Girl*, Franklin thought to himself, "*Yeah*, you remember back then, when we had *The Office* and *Parks and Rec*? When everybody loved TV? Remember that?" Around that time, he was out on the picket lines fighting alongside the Writers Guild of America over, among other things, the gutting of writers' rooms.

"See, everybody still likes those shows where we had a whole writers' room and we had a full season that was more than six episodes," he told me. "And it sort of gave a lot of meaning to that time in my life where I was doing all those shows. People care about that stuff, and they miss it."

But why *do* we care about *New Girl*? Why do we miss it enough to keep watching it, reliving the moments we've already seen, over and over again?

My own personal answer boils down to toilet paper. It's a tiny moment in the Season Five episode "Wig," which involves Nick spiraling over how to interact with his new crush, Reagan. As he sloppily shoves a large burrito in his mouth, he informs her, apropos of nothing, "There's extra toilet paper in the bathroom if you need it!"

Schmidt turns to him with a note of concern. "Are you hiding toilet paper again?"

Yes, it's a simple throwaway line, and Nick's toilet-paper hoarding is never referenced again, but that small back-and-forth made me think, "*Oh*, this is why this show is so special." Strange but deeply character-specific moments were allowed to live on the fringes of an otherwise by-the-books hangout show, the kind of off-kilter humor that takes you by surprise and also feels deeply real to who these fictional people are. Over and over again, we were given toilet paper–like gifts. They might have cost the cast and crew their sleep and sanity, but the willingness to—as Greenfield once said—go to outer space makes *New Girl* the type of show that has stayed fresh and so very alive no matter how many times you rewatch it.

Jake Johnson's daughters were born while he was filming Season Three's "Thanksgiving III" episode. "Oh fuck," he thought. "I don't want to be an actor anymore now that I'm a dad. I don't want to be recognized, I don't want to be the center of attention. This was a huge mistake, their childhood is going to be weird."

A funny thing changed the framing of that feeling.

Johnson was on a hike with his children and his mother-in-law when a group of *New Girl* fans stopped them to snap a photo with the actor. Afterward, Johnson's mother-in-law tried to gauge how his kids were feeling about the interaction. His daughter meant to say, "Somebody wanted a photo because my daddy's famous" . . . but instead she said, "Somebody wanted a photo because my daddy's familiar." That word, Johnson told me, changed his soul.

Familiar—that's what he is to people. The other day, he was out to lunch and the waitress came over to the table and was so friendly and nice. It felt like, from the first second, they knew each other. They started doing bits, talked about fasting, and she shared that she was on day twelve of quitting weed.

When she walked away from the table, Johnson realized how normal it felt to get so personal with strangers so quickly. Later, as he walked out of the restaurant, the waitress told him, "I just want to say, I love you, I love *New Girl*, you must have fallen in love with Jess in real life because she's incredible."

"We all fell in love with Jess," Johnson replied, and the two shared a big smile.

New Girl made the world familiar to him, Johnson realized. If he's in an airport, he knows a fifth of the people there. When he goes to a Dodgers game, people will call out, "Nick!" and he'll wave back. They'll quickly correct themselves and say, "Sorry! Jake!" That name distinction doesn't matter to Johnson. Plus, they don't want to bother him, they just want to say hi.

"I don't want to be famous, famous feels so lame to me, that's nothing interesting," Johnson said. "But I *do* want to be familiar."

Years ago, Liz Meriwether sat down to write a pitch for a pilot called *Chicks and Dicks,* setting out to tell the story of a bunch of lovable weirdos who found each other when they needed one another most. She wanted Jess, fresh off a debilitating breakup, to learn to stand up for herself and become confident in life and love. She wanted to show what the slow path to adulthood looked like. There was no road map of anything else to come, other than that Meriwether knew she wanted her endlessly optimistic heroine and the cranky bartender to end up together.

At that, and so much more, she succeeded.

While filming the final season of the show, Meriwether did a Netflix binge of the series. It turned out to be a mixed bag of emotions. As she watched her show, she was reminded of the stories she thought they screwed up and the scenes that had racked up twelve hours in the edit bay. But there was an unexpected joy in watching, too. She found herself appreciating the comedy without fixating on every joke that didn't make the cut. There were times when she could push past the grueling work that went into each episode and just enjoy what was on her screen.

So much had changed in the intervening years. Meriwether was twenty-nine when she filmed the pilot and was thrown into the bizarre deep end of making and sustaining a television series. As the show ended, she told *The New York Times* that she viewed herself as somewhere between *The Lord of the Rings'* Gandalf and a network hack.

An important change had happened as time went on in the writers' room. Meriwether started to hear something that almost felt like a click in her head. "That's it, that's right," the click would tell her. She got better at trusting that feeling.

Seeing the rebirth of *New Girl* has been, as Meriwether put it to me, genuinely moving. "My experience of making the show was feeling like I was failing constantly—so much of my experience was just stressed out and feeling like I had failed," she said. "I had really genuinely no idea that people would still watch it and love it. As it was ending, I think my greatest fear was . . . we did all this and it's just going to be gone." It blows her mind, and moves her, that people are still discovering the series now.

She added, "We loved it. We all loved it so much. I think we all felt it was really hard and dark sometimes, but we all loved the show, and loved the characters. It's just so gratifying that people still care about it."

When the series took its final bow, the writer hoped that she had wrapped it all up in a way that made everybody feel good and happy. "I'm sure there are things that people wanted us to have done, but hopefully the end of the show feels like a good ending," she said as she did her last press interviews for *New Girl*. "If it doesn't, please don't come at me on Twitter."

In the words of Jessica Day, as she bid farewell to the loft that changed her life forever, I think it was just right.

Acknowledgments

I STILL CAN'T QUITE BELIEVE I got to spend an entire year writing about a show I love so much, and I have many, many people to thank for making that happen.

A very big and appreciative thank-you to Linda Konner, my agent and my friend, who is always unbelievably quick, thorough, and just an incredible force of nature. My editor Hannah Pierdolla was a complete joy to work with—thank you so much for your endless amount of support, smarts, kindness, encouragement, thoughtful guidance, and—last but certainly not least—being a True American aficionado. Thank you so much to Laura Clark and the team at St. Martin's Press for believing in this book and for being so warm and enthusiastic throughout it all.

I am so grateful to every single person from the *New Girl* world who took the time to speak to me. They rewatched old episodes, dug through their archives for mementos, didn't bat an eye at all of the very, very specific questions, and were complete joys to interview. There would be no book without them:

Nick Adams, Russ T. Alsobrook, Michael Andrews, Alec Berg, Michael Budge, Zooey Deschanel, Jorjee Douglass, Joe Earley, Nelson Franklin, Matt Fusfeld, Josh Gad, Christine Gernon, Robin Glaser, Eliot Glazer, Fred Goss, Max Greenfield, David Iserson, Berkley Johnson, Jake Johnson, Jake Kasdan, Sophia Lear, Zoe Lister-Jones, Justin Long, Megan Mascena, Debra McGuire, Liz Meriwether, Julian Morris, Lamorne Morris, Giselle Murillo, Trent O'Donnell, Erin O'Malley, Nasim Pedrad, Jesse Peretz, Katherine Pope, Bill Purple, Rob Riggle, Michael Risoli, Rob Rosell, Kim Rosenstock, Hugh Ross, Jeff Sage, Lorene Scafaria, Jane Shirkes, Hannah Simone, Michael Spiller, Steven Tsuchida, David Walton, Steve Welch, Michael Whetstone, Jason Winer, Max Winkler, Lamar Woods, and Seth Yanklewitz.

So much thanks and appreciation goes to Liz, Zooey, Lamorne, Hannah, Max, and Jake, who were incredibly generous with their time and memories. It meant the world.

I am so grateful to the many assistants, managers, publicists, and agents who helped connect me and coordinated interviews. An extra big thank-you to Meghan Dresdner, Myles Goldman, and Samantha Shipp, who were so thoughtful and helpful.

Berkley, there are not enough words. Thank you for so patiently putting up with me over the past year, for answering every single one of my (many, many) questions, and for being wonderfully kind throughout it all. It would be a far lesser book without you. Michael Risoli, thank you for sharing wonderful photos and such incredible stories—you were beyond helpful throughout this whole process. Michael Budge, you answered all my wildly specific *New Girl* emails—thank you for lending a generous hand so many times. Jorjee Douglass, Robin Glaser, Hugh Ross, and Michael Whetstone, thank you for taking the time to send me such a wealth of amazing photos and videos. I'm really grateful to Violet Li, Erin O'Malley, David Walton, Anita Mukherji, Ava Tramer, Max Gaspin, Todd Milliner, and Matt Fusfeld for so kindly reaching out to *New Girl* friends and colleagues on my behalf. Jeff Sage, thank you for talking to me multiple times over the years—it's been such a pleasure. Beatriz Chahin, thank you so much for hopping on the phone with me to talk about the *Brooklyn Nine-Nine / New Girl* crossover.

My deep thanks to Kirthana Ramisetti, Jennifer Keishin Armstrong, Saul Austerlitz, and Erin Carlson, the best and wisest author group, who are also such wonderful friends and colleagues.

Rebecca, I wish I could put into proper sentences just how much I appreciate you being there every step of the way, this year and every year. You make *everything* brighter, and I feel so very lucky to get to have you as a friend. Louisa, thank you so much for reading the book and offering such incredibly smart, helpful, thorough, and encouraging feedback—it really made such a difference. Tessa, my *New Girl* lifeline, I'm very grateful to you.

All my love and appreciation to Rima, Molly, and Abigail: Thank you so much for somehow never tiring of reading the countless drafts of emails I texted you, looking at chapters, and being such a wonderful support system, now and always.

To Mom, Dad, and Kira, whom I love so much. You are my lifeline and my first call for everything. Thank you for always being there and always making life better. And to my mom, who has never seen an episode of *New Girl* but was my most dedicated reader as I was writing this book. When the project was coming to an end, she sent a group text to the family saying: "I would like to watch new girl can someone give me a password? Tu." I think she's going to really like Winston.

Ben, it takes a certain level of patience and kindness to listen to me read my very large manuscript out loud to you, time and time again, but you always did it, no questions asked. As Nick Miller once said, I fell in love with you the moment you walked through the door—and I've loved you every day since. Thank you for all the warmth, joy, and happiness.

Bibliography

Introduction

Meriwether, Liz. "Pitch Doc."

Meriwether, Liz. "Why Hating L.A. Is Good for My Comedy." *Vulture*, February 18, 2016. www.vulture.com/2016/02/liz-meriwether-los-angeles-hate-is-good-for-comedy.html.

Meriwether, Liz, Brett Baer, and Dave Finkel. "The New Girl and Her Guys." Moderated by Jan Oxenberg. *Written By* magazine, Summer 2012. www.mydigitalpublication.com/summer-2012?i=113611&p=10&view=issueViewer.

Perez, Maya, and Barbara Morgan, eds. *On Story—The Golden Age of Television* (University of Texas Press, 2018). "New Girl: A Conversation with Elizabeth Meriwether, Moderated by Beau Willimon (2016)."

1: Chicks and Dicks

Adams, Erik. "The *New Girl* showrunners on some of season 2's biggest challenges." *AV Club*, May 10, 2013. www.avclub.com/the-new-girl-showrunners-on-some-of-season-2-s-biggest-1798238544.

Associated Press. "'No Strings' Attaches to No. 1 Box Office Spot." January 24, 2011. www.cbsnews.com/news/no-strings-attaches-to-no-1-box-office-spot/.

Blacker, Ben, host. *Nerdist Writers Panel*, podcast, "#23: Liz Meriwether, Liz Craft and Sarah Fain & Angela Kang." *Nerdist*, January 26, 2012. archive.nerdist.com/nerdist-writers-panel-23-liz-meriwether-liz-craft-and-sarah-fain-angela-kang/.

Fox, Jesse David, host. *Good One: A Podcast About Jokes*, podcast, "Liz Meriwether's

Evolution from New Girl to The Dropout." *Vulture*, June 16, 2022. open.spotify.com/episode/6zKCdlwZgSMxvFEgnnOWAA.

Frankel, Daniel. "Final 'Bridesmaids' Weekend Tally: $26.2M." *TheWrap*, May 16, 2011. www.thewrap.com/final-bridesmaids-weekend-tally-262m-27446/.

Goss, Fred. Interview by author.

Kasdan, Jake. Interview by author.

Kasdan, Jake. "Pilot Crazy." *DGA Quarterly*, Spring 2013. www.dga.org/craft/dgaq/issues/1302-spring-2013/funny-business-jake-kasdan.

Lovece, Frank. "'No Strings Attached' Makes the Rounds." *Film Festival Traveler*, January 21, 2011. filmfestivaltraveler.com/film-arts/film-arts-interviews/1140-no-strings-attached-roundtable.

Malone, Noreen. "Not That Kind of Girl." *The New Republic*, May 10, 2013. newrepublic.com/article/113170/liz-meriwether-new-girl-creator-anti-lena-dunham.

Meriwether, Liz. Interview by author.

Meriwether, Liz. "Pitch Doc."

Meriwether, Liz. "Why Hating L.A. Is Good for My Comedy." *Vulture*, February 18, 2016. www.vulture.com/2016/02/liz-meriwether-los-angeles-hate-is-good-for-comedy.html.

Nelson, Steffie. "10 Screenwriters to Watch: Liz Meriwether." *Variety*, July 28, 2009. variety.com/2009/scene/markets-festivals/liz-meriwether-1118006587/.

New Girl: The Complete First Season, DVD, bonus material, 20th Century Fox, 2012.

Paskin, Willa. "'New Girl' creator Liz Meriwether: 'I don't think the show is adorkable.'" *Salon*, May 15, 2013. www.salon.com/2013/05/15/new_girl_creator_liz_meriwether_i_dont_think_the_show_is_adorkable/.

Perez, Maya, and Barbara Morgan, eds. *On Story—The Golden Age of Television* (University of Texas Press, 2018). "New Girl: A Conversation with Elizabeth Meriwether, Moderated by Beau Willimon (2016)."

Pope, Katherine. Interview by author.

Press, Joy. *Stealing the Show: How Women Are Revolutionizing Television* (Atria Books, 2018).

Radloff, Jessica. "'New Girl' Was Never Meant to Be 'Adorkable'—but We Fell for It Anyway." *Glamour*, April 10, 2018. www.glamour.com/story/new-girl-final-season.

Rochlin, Margy. "On the Air-New Girl." *DGA Quarterly*, Spring 2015. www.dga.org/craft/dgaq/issues/1502-spring-2015/on-the-air-new-girl.

Rooney, David. "Making a Success of Her Messiness on Two Coasts." *The New York Times*, May 5, 2010. www.nytimes.com/2010/05/09/theater/09meriwether.html.

Schneider, Michael, "'New Girl' Creator's Real-Life Eye Mishap Inspired the Show's 'Adorkable' Wedding Finale," *IndieWire*, May 15, 2018. www.indiewire.com/features/general/new-girl-series-finale-wedding-liz-meriwether-zooey-deschanel-1201964906/.

Schoeneman, Deborah. "An Entourage of Their Own." *The New York Times*, March 20, 2009. www.nytimes.com/2009/03/22/fashion/22fempire.html.

Stasio, Marilyn. "The Mistakes Madeline Made." *Variety*, April 23, 2006. variety.com/2006/legit/reviews/the-mistakes-madeline-made-1200516795/.

Straub, Emma. "Why Can't I Be You: Liz Meriwether." *Rookie*, November 26, 2012. www.rookiemag.com/2012/11/wciby-liz-meriwether/.

Villarreal, Yvonne. "Elizabeth Holmes' wild trial almost remade 'The Dropout.' Here's why it was left out." *Los Angeles Times*, March 3, 2022. www.latimes.com/entertainment-arts/tv/story/2022–03–03/the-dropout-hulu-elizabeth-holmes-liz-meriwether-new-girl.

Winer, Jason. Interview by author.

Yale Daily News. "Spotlight on Liz Meriwether." December 11, 2002. yaledailynews.com/blog/2002/12/11/spotlight-on-liz-meriwether/.

Young, John. "Box office report: 'No Strings Attached' grabs first place with $20.3 mil." *Entertainment Weekly*, January 23, 2011. ew.com/article/2011/01/23/box-office-report-no-strings-attached/.

2: Finding Apartment 4D

Andrews-Dyer, Helena. "For his biggest role yet, Lamorne Morris is once again 'the Black dude.'" *The Washington Post*, October 15, 2024. www.washingtonpost.com/entertainment/movies/2024/10/15/lamorne-morris-saturday-night/.

Barton, Laura. "Zooey Deschanel: Funny Girl." *The Guardian*, March 6, 2012. www.theguardian.com/tv-and-radio/2012/mar/06/zooey-deschanel-funny-girl.

Deschanel, Zooey. Interview by author.

Deschanel, Zooey. "Zooey Deschanel: How To LET GO Of Others' Opinions & ALIGN With Your Most AUTHENTIC TRUTH!" Interview by Lewis Howes. YouTube, March 18, 2024. www.youtube.com/watch?v=z9qpo0Qfuh8.

Finkel, David. "A Special Convo with David Finkel, Producer/Writer of 'New Girl' & '30 Rock.'" Interview by Kyrus Keenan Westcott. *The Vibe with Ky*. YouTube, October 5, 2021. www.youtube.com/watch?v=oqTt31cdPBg.

Greenfield, Max. Interview by author.

Johnson, Jake. Interview by author.

Johnson, Jake. "Jake Johnson Got Turned Down from an Audition After 45 Seconds." KFC Radio. YouTube, March 16, 2022. www.youtube.com/watch?v=RRweY3tNk5s.

Johnson, Jake. "New Girl's Jake Johnson Loves Drunk Acting." Interview by Paul F. Tompkins. *Made Man*. YouTube, April 22, 2013. www.youtube.com/watch?v=54eCmg_f3YQ.

Kasdan, Jake. "Pilot Crazy." *DGA Quarterly*, Spring 2013. www.dga.org/craft/dgaq/issues/1302-spring-2013/funny-business-jake-kasdan.

Moore, Frazier. "Zooey Deschanel Is Fox's 'New Girl.'" *The Seattle Times*, September 20, 2011. www.seattletimes.com/entertainment/tv/zooey-deschanel-is-foxs-new-girl/.

Morris, Lamorne. Interview by author.

Perez, Maya, and Barbara Morgan, eds. *On Story—The Golden Age of Television* (University of Texas Press, 2018). "New Girl: A Conversation with Elizabeth Meriwether, Moderated by Beau Willimon (2016)."

Pope, Katherine. Interview by author.

Rankin, Seija. "Lamorne Morris Finally Lands a Gig on 'SNL' (Sort Of)." *The Hollywood Reporter*, October 11, 2024. www.hollywoodreporter.com/movies/movie-features/lamorne-morris-interview-saturday-night-snl-new-girl-1236027022/.

Reynolds, Gareth, and Jake Johnson, hosts. *We're Here to Help*, podcast. "Bathroom Trash is Private with Hannah Simone," May 6, 2024. podcasts.apple.com/podcast/bathroom-trash-is-private-with-hannah-simone/id1702753838?i=1000654644133.

Simone, Hannah. Interview by author.

Simone, Hannah and Lamorne Morris, hosts. *Welcome to Our Show*, podcast. "105: Cece Crashes." iHeartPodcasts, February 21, 2022. www.globalplayer.com/podcasts/episodes/7DrdhXg/.

Simone, Hannah, and Lamorne Morris, hosts. *Welcome to Our Show*, podcast. "Rerun: A Conversation with Jake Kasdan." iHeartPodcasts, January 24, 2022. www.globalplayer.com/podcasts/episodes/7DrejXV/.

Snierson, Dan. "Zooey Deschanel on her 'New Girl' role: 'If I had read this character in a movie script, I would've jumped on board immediately.'" *Entertainment Weekly*, September 14, 2011. ew.com/article/2011/09/14/zooey-deschanel-new-girl/.

Villarreal, Yvonne. "Damon Wayans Jr., pilot season's most in-demand actor, on his 'Living Color' childhood—plus, a 'Happy Endings' movie?" *Los Angeles Times*, October 11, 2018. www.latimes.com/entertainment/tv/la-et-st-damon-wayans-jr-sunday-conversation-20181011-story.html.

Volpe, Allie. "How Lamorne Morris Turned a Bad Audition Into a Role on 'New Girl.'" *Backstage*, June 17, 2020. www.backstage.com/magazine/article/lamorne-morris-turned-bad-audition-role-new-girl-1–1856/.

Winkler, Max. Interview by author.

The Writers Guild Foundation. "Inside the Writers Room with NEW GIRL." June 12, 2014.

Yanklewitz, Seth. Interview by author.

Yuan, Jada. "The Pinup of Williamsburg." *New York*, September 9, 2011. nymag.com/arts/tv/profiles/zooey-deschanel-2011–9/.

Zakarin, Jordan. "Max Greenfield Almost Quit Acting to Become Writer Before 'New Girl.'" *TheWrap*, April 21, 2014. www.thewrap.com/max-greenfield-almost-quit-acting-become-writer-new-girl/.

3: The Pilot

Adewunmi, Bim, and Nichole Perkins, hosts. *Thirst Aid Kit*, podcast. "A 'Two Appetizers' Kinda Guy (feat. Jake Johnson)." *Slate*, August 20, 2020. slate.com/podcasts/thirst-aid-kit/2020/08/jake-johnson-talks-with-tak.

Andrews, Michael. Interview by author.

Baum, Gary. "'New Girl' Tagline 'Adorkable' Makes the Dictionary." *The Hollywood Reporter*, June 20, 2014. www.hollywoodreporter.com/tv/tv-news/new-girl-tagline-adorkable-makes-713608/.

Deschanel, Zooey. Interview by author.

Douglass, Jorjee, and Robin Glaser. Interview by author.

Earley, John. Interview by author.

Egner, Jeremy. "Elizabeth Meriwether Answers Your 'New Girl' Questions." *ArtsBeat* (blog). *The New York Times*, February 5, 2013. archive.nytimes.com/artsbeat.blogs.nytimes.com/2013/02/05/elizabeth-meriwether-answers-your-new-girl-questions/.

Glamour. "Meet the Women Who Run Your Favorite Movies and TV Shows," August 7, 2013. www.glamour.com/gallery/meet-the-women-who-run-your-favorite-movies-and-tv-shows.

Douglass, Jorjee, and Robin Glaser. Interview by author.

Glassman, Thea. *Freaks, Gleeks & Dawson's Creek* (Running Press, 2023).

Goodman, Jillian. "Why Is *New Girl* Shooting Up Vulture's Anticipation Index While *2 Broke Girls* Languishes?" September 16, 2011. www.vulture.com/2011/09/how_important_is_twitter_to_yo.html.

Hibberd, James. "Zooey Deschanel's New Girl opens big." *Entertainment Weekly*, September 21, 2011. ew.com/article/2011/09/21/fox-new-girl/.

Kasdan, Jake. Interview by author.

Maerz, Melissa. "'New Girl' gets a new attitude." *Entertainment Weekly*, March 16, 2012. ew.com/article/2012/03/16/new-girl-gets-new-attitude/.

Mascena, Megan. Interview by author.

McGuire, Debra. Interview by author.

McGuire, Debra. Interview. in *New Girl: The Complete First Season*, DVD, 20th Century Fox, 2012.

Meriwether, Liz. Interview by author.

Meriwether, Liz. Original *New Girl* pilot script.

Paskin, Willa. "New Girl's Max Greenfield on Playing Schmidt, Liking Rihanna, and Loving Ray Romano." *Vulture*, December 6, 2011. www.vulture.com/2011/12/new-girls-max-greenfield-on-playing-schmidt-liking-rihanna-and-loving-ray-romano.html.

Pope, Katherine. Interview by author.

Press, Joy. *Stealing the Show: How Women Are Revolutionizing Television* (Atria Books, 2018).

Price, Leslie. "The Costume Designer Behind Fox's Newly-Renewed New Girl." *Racked*, March 4, 2013. la.racked.com/2013/3/4/7684729/new-girl-costume-designer-debr.

Purple, Bill. Interview by author.

Radloff, Jessica. "'New Girl' Was Never Meant to Be 'Adorkable'—but We Fell for It Anyway." *Glamour*, April 10, 2018. www.glamour.com/story/new-girl-final-season.

Rancilio, Alicia. "Max Greenfield of 'New Girl' isn't worried he'll be typecast because of over-the-top TV role." *Times Colonist*, February 26, 2013. www.timescolonist.com/entertainment/max-greenfield-of-new-girl-isnt-worried-hell-be-typecast-because-of-over-the-top-tv-role-4580204.

Rushfield, Richard. "A Fancy Evening with the Cast and Crew of New Girl." *Grantland*, June 11, 2012. grantland.com/hollywood-prospectus/an-fancy-evening-with-the-cast-and-crew-ofnew-girl/.

Sage, Jefferson. Interview by author.

Sepinwall, Alan. "FOX's 'New Girl' showcases Zooey Deschanel." *Uproxx*, September 20, 2011. uproxx.com/sepinwall/review-foxs-new-girl-showcases-zooey-deschanel/.

Simone, Hannah. Interview by author.

Snierson, Dan. "A New Perspective on 'New Girl.'" *Entertainment Weekly*, August 9, 2013. ew .com/article/2013/08/09/new-perspective-new-girl/.

Stuever, Hank. "Fox's 'New Girl' goes Zooey kablooey." *The Washington Post*, September 19, 2011. www.washingtonpost.com/lifestyle/style/foxs-new-girl-goes-zooey-kablooey-cbss-unforgettable -seems-a-tad-familiar/2011/09/18/gIQAWQcRgK_story.html.

USA Today. "Max Greenfield of 'New Girl' steers shallows of Schmidt." November 26, 2012. usatoday.com/story/life/tv/2012/11/26/max-greenfield-schmidt-new-girl/1707309/.

Welch, Steve. Interview by author.

4: Welcome to the Loft, Part I

Adalian, Josef. "Zooey Deschanel Relieved to Get 'New Girl's Jess/Nick Romance Going Already." *Vulture*, August 5, 2013. www.vulture.com/2013/08/zooey-deschanel-on-season-3-of -new-girl.html.

Adams, Erik. "Comedy Showrunners Week: *New Girl* creator Elizabeth Meriwether laughs at her characters' pain." *AV Club*, September 25, 2012. www.avclub.com/comedy-showrunners-week -new-girl-creator-elizabeth-mer-1798233599.

Adams, Erik. "*New Girl*: 'Injured.'" *AV Club*, March 7, 2012. www.avclub.com/new-girl-injured -1798171854.

Adams, Nick. Interview by author.

Carter, Bill. "Fox Quickly Endorses 'New Girl.'" *Media Decoder* (blog). *The New York Times*, September 28, 2011. archive.nytimes.com/mediadecoder.blogs.nytimes.com/2011/09/28/fox-quickly -endorses-new-girl/.

Cueto, Mauricio. "'Happy Endings' Deserved Better." *Collider*, August 22, 2024. collider.com /happy-endings-cancelled/.

Fox, Jesse David, host. *Good One: A Podcast About Jokes*, podcast. "Liz Meriwether's Evolution from New Girl to The Dropout." *Vulture*, June 16, 2022.

Kasdan, Jake. Interview by author.

Meriwether, Liz, Brett Baer, and Dave Finkel. "The New Girl and Her Guys." Moderated by Jan Oxenberg. *Written By* magazine, Summer 2012. www.mydigitalpublication.com/summer-2012 ?i=113611&p=10&view=issueViewer.

Reynolds, Gareth, and Jake Johnson, hosts. *We're Here to Help,* podcast. "Look at MY Goatee with Lamar Woods." February 12, 2024. podcasts.apple.com/podcast/look-at-my-goatee-with -lamar-woods/id1702753838?i=1000645006473.

Risoli, Michael. Interview by author.

Storey, Kate. "Damon Wayans Jr. gets his job back on 'New Girl.'" *New York Post*, November 9, 2013. nypost.com/2013/11/09/damon-wayans-jr-gets-his-job-back-on-new-girl/.

Welch, Steve. Interview by author.

Wightman, Catriona. "Lamorne Morris joins Fox's 'New Girl.'" *Digital Spy*, July 11, 2011. www .digitalspy.com/tv/ustv/a329279/lamorne-morris-joins-foxs-new-girl/.

Winer, Jason. Interview by author.

The Writers Guild Foundation. "Inside the Writers Room with NEW GIRL," June 12, 2014.

Yanklewitz, Seth. Interview by author.

5: Welcome to the Loft, Part II

Adams, Nick. Interview by author.

Baum, Gary. "'New Girl' Tagline 'Adorkable' Makes the Dictionary." *The Hollywood Reporter*, June 20, 2014. www.hollywoodreporter.com/tv/tv-news/new-girl-tagline-adorkable-makes-713608/.

Budge, Michael. Interview by author.

Carter, Bill. "In a Gloomy Economy, TV Sitcoms Are Making a Comeback." *The New York Times*, October 23, 2011. www.nytimes.com/2011/10/24/business/media/in-a-gloomy-economy-tv-sitcoms-are-making-a-comeback.html.

Deschanel, Zooey. Interview by author.

Glamour. "5 of Our Favorite Things Zooey Deschanel (Glamour's February Cover Star!) Shared with Us," January 2, 2013. www.glamour.com/story/5-of-our-favorite-things-zooey.

Goodman, Jessica. "How a Nonsensical Drinking Game Became *New Girl*'s Most Beloved Bit." *Bustle*, April 14, 2022. www.bustle.com/entertainment/new-girl-true-american-an-oral-history-of-the-game-without-rules.

Greenfield, Max. Interview by author.

Handy, Bruce, and Juli Weiner. "Male and Female Perspectives on Zooey Deschanel's New Girl: The Starr Report, Sex Advice, and Jimmy Stewart." *Vanity Fair*, December 7, 2011. www.vanityfair.com/news/2011/12/Zooey-Deschanel-on-emNew-Girlem-Male-and-Female-PerspectivesThis-Week-The-Starr-Report-Sex-Advice-and-Jimmy-Stewart.

Iserson, David. Interview by author.

Johnson, Berkley. Interview by author.

Johnson, Jake. Interview by author.

Keveney, Bill. "Greenfield finds the soft side to his 'New Girl' character." *Trib Live*, November 30, 2012. archive.triblive.com/aande/more-a-and-e/greenfield-finds-the-soft-side-to-his-new-girl-character/.

Klausner, Julie. "Don't Fear the Dowager: A Valentine to Maturity." *Tumblr*, June 8, 2011. web.archive.org/web/20250309151825/http://julieklausner.tumblr.com/post/6331886267/dont-fear-the-dowager-a-valentine-to-maturity-an.

Lacob, Jace. "'New Girl' Creator Liz Meriwether on Jess, Sexuality, Schmidt & More." *The Daily Beast*, May 8, 2012. www.thedailybeast.com/new-girl-creator-liz-meriwether-on-jess-sexuality-schmidt-and-more/.

Lee, Ashley. "*New Girl* is moving in for good—Fox orders second season." *SheKnows*, April 9, 2012. www.sheknows.com/entertainment/articles/956599/new-girl-renewed-for-second-season/.

Long, Justin. Interview by author.

Maerz, Melissa. "'New Girl' gets a new attitude." *Entertainment Weekly*, March 16, 2012. ew.com/article/2012/03/16/new-girl-gets-new-attitude/.

Martin, Denise. "Behind the Scenes: 10 Odd Items from the *New Girl* Set, Explained." *Vulture*, May 7, 2013. www.vulture.com/2013/05/behind-the-scenes-10-odd-items-from-the-new-girl-set.html.

Meriwether, Liz, Brett Baer, and Dave Finkel. "The New Girl and Her Guys." Moderated by Jan Oxenberg. *Written By* magazine, Summer 2012. www.mydigitalpublication.com/summer-2012?i=113611&p=10&view=issueViewer.

New Girl: The Complete First Season, DVD, "Bad in Bed" commentary, 20th Century Fox, 2012.

New Girl: The Complete First Season, DVD, "Evolution of an Episode," 20th Century Fox, 2012.

Peretz, Jesse. Interview by author.

Rorke, Robert. "'New Girl's' Dude." *New York Post*, April 8, 2012. nypost.com/2012/04/08/new-girls-dude/.

Sepinwall, Alan. "Interview: 'New Girl' creator Liz Meriwether post-mortems season 1." *Uproxx*, May 8, 2012. uproxx.com/sepinwall/interview-new-girl-creator-liz-meriwether-post-mortems-season-1/.

Seyward, Darby. "Enough Quirkiness! Why I Can't Stand Zooey Deschanel." *The New Republic*, November 1, 2011. newrepublic.com/article/96904/zooey-deschanel-new-girl-annoying.

Shirkes, Jane. Interview by author.

Simone, Hannah. Interview by author.

Spiller, Michael. Interview by author.

Toomer, Jessica. "Hannah Simone Has No Plans to Stop After 'New Girl.'" *Uproxx*, April 24, 2018. uproxx.com/tv/hannah-simone-new-girl-ending-greatest-american-hero-interview/.

USA Today. "Max Greenfield of 'New Girl' steers shallows of Schmidt." November 26, 2012. usatoday.com/story/life/tv/2012/11/26/max-greenfield-schmidt-new-girl/1707309/.

Welch, Steve. Interview by author.

Williams, Mary Elizabeth. "Zooey Deschanel declares her feminism." *Salon*, January 4, 2013. www.salon.com/2013/01/04/zooey_deschanel_declares_her_feminism/.

Winer, Jason. Interview by author.

Whetstone, Michael. Interview by author.

The Making of True American

Goodman, Jessica. "How a Nonsensical Drinking Game Became *New Girl*'s Most Beloved Bit." *Bustle*, April 14, 2022. www.bustle.com/entertainment/new-girl-true-american-an-oral-history-of-the-game-without-rules.

Johnson, Berkley. Interview by author.

Murillo, Giselle. Interview by author.

6: The *New Girl* Lab, Part I

Adams, Erik. "The *New Girl* showrunners on topping season two's big kiss." *AV Club*, May 15, 2013. www.avclub.com/the-new-girl-showrunners-on-topping-season-two-s-big-ki-1798238429.

Adams, Nick. Interview by author.

Ballhaus, Louisa. "*New Girl* Creator Liz Meriwether Wanted *The Dropout* to Explore What Happens After Women Get Power." *SheKnows*, July 12, 2022. www.sheknows.com/feature/the-dropout-liz-meriwether-elizabeth-holmes-women-in-power-2541399/.

Beard, Lanford. "Taylor Swift: First Look at 'New Girl' cameo with Zooey Deschanel." *Entertainment Weekly*, May 1, 2013. web.archive.org/web/20191130215139/https://ew.com/article/2013/05/01/taylor-swift-new-girl-first-look/.

Berg, Alec. Interview by author.

Charles, Tina. "Hiatus Helper Exclusive: 'New Girl's Lamorne Morris Q&A." *TV Goodness*, July 2, 2013. www.tvgoodness.com/2013/07/02/hiatus-helper-new-girls-lamorne-morris-qa-interview/.

Deschanel, Zooey. Interview by author.

Fast Company. "'New Girl' Creator Brett Baer, Executive Producers Liz Meriwether, Dave Finkel on Embracing Groupthink." May 13, 2013. www.fastcompany.com/3009660/new-girl-creator-brett-baer-executive-producers-liz-meriwether-dav.

Franklin, Nelson. Interview by author.

Fusfeld, Matt. Interview by author.

Glazer, Eliot. Interview by author.

Greenfield, Max. Interview by author.

Greenfield, Max. "Max Greenfield on His Best Day Ever: Working with Taylor Swift on *New Girl*." *Vulture*, May 14, 2013. www.vulture.com/2013/05/max-greenfield-taylor-swift-diary-new-girl.html.

Iserson, David. Interview by author.

Johnson, Berkley. Interview by author.

Johnson, Jake. "BECOMING: Jake Johnson-Part 2," *BECOMINGSeries*, October 4, 2012. www.youtube.com/watch?v=yYwieXd93bw.

Johnson, Jake. Interview by author.

Lear, Sophia. Interview by author.

Lindbergh, Ben. "How 'New Girl' Never Gets Old." *The Ringer*, February 17, 2017. www.theringer.com/2017/02/17/tv/how-new-girl-never-gets-old-f15a6e3e347.

Long, Justin, host. *Life Is Short with Justin Long*, podcast. "Max Greenfield." Wondery, August 27, 2019. wondery.com/shows/justin-long/episode/5779-max-greenfield/.

Martin, Denise. "Vulture Visits the Set of *New Girl*, Where Things Are Getting Weird." *Vulture*, September 6, 2012. www.vulture.com/2012/09/vulture-visits-the-set-of-new-girl.html.

McHenry, Jackson. "Elizabeth Meriwether Wants to Complicate Your Diagnosis of Elizabeth Holmes." *Vulture*, April 7, 2022. www.vulture.com/article/elizabeth-meriwether-the-dropout-finale-interview.html.

Meriwether, Liz. Interview by author.

Meriwether, Liz. "Why Hating L.A. Is Good for My Comedy." *Vulture*, February 18, 2016. www.vulture.com/2016/02/liz-meriwether-los-angeles-hate-is-good-for-comedy.html.

Meriwether, Liz, Brett Baer, and Dave Finkel. "The New Girl and Her Guys." Moderated by Jan Oxenberg. *Written By* magazine, Summer 2012. www.mydigitalpublication.com/summer-2012?i=113611&p=10&view=issueViewer.

Moraski, Lauren. "Yep, Jake Johnson Would Be Sad to Say Goodbye to 'New Girl,' Too." *HuffPost,* April 4, 2017. www.huffingtonpost.co.uk/entry/jake-johnson-new-girl-finale_n_58e2b9d7e4b0d0b7e163d472.

Morris, Lamorne. Interview by author.

O'Malley, Erin. Interview by author.

Perez, Maya, and Barbara Morgan, eds. *On Story—The Golden Age of Television* (University of Texas Press, 2018). "New Girl: A Conversation with Elizabeth Meriwether. Moderated by Beau Willimon (2016)."

Press, Joy. *Stealing the Show: How Women Are Revolutionizing Television* (Atria Books, 2018).

Rash, Jim, host. *The Writers' Room*, podcast. "New Girl." SundanceTV, November 4, 2014. www.youtube.com/watch?v=qZ5a5q89dT0.

Raz, Guy, host. *The Great Creators with Guy Raz*, podcast. "Jake Johnson: His Creative Crisis on 'New Girl', Anna Kendrick Chemistry, and the 'Dog' Mentality that Carried Him from Drop-out to Director." January 23, 2024. www.thegreatcreators.com/episodes/johnson.

Riggle, Rob. Interview by author.

Risoli, Michael. Interview by author.

Rosenstock, Kim. Interview by author.

Scafaria, Lorene. Interview by author.

Sepinwall, Alan. "'New Girl' creator Liz Meriwether on Nick and Jess, Schmidt's choice, and the fun of season 2." *Uproxx*, May 14, 2013. uproxx.com/sepinwall/new-girl-creator-liz-meriwether-on-nick-and-jess-schmidts-choice-and-the-fun-of-season-2/.

Stern, Marlow. "Jake Johnson Talks His Gonzo Directorial Debut, 'Self Reliance.'" *Rolling Stone*, December 5, 2023. www.rollingstone.com/tv-movies/tv-movie-features/jake-johnson-interview-olivia-rodrigo-new-girl-residuals-taylor-swift-self-reliance-1234910551/.

Travers, Ben. "'New Girl': Max Greenfield Made Schmidt the Richest, Funniest Supporting Sitcom Star Since Joey." *IndieWire*, May 16, 2018. www.indiewire.com/awards/consider-this/new-girl-schmidt-max-greenfield-best-character-1201965337/.

Travers, Peter. *Popcorn with Peter Travers*, podcast. "Jake Johnson on Saying Goodbye to Nick Miller from 'New Girl' . . ." ABC News, July 11, 2018. abcnews.go.com/GMA/Culture/video/jake-johnson-goodbye-nick-miller-girl-56498188.

Visram, Talib. "The One Where I Counted the Jokes in Popular Sitcoms." *The Atlantic*, November 28, 2014. www.theatlantic.com/entertainment/archive/2014/11/jokes-per-minute-sitcom-ratings-link/382734/.

Winkler, Max. Interview by author.

The Writers Guild Foundation. "Inside the Writers Room with NEW GIRL." June 12, 2014.

Zaragoza, Alex. "The Single Person Answer to Thanksgiving May Be Bangsgiving." *Vice*, November 21, 2018. www.vice.com/en/article/the-single-person-answer-to-thanksgiving-may-be-bangsgiving/.

7: Nick and Jess

Adams, Erik. "The *New Girl* showrunners on topping season two's big kiss." *AV Club*, May 15, 2013. www.avclub.com/the-new-girl-showrunners-on-topping-season-two-s-big-ki-1798238429.

Adams, Nick. Interview by author.

Beard, Lanford. "'New Girl': Jake Johnson talks [SPOILER] scene with Zooey Deschanel." *Entertainment Weekly*, May 1, 2013. ew.com/article/2013/05/01/new-girl-jake-johnson-liz-meriwether-virgins/.

Berg, Alec. Interview by author.

Deschanel, Zooey. Interview by author.

Douglass, Jorjee, and Robin Glaser. Interview by author.

Egner, Jeremy. "Elizabeth Meriwether Answers Your 'New Girl' Questions." *ArtsBeat* (blog). *The New York Times*, February 5, 2013. archive.nytimes.com/artsbeat.blogs.nytimes.com/2013/02/05/elizabeth-meriwether-answers-your-new-girl-questions/.

Fusfeld, Matt. Interview by author.

Glassman, Thea. "How *New Girl* Plans to Make Things Right in Its Final Season." *Vanity Fair*, April 10, 2018. www.vanityfair.com/hollywood/2018/04/how-new-girl-plans-to-make-things-right-in-its-final-season.

Gopaldas, Reshma. "Jake Johnson Talks Bad Advice, *New Girl* Memories & Why He Doesn't Want to Talk to Famous People." *SheKnows*, December 31, 2023. www.sheknows.com/entertainment/articles/2925939/jake-johnson-podcast-new-girl-zooey-deschanel/.

Hunt, Stacey Wilson, and Lacey Rose. "THR Emmy Roundtable: 'New Girl,' 'Big Bang' Showrunners on Dropping F-Bombs and Comedy's Tough Year." *The Hollywood Reporter*, June 10, 2013. www.hollywoodreporter.com/tv/tv-news/emmys-new-girl-big-bang-564293/.

Iserson, David. Interview by author.

Johnson, Berkley. Interview by author.

Johnson, Jake. "Jake Johnson Discusses *THAT* New Girl Kissing Scene." *Bustle*, January 30, 2024. www.youtube.com/shorts/MMDgPSHPBYo.

Kasdan, Jake. Interview by author.

Leach, Samantha, "Zooey Deschanel Can't Be Anyone But Herself." *Bustle*, June 29, 2022. www.bustle.com/entertainment/zooey-deschanel-profile-new-girl-podcast-she-and-him.

Martin, Denise. "*New Girl* Showrunners Go Deep on Nick and Jess, and Tease a Season 4 Reset." *Vulture*, May 7, 2014. www.vulture.com/2014/05/new-girls-showrunners-talk-jess-nick-season-4.html.

Meriwether, Liz. Interview by author.

Paskin, Willa. "'New Girl' creator Liz Meriwether: 'I don't think the show is adorkable.'" *Salon*, May 15, 2013. www.salon.com/2013/05/15/new_girl_creator_liz_meriwether_i_dont_think_the_show_is_adorkable/.

Pope, Katherine. Interview by author.

Risoli, Michael. Interview by author.

Rosenstock, Kim. Interview by author.

Ross, Hugh. Interview by author.

Scafaria, Lorene. Interview by author.

Sepinwall, Alan. "'New Girl' creator looks back: 'You win some, you lose some.'" *Uproxx*, September 9, 2014. uproxx.com/sepinwall/new-girl-creator-liz-meriwether-looks-back-and-forward-you-win-some-you-lose-some/.

Tsuchida, Steven. Interview by author.

Walton, David. Interview by author.

Welch, Steve. Interview by author.

Winkler, Max. Interview by author.

An Ode to Bearclaw

Gad, Josh. Interview by author.

Gernon, Christine. Interview by author.

8: Prince

Adams, Erik. "*New Girl*: 'Prince.'" *AV Club*, February 3, 2014. www.avclub.com/new-girl-prince-1798179394.

Al-Ghamdi, Abdullah. "'It Wasn't a Loved Show": New Girl's Decline & End Before Netflix Era Relived in Detail by Star." *Screenrant*, January 19, 2024. screenrant.com/new-girl-popularity-decline-jake-johnson-reaction/.

Angelo, Megan. "From a 'New Girl' to the Next One's Champion." *The New York Times*, May 11, 2018. www.nytimes.com/2018/05/11/arts/television/elizabeth-meriwether-new-girl.html.

Beard, Lanford. "'New Girl' recap: 'Double Date' spells double trouble for Schmidt." *Entertainment Weekly*, October 2, 2013. ew.com/article/2013/10/02/new-girl-season-3-episode-3-recap-double-date/.

Carter, Bill. "How 'New Girl' on Fox Lost Its Ratings Mojo." *Media Decoder* (blog). *The New York Times*, March 28, 2012. archive.nytimes.com/mediadecoder.blogs.nytimes.com/2012/03/28/how-new-girl-on-fox-lost-its-ratings-mojo/.

The Columbus Dispatch. "Damon Wayans Jr.'s familiar face revisits role on 'New Girl.'" November 15, 2013. dispatch.com/story/entertainment/television/2013/11/05/damon-wayans-jr-s-familiar/23425538007/.

Deschanel, Zooey. Interview by author.

Dockterman, Eliana. "Dear Guys, It's Okay to Watch *New Girl*." *Time*, October 1, 2013. entertainment.time.com/2013/10/01/dear-guys-its-okay-to-watch-new-girl/.

Douglass, Jorjee, and Robin Glaser. Interview by author.

Fallon, Kevin. "The Return of New Girl's Coach . . . and of Faith in the Still-Great Comedy." *The Daily Beast*, November 5, 2013. www.thedailybeast.com/the-return-of-new-girls-coachand-of-faith-in-the-still-great-comedy/.

Fox, Jesse David, host. *Good One: A Podcast About Jokes*, podcast. "Liz Meriwether's Evolution from New Girl to The Dropout." *Vulture*, June 16, 2022. open.spotify.com/episode/6zKCdlwZgSMxvFEgnnOWAA.

Fusfeld, Matt. Interview by author.

Gary, Brian, host. *3rd and Fairfax: The WGAW Podcast*, podcast. "Liz Meriwether." Writers Guild of America West, August 30, 2022. podcasts.apple.com/podcast/liz-meriwether/id1001323963?i=1000577737684.

Gondelman, Josh. "*New Girl* Recap: Schmidt Is the Danger." *Vulture*, October 2, 2013. www.vulture.com/2013/10/new-girl-recap-season-3-double-date.html.

Goss, Fred. Interview by author.

Greenfield, Max. Interview by author.

Greenfield, Max. "Max Greenfield on Meeting Prince." Interview by Ellen DeGeneres. *TheEllenShow*, January 13, 2014. www.youtube.com/watch?v=MGQvnzOdlbg.

Grossbart, Sarah. "21 Facts About *New Girl* That Will Leave You Wistful for the Loft." *E! News*, September 20, 2021. www.eonline.com/news/1302848/21-facts-about-new-girl-that-will-leave-you-wistful-for-the-loft.

Johnson, Berkley. Interview by author.

Johnson, Jake. Interview by author.

Kasdan, Jake. Interview by author.

Leach, Samantha. "Jake Johnson Is in a Long-Term Relationship with His Fans." *Bustle*, January 9, 2024. www.bustle.com/entertainment/jake-johnson-self-reliance-interview.

Martin, Denise. "Jake Johnson on Nick Miller's Craziest Moves—in GIF Form." *Vulture*, February 19, 2013. www.vulture.com/2013/02/jake-johnson-on-nick-millers-craziest-moves.html.

Mascena, Megan. Interview by author.

Meriwether, Liz. Interview by author.

Meriwether, Liz. "'Isn't This Funnier?' *New Girl* Creator Liz Meriwether Recalls the Making of the Prince Episode." *Vulture*, April 26, 2016. www.vulture.com/2016/04/new-girl-liz-meriwether-prince.html.

O'Connell, Mikey. "'New Girl' Creator Liz Meriwether on Accidental Love Triangles, Reintroducing Damon Wayans." *The Hollywood Reporter*, September 17, 2013. www.hollywoodreporter.com/tv/tv-news/new-girl-creator-liz-meriwether-2–630723/.

Paskin, Willa. "'New Girl' creator Liz Meriwether: 'I don't think the show is adorkable.'" *Salon*, May 15, 2013. www.salon.com/2013/05/15/new_girl_creator_liz_meriwether_i_dont_think_the_show_is_adorkable/.

Pope, Katherine. Interview by author.

Press, Joy. *Stealing the Show: How Women Are Revolutionizing Television* (Atria Books, 2018).

Purple, Bill. Interview by author.

Risoli, Michael. Interview by author.

Sepinwall, Alan. "'New Girl' creator looks back: 'You win some, you lose some.'" *Uproxx*, September 9, 2014. uproxx.com/sepinwall/new-girl-creator-liz-meriwether-looks-back-and-forward-you-win-some-you-lose-some/.

Simone, Hannah. Interview by author.

Simone, Hannah, and Lamorne Morris, hosts. *The Mess Around*, podcast. "Coach (Damon Wayans Jr) Answers Your Prince Questions." iHeartPodcasts, January 23, 2025. www.globalplayer.com/podcasts/episodes/7DroeNa/.

Skipper, Clay. "Max Greenfield, TV's Most Lovable Narcissist, Is Nothing But Lovable Offscreen." *GQ*, October 4, 2016. www.gq.com/story/max-greenfield-interview-schmidt-new-girl.

Valiente, Alexa. "Jake Johnson shares stories from the set of 'New Girl' and what his life is like since the series finale." *Good Morning America*, July 11, 2018. abcnews.go.com/GMA/jake-johnson-shares-stories-set-girl-life-series/story?id=56497601.

Welch, Steve. Interview by author.

Whetstone, Michael. Interview by author.

Wieselman, Jarett. "How 'New Girl' Lost Its Way and Found Itself Again." *BuzzFeed News*, November 3, 2014. www.buzzfeednews.com/article/jarettwieselman/how-new-girl-lost-its-way-and-found-itself-again-in-season-4.

Wilstein, Matt. "'New Girl's' Jake Johnson Is Ready to Be a Movie Star." *The Daily Beast*, April 4, 2017. www.thedailybeast.com/new-girls-jake-johnson-is-ready-to-be-a-movie-star/.

9: How Winston Became Winston: an Investigation

Adams, Erik. "*New Girl*'s Lamorne Morris on introducing the world to Theodore K. Mullins." *AV Club*, September 17, 2013. www.avclub.com/new-girl-s-lamorne-morris-on-introducing-the-world-to-t-1798240608.

Beard, Lanford. "'New Girl' recap: Abby moves out (to Schmidt's), Winston moves forward." *Entertainment Weekly*, February 26, 2014. ew.com/article/2014/02/26/new-girl-recap-season-3-episode-17-sister-ii/.

Canfield, David. "Lamorne Morris Levels Up: 'I Want to Be Morgan Freeman.'" *Vanity Fair*, August 12, 2024. www.vanityfair.com/hollywood/story/lamorne-morris-fargo-saturday-night-emmys-awards-insider.

Fusfeld, Matt. Interview by author.

Greenfield, Max. Interview by author.

Grossbart, Sarah. "21 Facts About *New Girl* That Will Leave You Wistful for the Loft." *E! News*, September 20, 2021. www.eonline.com/news/1302848/21-facts-about-new-girl-that-will-leave-you-wistful-for-the-loft.

Johnson, Berkley. Interview by author.

Morris, Lamorne. Interview by author.

Morris, Lamorne, and Kyle Shevrin, hosts. *The Lamorning After,* podcast. "Lamorne wins the Emmy." Headgum, September 25, 2024. headgum.com/the-lamorning-after/tla-29-lamorne-wins-the-emmy.

Pedrad, Nasim. Interview by author.

Radloff, Jessica. "On a Date with New Girl's Lamorne Morris: Talking Expectations, Rom Coms, and the Question That Drives Him Crazy." *Glamour*, February 9, 2016. www.glamour.com/story/on-a-date-with-new-girls-lamor.

Sepinwall, Alan. "'New Girl' creator looks back: 'You win some, you lose some.'" *Uproxx*, September 9, 2014. uproxx.com/sepinwall/new-girl-creator-liz-meriwether-looks-back-and-forward-you-win-some-you-lose-some/.

Tedder, Michael. "Lamorne Morris Is Waking Up." *The Ringer*, September 9, 2020. www.theringer.com/2020/09/09/tv/lamorne-morris-woke-hulu-interview-racism.

Victorian, Brande, "Lamorne Morris Relates to Garrett Morris' Experience as the First Black Cast Member of 'SNL,'" *The Hollywood Reporter*, September 29, 2024. www.hollywoodreporter.com/movies/movie-features/lamorne-morris-garrett-morris-saturday-night-1236005715/.

Vulture, "The 'New Girl' Guys Recall the Horrible Questions Asked About Coach and Winston," October 27, 2020. www.youtube.com/watch?v=AACKTtWo6no.

Woods, Lamar. Interview by author.

When Nick Met Tran

Adams, Erik. "The *New Girl* showrunners on some of season 2's biggest challenges." *AV Club*, May 10, 2013. www.avclub.com/the-new-girl-showrunners-on-some-of-season-2-s-biggest-1798238544.

Johnson, Jake (@mrjakejohnson). "RIP. So much fun to work with." Instagram, February 28, 2022. www.instagram.com/mrjakejohnson/p/CaiOsXnPdet/.

Raz, Guy, host. *The Great Creators with Guy Raz*, podcast. "Jake Johnson: His Creative Crisis on 'New Girl', Anna Kendrick Chemistry, and the 'Dog' Mentality that Carried Him from Dropout to Director." January 23, 2024. www.thegreatcreators.com/episodes/johnson.

Rosenstock, Kim. Interview by author.

10: The *New Girl* Lab, Part II

Adams, Erik. "The *New Girl* showrunners on some of season 2's biggest challenges." *AV Club*, May 10, 2013. www.avclub.com/the-new-girl-showrunners-on-some-of-season-2-s-biggest-1798238544.

Deschanel, Zooey. Interview by author.

FitzSimons, Amanda. "*New Girl* Creator Liz Meriwether's Home Is Ready for Its Star Turn." *Elle*, October 23, 2013. www.elle.com/fashion/personal-style/a12601/new-girl-creator-liz-meriwether-interview/.

Fox, Jesse David, host. *Good One: A Podcast About Jokes*, podcast. "Liz Meriwether's Evolution from New Girl to The Dropout." *Vulture*, June 16, 2022. open.spotify.com/episode/6zKCdlwZgSMxvFEgnnOWAA.

Gary, Brian, host. *3rd and Fairfax: The WGAW Podcast*, podcast. "Liz Meriwether." Writers Guild of America West, August 30, 2022. podcasts.apple.com/podcast/liz-meriwether/id1001323963?i=1000577737684.

Iserson, David. Interview by author.

Jaffe, Jenny. "'New Girl' Season 4 Premiere Recap: Fridge People." *Vulture*, September 16, 2014. www.vulture.com/2014/09/new-girl-recap-season-4-premiere-jessica-biel.html.

Johnson, Jake. Interview by author.

Lindbergh, Ben. "How 'New Girl' Never Gets Old." *The Ringer*, February 17, 2017. www.theringer.com/2017/02/17/tv/how-new-girl-never-gets-old-f15a6e3e347.

Los Angeles Times. "Envelope Emmys Panel: Television show runners run with the ball." June 17, 2012. www.latimes.com/entertainment/tv/la-xpm-2012-jun-17-la-ca-showrunners-emmy-20120617-story.html.

Meriwether, Liz. Interview by author.

Morris, Julian. Interview by author.

Murillo, Giselle. Interview by author.

O'Connell, Mikey. "'New Girl' Creator Liz Meriwether Discusses the Finale and MIA Zooey Deschanel in Season 5 (Q&A)." *The Hollywood Reporter*, May 5, 2015. www.hollywoodreporter.com/tv/tv-news/new-girl-creator-liz-meriwether-4–793740/.

O'Connell, Mikey. "'New Girl' Showrunners Discuss the Fun and Frustration of Holiday Episodes." *The Hollywood Reporter*, November 25, 2014. www.hollywoodreporter.com/tv/tv-news/new-girl-showrunners-discuss-fun-752315/.

O'Connell, Mikey. "Showrunners 2012: 'New Girl's' Liz Meriwether, Brett Baer and David Finkel." *The Hollywood Reporter*, October 3, 2012. www.hollywoodreporter.com/news/general-news/showrunners-2012-new-girl-liz-meriwether-brett-baer-david-finkel-375619/.

Paskin, Willa. "'New Girl' creator Liz Meriwether: 'I don't think the show is adorkable.'" *Salon*, May 15, 2013. www.salon.com/2013/05/15/new_girl_creator_liz_meriwether_i_dont_think_the_show_is_adorkable/.

Perez, Maya, and Barbara Morgan, eds. *On Story—The Golden Age of Television* (University of Texas Press, 2018). "New Girl: A Conversation with Elizabeth Meriwether. Moderated by Beau Willimon (2016)."

Pope, Katherine. Interview by author.

Press, Joy. *Stealing the Show: How Women Are Revolutionizing Television* (Atria Books, 2018).

Purple, Bill. Interview by author.

Risoli, Michael. Interview by author.

Ross, Hugh. Interview by author.

Scafaria, Lorene. Interview by author.

Sepinwall, Alan. "How a 'New Girl' script gets made." *Uproxx*, February 27, 2013. uproxx.com/sepinwall/how-a-new-girl-script-gets-made-from-outline-to-final-cut-on-tinfinity/.

St. James, Emily. "*New Girl*'s editing team gave the show's comedy *and* drama its punch." *AV Club*, July 8, 2013. www.avclub.com/new-girl-s-editing-team-gave-the-show-s-comedy-and-dram-1798239062.

Walton, David. Interview by author.

Welch, Steve. Interview by author.

Zaragoza, Alex. "The Single Person Answer to Thanksgiving May Be Bangsgiving." *Vice*, November 21, 2018. www.vice.com/en/article/the-single-person-answer-to-thanksgiving-may-be-bangsgiving/.

11: Schmidt and Cece—Together at Last

Bricker, Tierney. "Why We Have Zooey Deschanel's Pregnancy to Thank for That Epic *New Girl* Proposal." *E! News*, May 5, 2015. www.eonline.com/news/653603/why-we-have-zooey-deschanel-s-pregnancy-to-thank-for-that-epic-new-girl-proposal.

Fusfeld, Matt. Interview by author.

Greenfield, Max. Interview by author.

Jaffee, Jenny. "Max Greenfield on the *New Girl* Finale, Being Too Schmidt-y, and Sia." *Vulture*, May 6, 2015. www.vulture.com/2015/05/new-girls-max-greenfield-on-being-too-schmidt-y.html.

Lister-Jones, Zoe. Interview by author.

Meriwether, Liz, Brett Baer, and Dave Finkel, "The New Girl and Her Guys," moderated by Jan Oxenberg, *Written By* magazine, Summer 2012, www.mydigitalpublication.com/summer-2012?i=113611&p=10&view=issueViewer.

Sepinwall, Alan. "Interview: 'New Girl' creator Liz Meriwether post-mortems season 1." *Uproxx*, May 8, 2012. uproxx.com/sepinwall/interview-new-girl-creator-liz-meriwether-post-mortems-season-1/.

Simone, Hannah. Interview by author.

12: No Girl

Bentley, Jean. "Megan Fox Replacing Zooey Deschanel on 'New Girl.'" *NBC CT*, September 18, 2015. www.nbcconnecticut.com/news/national-international/megan-fox-is-moving-to-new-girl-zooey-deschanel/1957523/.

Fusfeld, Matt. Interview by author.

Glazer, Eliot. Interview by author.

Johnson, Berkley. Interview by author.

Murillo, Giselle. Interview by author.

O'Connell, Mikey. "'New Girl's' Liz Meriwether Is Juggling the War on "Quiet Sexism" with Masking Baby Bumps." *The Hollywood Reporter*, January 5, 2016. www.hollywoodreporter.com/tv/tv-news/new-girls-liz-meriwether-is-852055/.

O'Donnell, Trent. Interview by author.

O'Malley, Erin. Interview by author.

Sepinwall, Alan. "'New Girl' creator on Megan Fox: 'She's funny in a cool way.'" *Uproxx*, February 8, 2016. uproxx.com/sepinwall/new-girl-creator-on-megan-fox-shes-funny-in-a-cool-way/.

Simone, Hannah. Interview by author.

Sims, David. "'New Girl' and the Power of Sitcom Shakeup." *The Atlantic*, March 9, 2016. www.theatlantic.com/entertainment/archive/2016/03/does-new-girl-need-zooey-deschanel-anymore/472926/.

Smith, C. Molly. "New Girl cast celebrates 100 episodes: 'It's surreal.'" *Entertainment Weekly*, March 8, 2016. ew.com/article/2016/03/08/new-girl-cast-100-episodes/.

Smith, C. Molly. "New Girl season 5 finale: Liz Meriwether unpacks 'surprising' ending." *Entertainment Weekly*, May 10, 2016. ew.com/article/2016/05/10/new-girl-season-5-finale-postmortem/.

That's IT LA. "Megan Fox Talks TMNT, Family and New Girl." June 3, 2016. thatsitla.com/megan-fox-talks-tmnt-family-new-girl/.

Walton, David. Interview by author.

Yanklewitz, Seth. Interview by author.

The Anatomy of the Popcorn Scene

Johnson, Berkley. Interview by author.

13: Sayonara, Sammy, Part I

Ausiello, Michael. "Jake Johnson Reveals How He Helped Save 'New Girl' from Cancellation." *TVLine*, November 24, 2017. www.yahoo.com/entertainment/jake-johnson-reveals-helped-save-000032828.html.

Deschanel, Zooey. Interview by author.

Fox, David Jesse. "What Was *New Girl*'s Legacy?" *Vulture*, May 15, 2018. www.vulture.com/2018/05/new-girl-legacy.html.

Franklin, Nelson. Interview by author.

Fusfeld, Matt. Interview by author.

Glassman, Thea. "How *New Girl* Plans to Make Things Right in Its Final Season." *Vanity Fair*, April 10, 2018. www.vanityfair.com/hollywood/2018/04/how-new-girl-plans-to-make-things-right-in-its-final-season.

Glazer, Eliot. Interview by author.

Greenfield, Max. Interview by author.

Heldman, Breanne L. "*New Girl* EPs answer pressing questions about the season finale." *Entertainment Weekly*, April 4, 2017. ew.com/tv/2017/04/04/new-girl-season-6-finale-interview/.

Johnson, Berkley. Interview by author.

Johnson, Jake. Interview by author.

Meriwether, Liz. Interview by author.

Morris, Lamorne. Interview by author.

Ng, Philiana. "'New Girl' Creator Says Final Season Is a 'Love Letter to the Fans.'" *ET*, January 4, 2018. www.etonline.com/new-girl-creator-says-final-season-love-letter-fans-93565.

O'Connell, Mikey. "'New Girl' Creator Explains the Season (Possibly Series) Finale." *The Holly-*

wood Reporter, April 4, 2017. www.hollywoodreporter.com/tv/tv-news/new-girl-season-6-finale-explained-990979/.

O'Connell, Mikey. "'New Girl' Creator Liz Meriwether on the Final Season That Almost Didn't Happen." *The Hollywood Reporter*, April 10, 2018. www.hollywoodreporter.com/tv/tv-news/new-girl-creator-liz-meriwether-final-season-almost-didnt-happen-1101149/.

O'Malley, Erin. Interview by author.

Rich, Katey. "Can a Short Seventh Season Give *New Girl* the Finale It Deserves?" *Vanity Fair*, May 15, 2017. www.vanityfair.com/hollywood/2017/05/new-girl-renewal-finale.

Sepinwall, Alan. "In Case This Was the 'New Girl' Series Finale, Producers Wanted [REDACTED] to Happen." *Uproxx*, April 4, 2017. uproxx.com/sepinwall/new-girl-finale-interview-jess-nick/.

Wilstein, Matt. "Jake Johnson: 'New Girl' Almost Definitely Ending After Season 6." *The Daily Beast*, March 12, 2017. www.thedailybeast.com/jake-johnson-new-girl-almost-definitely-ending-after-season-6/.

Woods, Lamar. Interview by author.

Zakarin, Jordan. "Max Greenfield Almost Quit Acting to Become Writer Before 'New Girl.'" *TheWrap*, April 21, 2014. www.thewrap.com/max-greenfield-almost-quit-acting-become-writer-new-girl/.

14: Sayonara, Sammy, Part II

Alsobrook, Russ T. Interview by author.

Chuba, Kirsten. "'New Girl' Cast Teases Finale, Reflects on 7 Seasons of Fox Comedy." *Variety*, May 9, 2018. variety.com/2018/tv/news/new-girl-cast-teases-finale-1202804021/.

Fox, Jesse David, host. *Good One: A Podcast About Jokes*, podcast. "Liz Meriwether's Evolution from New Girl to The Dropout." *Vulture*, June 16, 2022. open.spotify.com/episode/6zKCdlwZgSMxvFEgnnOWAA.

Franklin, Nelson. Interview by author.

Greenfield, Max. Interview by author.

Johnson, Berkley. Interview by author.

Li, Shirley. "*New Girl* creator Liz Meriwether on the series finale's biggest twists." *Entertainment Weekly*, May 15, 2018. ew.com/tv/2018/05/15/new-girl-series-finale-ending-liz-meriwether-interview/.

Li, Shirley. "*New Girl*: Jake Johnson reflects on Nick and Jess—and Nick and Schmidt." *Entertainment Weekly*, May 16, 2018. ew.com/tv/2018/05/16/new-girl-series-finale-jake-johnson-nick-jess-interview/.

Lister-Jones, Zoe. Interview by author.

Maas, Jennifer. "'New Girl' Series Finale: That Final Nick-Schmidt Bromance Flashback Was Totally Improvised." *TheWrap*, May 15, 2018. www.thewrap.com/new-girl-series-finale-nick-schmidt-jake-johnson-max-greenfield/.

Mascena, Megan. Interview by author.

O'Connell, Mikey. "'New Girl' Creator Liz Meriwether on the Final Season That Almost Didn't

Happen." *The Hollywood Reporter*, April 10, 2018. www.hollywoodreporter.com/tv/tv-news/new-girl-creator-liz-meriwether-final-season-almost-didnt-happen-1101149/.

O'Connell, Mikey. "'New Girl' Creator Talks Parting Shots from the Series Finale." *The Hollywood Reporter*, May 15, 2018. www.hollywoodreporter.com/tv/tv-news/new-girl-series-finale-creator-liz-meriwether-looks-back-fox-comedy-1110878/.

O'Malley, Erin. Interview by author.

Otterson, Joe. "TV Ratings: 'Roseanne' Stays on Top with 13.5 Million Viewers." *Variety*, April 11, 2018. variety.com/2018/tv/ratings/roseanne-ratings-abc-week-3–1202750318/.

Paige, Rachel. "In true Nick Miller fashion, Jake Johnson stole all his pants from *New Girl*." *HelloGiggles*, May 9, 2018. hellogiggles.com/jake-johnson-new-girl-pants/.

Risoli, Michael. Interview by author.

Schneider, Michael. "'New Girl' Creator's Real-Life Eye Mishap Inspired the Show's 'Adorkable' Wedding Finale." *IndieWire*, May 15, 2018. www.indiewire.com/features/general/new-girl-series-finale-wedding-liz-meriwether-zooey-deschanel-1201964906/.

Simone, Hannah. Interview by author.

Valiente, Alexa. "Jake Johnson shares stories from the set of 'New Girl' and what his life is like since the series finale." *Good Morning America*, July 11, 2018. abcnews.go.com/GMA/jake-johnson-shares-stories-set-girl-life-series/story?id=56497601.

Villarreal, Yvonne. "Elizabeth Holmes' wild trial almost remade 'The Dropout.' Here's why it was left out." *Los Angeles Times*, March 3, 2022. www.latimes.com/entertainment-arts/tv/story/2022–03–03/the-dropout-hulu-elizabeth-holmes-liz-meriwether-new-girl.

Walton, David. Interview by author.

Welch, Steve. Interview by author.

Whetstone, Michael. Interview by author.

Woods, Lamar. Interview by author.

15: Where the Road Goes

Angelo, Megan. "From a 'New Girl' to the Next One's Champion." *The New York Times*, May 11, 2018. www.nytimes.com/2018/05/11/arts/television/elizabeth-meriwether-new-girl.html.

Clark, Travis. "The most watched streaming TV shows and movies of 2020, according to Nielsen." *Business Insider*, January 12, 2021. www.businessinsider.com/most-watched-movies-shows-2020-on-netflix-disney-plus-nielsen-2021–1.

D'Souza, Shaad. "New Girl: screwball comedy gets funnier and smarter—and is best when binged." *The Guardian*, March 25, 2020. www.theguardian.com/culture/2020/mar/26/new-girl-screwball-comedy-gets-funnier-and-smarter-and-is-best-when-binged.

Franklin, Nelson. Interview by author.

Greenfield, Max. Interview by author.

Johnson, Jake. Interview by author.

Lawrence, Derek. "Why *New Girl* is the perfect quarantine comfort binge." *Entertainment Weekly*, March 31, 2020. ew.com/tv/new-girl-binge-watch-quarantine.

Li, Shirley. "*New Girl* creator Liz Meriwether on the series finale's biggest twists." *Entertainment Weekly*, May 15, 2018. ew.com/tv/2018/05/15/new-girl-series-finale-ending-liz-meriwether-interview/.

Lister-Jones, Zoe. Interview by author.

Long, Justin. Interview by author.

Longo, Joseph. "Nick Miller Was Always the One." *MEL*, June 23, 2020. melmagazine.com/en-us/story/nick-miller-new-girl-netflix.

Low, Elaine, and Natalie Jarvey. "Netflix is asking series creators for a female 'Jack Ryan,' a new 'New Girl,' or a fresh riff on 'The Voice,' according to Hollywood agency documents—and please, no 'sad coms.'" *Business Insider*, May 11, 2022. www.businessinsider.com/what-netflix-wants-new-series-writers-hollywood-agency-documents-2022–5.

Martin-Green, Sonequa. Via email.

Meriwether, Liz. Archival interview by author.

Meriwether, Liz. Interview by author.

Morris, Lamorne, and Kyle Shevrin, hosts. *The Lamorning After*, podcast. "Damon Moves out of the Loft . . . (Feat. Damon Wayans Jr)." Headgum, October 23, 2024. headgum.com/the-lamorning-after/damon-moves-out-of-the-loft-feat-damon-wayans-jr-re-release.

Pedrad, Nasim. Interview by author.

Toomer, Jessica. "'New Girl' Nailed the Art of a Slow-Burn TV Romance." *Uproxx*, June 17, 2020. uproxx.com/tv/new-girl-slow-burn-romance-jess-nick/.

Villarreal, Yvonne. "Elizabeth Holmes' wild trial almost remade 'The Dropout.' Here's why it was left out." *Los Angeles Times*, March 3, 2022. www.latimes.com/entertainment-arts/tv/story/2022–03–03/the-dropout-hulu-elizabeth-holmes-liz-meriwether-new-girl.

Walton, David. Interview by author.

Index

About the Author

Ben Leiken

THEA GLASSMAN is an entertainment journalist whose writing has appeared in *The New York Times*, *Vanity Fair*, *Architectural Digest*, and *Rolling Stone*. Her first book, *Freaks, Gleeks & Dawson's Creek*, went behind the scenes of seven groundbreaking teen television shows. She lives in New York City with her fiancé and their dog, Riggins, of *Friday Night Lights* fame.